THE DHARMA OF HEALING

The DHARMA *of* HEALING

··

The Path of Liberation from Stress, Pain, and Trauma

JUSTIN MICHELSON

Foreword by Rodney Smith

SHAMBHALA

Shambhala Publications, Inc.
2129 13th Street
Boulder, Colorado 80302
www.shambhala.com

Cover art: redstone/Shutterstock
Cover design: Daniel Urban-Brown
Interior design: Kate Huber-Parker

9 8 7 6 5 4 3 2 1

First Edition
Printed in the United States of America

Shambhala Publications makes every effort
to print on acid-free, recycled paper.
Shambhala Publications is distributed worldwide by
Penguin Random House, Inc.,
and its subsidiaries.

Library of Congress Cataloging-in-Publication Data
Names: Michelson, Justin, author. | Smith, Rodney, writer of foreword.
Title: The dharma of healing: the path of liberation from stress, pain, and trauma /
Justin Michelson; foreword by Rodney Smith.
Description: First edition. | Boulder, Colorado: Shambhala, [2025] |
Includes bibliographical references.
Identifiers: LCCN 2024031788 | ISBN 9781645473640 (trade paperback)
Subjects: LCSH: Compassion. | Healing—Psychological aspects. |
Mindfulness (Psychology) | Meditation.
Classification: LCC BJ1475 .M53 2025 | DDC 203/.1—dc23/eng/20241025
LC record available at https://lccn.loc.gov/2024031788

The authorized representative in the EU for product safety and compliance is eucomply OÜ,
Pärnu mnt 139b-14, 11317 Tallinn, Estonia, hello@eucompliancepartner.com.

Contents

Part Three

THE REALIZATION

Foreword

The Dharma of Healing is about the healing powers of the spiritual heart, written by Justin Michelson, who courageously shares his own exploration with depth and insight. This book is a wonderfully fresh and nicely crafted investigation into the benefits and constraints of opening our hearts and minds to the truth revealed by pure awareness. Justin encourages the modalities of mindfulness and self-compassion as reliable and proven methods to ground and stabilize our path forward. When these methods are combined with a determined and persistent investigation into the nuances of our own minds, it lays bare the path of self-actualization as the full integration of the sense of self within the entirety of life. In Justin's words, "We apply the process to every layer of our psyche—including all the parts that don't feel compassionate or safe—all the way back to the first time we turned away. . . . Eventually, all parts of us are reintegrated, first into our psyches and then into the fabric of life itself."

I have known Justin since his midteens when he entered a mindfulness class for young people that I was leading. He was cautious but excited about meditation, and I could see in him, even then, the early stirrings of a life that would be captured by the Dharma.

Justin's dharma path is revealed through the exploration of his woundedness, the deep areas of our collective and individual psyches where history has imbedded the scar tissues of the past. To provide a present-day orientation to the ancient subject of healing, Justin uses the term *self-compassion*. This expresses the fundamental love and warmth toward all aspects of ourselves as the overriding force that can potentially heal our inward traumas. He emphasizes that his self-revelations were often guided, grounded, and held within this ageless internal resource. Throughout the book he challenges many of our cultural assumptions that unconsciously maintain woundedness, including the conventional way we understand ourselves as separate and isolated entities. Justin urges us to evolve out of this conditioned way of seeing into the intrinsic interconnectedness of all existence.

While self-compassion can be cultivated, Justin also points out that it is a natural component of awareness. When our psychological selves heal and transform, true compassion can shine forth. In this way, Justin skillfully connects healing to self-realization.

One of the central tools used by Justin is wisdom application, also known as skillful means. For instance, we might encourage our wholesome emotions to offset challenges that unwholesome emotions evoke. These healthier effects of mind can offer space and counterbalance to our troublesome self-doubt. To aid the reader into a full realized understanding, he adds a synthesis of diagrams, tables, reflections, journal prompts, and guided inquiries, and uses these devices to break complicated terms into easily understandable parts and inch us forward into a full assimilation of his themes. Although some may interpret this as too analytical and scholarly, this approach can provide a valuable way to further our investigation and deepen our wisdom.

However, substituting one set of conditions for another or breaking complicated phrases into digestible parts does not end our conflicts. To end suffering we must release, surrender, and let ourselves be. We must be wise and conscious enough to leave ourselves alone, no longer viewing ourselves as a problem to fix, and be able to relax and bathe in our innate goodness without moral prodding. Living completely exposed, unafraid of the propensities of the mind, is the definition of freedom, and Justin's book moves us toward that clear seeing.

Likewise, knowing the subject intellectually and/or practicing specific exercises do not suffice on their own. To move into the truth, we have to dive in and allow our heart free rein to direct us toward its yearning, which is in the direction of more inclusivity, intimacy, and depth, taking us forever into the curiosity and grounded assurance of wisdom. Our path is uniquely our own, unlike anyone else who has ever traversed this landscape. It is not even "our path" since we are neither the owners of it nor do we empower it forward. It is all unfolding from the timeless and ineffable mystery. Wisdom can only arise when we remember to follow our intrinsic wonder and curiosity. If we divert our direction and follow another's path, we may momentarily lighten our self-doubt, but we will have, most assuredly, lost our way.

The final sections of *The Dharma of Healing* are a guidance through holistic action, where the action comes from a growing realization of our interdependence. Whether that action comes from simple listening, relational living, or social activism, these actions will be less and less self-centered. A kind of thinning of self takes place as we become more aware of our intrinsic emptiness. As we become more translucent, there is a natural response toward compassionate actions. Yes, we will still be confronted by our egoic impulses, but slowly over time, as we learn to hold and address these remaining conditioned tendencies, we evolve out of the perception of isolation into a field of interconnection. This evolution out of egocentrism changes everything and is accompanied by a new perception of reality. This new perception has us moving in love, through love, as love. In fact, it might be said that we become the nobody we are by loving ourselves out of existence.

What we discover after all this inquiry and exploration into our woundedness is the vast beauty of our own being. I encourage a full and heartfelt reading of *The Dharma of Healing*. Let it deepen the mystery that has already begun.

Rodney Smith
Seattle, Washington
May 2024

How to Use This Book

The Dharma of Healing is a handbook for spiritual freedom in an age of global crisis. The text offers a description of the theory (part 1), the practices (part 2), and the realizations (part 3) we can experience. Just as important, however, are the journal prompts and guided meditations that are a companion to the book and that invite the reader into an intimate personal understanding of this unique path and practice.

At the end of each chapter, you'll find journal prompts and short guided reflections or meditations in linked online audio recordings. These are intended to be explored sequentially as you make your way through the book. The core *Dharma of Healing* practices are in part 2. There you'll find a comprehensive system of preparatory reflections and guided meditations that gently lead you into the heart of the embodied experience of spiritual healing and freedom. These twenty-four meditations are divided into foundational practices to acquire the prerequisite skills and four progressive levels of meditative exploration, described as the *four turnings of the wheel of healing*. They can be experienced successively as you read through part 2 or after reading through the full book. They are intended to be returned to again and again as we "turn the wheel of healing" throughout our lives.

The audio recordings for both end-of-chapter meditations and the core progression of the four turnings are located at www.justinmichelsondharma .com/thedharmaofhealing/practices and www.shambhala.com/dharmaof healingpractices.

Please take the opportunity to explore for yourself the special and powerful journey that is the Dharma of Healing: the path of liberation from stress, pain, and trauma.

THE DHARMA OF HEALING

Introduction

For me, living within this age of crisis has been a great challenge at times. By elementary school, I had learned about the disappearing rainforests and dwindling species. By middle school, I had read about the vast disparities in wealth and the needless poverty around the globe. By high school, I had begun to understand the mechanisms of endless wars, corruption, and oppression that humans impose on one another. Each time I discovered a new aspect of the troubled nature of our world, my heart would sink. It was only in hindsight that I would realize each painful discovery also ripened me, guiding me deeper and deeper into a profound personal exploration, determined to discover the root cause of this suffering and to establish an inner refuge amid the storm.

Today, everyone is affected, directly or indirectly, by the colliding disasters of climate change, environmental degradation, resource scarcity, and pandemics, not to mention growing wealth inequality, war, systemic injustice, and social unrest. We're all bombarded by the endless news cycles of one crisis after the next. According to a recent Gallup poll, 2022 and 2023 marked the peak of a steady global rise in negative emotional experiences.[1]

While these collective conditions are undesirable, even tragic, the increasing challenge is likely catalyzing more and more of us to explore topics like mindfulness,[2] spirituality,[3] and overall wellness.[4] That makes sense; these are solutions that we can control and that can support us no matter what conditions we find ourselves in. However, for many of us, the first challenge is carving out the space and time to devote our attention to ourselves. Simply managing the fundamentals of work and family is often more than enough already. When we do, we naturally begin to feel more ease and clarity. However, to our disappointment, even with regular practice, most of us find our deeper disruptive patterns persist. The anxiety, the depression, the self-judgment, the loneliness—these stronger feelings under the surface—and, in particular, our responses to them keep us feeling stuck or overwhelmed and affect our relationships.

Even when we attend workshops or retreats that help us break through and reach new depths of healing and insight, many of us discover the patterns we released readily grow back. We touch something real and important, but we struggle to understand it in our lives. Deeper down, we can compare ourselves to others and feel like we're failing somehow, not quite able to apprehend the elusive contentment we hear about.

Each of these struggles are totally understandable, even expected. Immersed in, or surrounded by, the fast-paced, high-pressure, and distraction-rich environment of the twenty-first-century culture of materialism, status-seeking, and instant gratification, it can be challenging for even the most dedicated among us to sustain a spiritual outlook, let alone embodied wisdom. However, that inherent challenge can be amplified or soothed depending on the approach we take to our healing and spiritual path. Many of the people I meet are missing something vital.

On the broadest level, a spiritual practice may be missing a healing dimension, or a healing practice may be missing a spiritual understanding. Either could be missing a clear application in our work lives, relationships, or service in the world. On the level of technique, we may be applying certain strategies at the expense of others. Restoring balance and wholeness to our path is often the key that unlocks truly fulfilling growth.

Most of us know about mindfulness. It's a potent aspect of many self-help methods, offering a wide range of benefits, from reduced negative affect to increased performance and health.[5] It's also a powerful part of many spiritual traditions, cultivating relaxation and wisdom, including clear seeing into the habit patterns of our own hearts and minds. It's also a critical component of wise engagement in the world, as service work requires great intimacy, attentiveness, and responsiveness. In this way, mindfulness bridges healing, spirituality, and engagement, making it an essential foundational element to any spiritual path.

However, there is a limit to what mindfulness can do. Like many of my colleagues, I had to discover this the hard way. After a few years of regular meditation practice, I had developed the skill to be mindful: I could let a thought go by or an emotion pass; I could even surrender into the deep stillness and spaciousness of my heart. I presumed these things were enough to embody deep spiritual truths and, ultimately, live a peaceful and happy life.

I wasn't aware that underneath my mindful attention lived an even deeper, hidden world of psychological wounding. And after a year of intensive practice at retreat centers, when the stored pain rose into my awareness, my practice and life became paralyzed in its grip. It was then I began to see that my mindfulness alone was helpless in the face of the deepest terrors, shames, and doubts lodged in my body. My practice, the dearest thing to me, had stopped working, and I was left confused, hopeless, anxious, and exhausted. Eventually, I was forced to surrender my stubbornness and accept that my pain needed a different kind of attention from me. It didn't require a new technique or a new teacher to try to fix it or make it go away. My pain needed a sincere presence of heart—a force both stronger and somehow softer than mindfulness alone.

Over the years, I've explored the amazing capacities of this essential human treasure we each contain. Each wholesome quality of heart—its curiosity, joy, love, gratitude—has a profound and powerful genius. Curiosity opens us to learn, while joy celebrates connection. Love opens us to intimacy, while gratitude avails us of contentment.

However, there was one more quality of heart in particular that rose to the top as the clear choice to spearhead my journey of healing and insight. This heart quality can be soft and strong, focused and expansive. It can disarm and transform our toughest patterns, letting lessons and insights integrate in their place. It can elevate us to spiritual heights while keeping us grounded and connected. Moreover, it can adapt skillfully to the needs of our one-of-a-kind life and heart. Sourced from an ancient instinct within us, it's a most precious jewel of our earthly evolution.

Today, in my experience as a teacher, it seems to be the most relevant spiritual companion we could hope for in this troubled world. It redeems us and confirms our essential goodness, even when everything else is falling apart. It keeps us centered and connected in the face of challenge. We could call it a technique, but it's more an innate home we can inhabit. It is none other than the jewel of *compassion*.

You can tell that I'm not describing just any type of compassion here. I'm referring to a thorough and wholehearted expression that, while inherent to each of us, takes some careful coaxing to come alive. More importantly, I'm referring to the power of that radiance when it is shined *back onto ourselves*. This radical act catalyzes a profound inner and outer maturation that restores wholeness to our lives. Eventually, we can grow in strength and resilience to such a degree that even our and the world's immense challenges can't crush us. Instead, they become opportunities to expand even further.

· ·

The Dharma of Healing is a system of spiritual practice for the modern seeker. Through a series of fresh perspectives, principles, and practices, it repositions psychological healing as central to both spiritual development and maturation as well as effective engagement in the world. Synergizing the liberating wisdom of insight meditation with the therapeutic power of self-compassion, it is a pathway of practice rooted in an ancient and proven wisdom tradition that can bear fruit within our modern minds and lives. This synergy of spirituality, healing, and engagement naturally emerged from the evolution of my own personal journey.

When I met my teacher Rodney Smith at a class for teens, I was just a high school kid. I had no idea what meditation or mindfulness was; I'd certainly never heard of insight meditation. However, it was partly this innocence of heart that made my first experiences so profound. In that first class, sitting silently was the most refreshingly simple thing I'd ever done. I could feel myself like the great, old fir trees that towered near my childhood home. They just were what they were, whether sick and broken or healthy and tall; they were unshakably confident in their essential authenticity, aware and connected to everything around them. To my surprise, I had that in me, too.

For many years after that class, I followed the Dharma wherever it took me. Through practice and study, I learned more and more about the Buddha's teachings and their expressions in the insight, Zen, and Tibetan lineages. However, the insight tradition seemed to paint the clearest picture of our universal human condition and the path to experiencing freedom within it.

Insight meditation, also known as the vipassana movement, is a Western derivative of Theravada Buddhism and originated from teachers within Burma and Thailand starting in the nineteenth century. The name *insight* is simply a translation of the Pali word *vipassana* and speaks to the idea that liberation comes from seeing into the true nature of reality. As it came to the West, it was popularized by various teachers with their own styles, such as Jack Kornfield and Joseph Goldstein and the retreat centers of Spirit Rock and Insight Meditation Society that they founded. In the process, many of the religious elements were set aside, yet the foundation of Theravada Buddhist teachings remains.

Even though I would find a home in this lineage, my own path never felt confined to one method, teaching, or tradition. Over the past twenty-five years, in addition to practicing in the Zen and Tibetan traditions, I've studied secular forms of mindfulness, such as Mindfulness-Based Stress Reduction or MBSR and mindful self-compassion, as well as trauma-informed and nature-based mindfulness. I've found personal healing through modalities such as somatic therapy, improvisational dance, and Internal Family Systems. I've also committed decades to integrating spiritual concepts into environmental education and community service work, including sharing the Dharma in creative ways with others.

While insight meditation has great strengths, it also lacked some critical support I needed at times. For example, it wasn't until I adopted the compassionate and relational emphases of approaches like Internal Family Systems (IFS) that I began to feel safe enough to integrate and embody the deeper truths of insight meditation in my daily life. As I learned to fully embrace my vulnerable humanness alongside my expansive spiritual experiences, I felt an even greater sense of wholeness inside. This made it easier to engage with my service work in the world without losing my clarity, ease, and conviction.

This was also the beginning of an ever-deepening answer to the core inquiries I'd painstakingly pursued since my early twenties. At that time, my spiritual longing was overwhelming, although in an emotional choice I would ultimately decide against pursuing a monastic life. I couldn't leave this world behind when it needed so much, but I couldn't leave my devotion to awakening either. So I had to know: What was the meeting place of spirituality, healing, and activism? How could I awaken *within* an active life of service in this chaotic world? Many years later, this book is an answer to those early questions—ultimately proposing a unified theory, practice, and path to realization based in true compassion.

For those Westerners already immersed in the Dharma, I propose what may be a significant shift in focus: the fundamental importance of thorough psychological healing to the progression of the spiritual path. A spiritual journey without healing will likely remain disconnected and conflictual, even if only at a subtle level of mind. To remedy this, I place engaged heart practices and compassionate self-inquiry as a prerequisite for—and an ongoing companion to—traditional wisdom or concentration practices. The healing they bring activates and integrates the wisdom we seek. Along the way, I work to reconcile numerous paradoxes, including that between the personal healing of the self and the deeper liberating truths of impermanence and nonself.

For those arriving from a secular or psychological background, I offer the often-missing spiritual depth that can alchemize and awaken modern Western psychological approaches. Healing will always feel incomplete unless it includes a radical reconnection to something far greater than ourselves. Or to put it another way: understanding the true nature of our suffering is just as important as healing it. Hence, a healing journey without the spiritual dimension will likely remain confining and ultimately not entirely satisfying. To remedy this, I elevate and expand the healing capacities of the human heart out of the merely personal and place them within a larger expression of collective and universal unfolding. Doing so, I point toward the more profound spiritual purpose of healing and propose a meditative framework through which to experience it.

For those arriving from the front lines of activism, I suggest a renewed devotion to the self-focused practices that create a foundation for sustainable engagement. A life of service without a solid foundation in healing and spirituality will likely lose its purity of intention and, thus, its effectiveness—not to mention the courage, energy, and wisdom needed to persevere. It's all too easy to act from our unresolved fear and judgment, taking sides and increasing division instead of transforming into the more compassionate and wise beings that the world dearly needs. To remedy this, I describe a radical practice of activism that flows forth as an outpouring of a full and nourished heart—one that can liberate ourselves and others in the process.

• •

As I explore these topics, I reference a *healing path* and a *spiritual path* many times. For clarity, when I refer to healing or the healing path, I'm essentially discussing the process of releasing, or better yet, *transforming* painful patterns of thought and emotion often stored in the body. For example, we can learn to alchemize sadness into joy, self-judgment into self-compassion, tension into ease, anxiety into inner safety, and ultimately, ill-being into well-being. When done skillfully, this process restores internal connectivity and, thus, a sense of wholeness within us. When I reference the spiritual path, I'm generally talking about the understandings and practices that serve to restore a transformative interconnection between ourselves and the greater essence of life—initiating a radical re-perception of our lives. In this way, spirituality also restores a sense of wholeness, just in a more expansive and inclusive way.

Both paths naturally synergize and support one another. Their fruition depends on the unconditional embrace of our emotional and mental lives. In service to this, you'll notice I often personify emotions and thoughts to bring them to life, increase our sense of intimacy with them, and aid in the process of transformative healing. Paradoxically, many find that by embracing them in this way, they actually liberate into their more than personal forms. You may intuitively resonate with this personified approach, but if not, you are welcome to translate the descriptions into a more impersonal framing.

Both pathways of healing and spirituality also rely on the same guiding principle: the subjective feeling of *connection*—within and without. I also describe this as an inner intimacy or even a sense of inner belonging or kinship. When this felt, embodied connection to oneself, others, or the world is supportive and strong, it leads to a felt sense of safety inside. This allows us to relax, feel OK in ourselves, and open to something greater than us. In this way, felt connection and safety provide the container within which the pain and confusion of life can be metabolized and help us discover the deeper truths of our interconnected universe.

Ultimately, all spirituality guides us toward the source or essence of life, called by many names. We might say God, Spirit, or Presence. In the insight tradition, it's often called *emptiness* or our *true nature*. In this book, I most often call it *life itself* as a reference to the interconnected totality of things. When speaking about our meditative experience, I call it *awareness*—as our attention itself can be seen as a doorway to, and manifestation of, this spiritual dimension of ourselves (more on this later).

In addition, I'll be using other words that might be new to you. For example, *Dharma* is a word that means multiple things. It means "the true nature of things" (as used in the book title) and also "the teachings of the Buddha" (as used in this introduction). You'll also notice me referring to our *heart-mind* because, in the insight tradition, our emotional and mental lives are not considered separate but as part of a singular process. In specific chapters, I'll refer to some basic Buddhist teachings like the four noble truths, the *brahmaviharas* ("divine abodes"), or more abstract teachings like that of nonself. Don't worry if they're new to you. Each of them will be explained to the extent necessary.

..

My deepest wish for all of us is to feel that we are safe and connected inside *no matter what*. Even if in the moment we seem broken or lost or abandoned, even if our deepest worldly dreams have fallen apart, even if our existential fears for ourselves or the world come to pass—now or in the future—may we rest in the embodied knowing that we are always whole and complete at our core. Feeling this safety and connection in our bones is the eventual promise of compassionate devotion to ourselves as laid forth in this book.

In this way, my deepest wish is not for you to cling to a particular practice or always act in a certain compassionate way. It's to form an unshakable foundation from which you can live fully and fearlessly with an open heart while you're here and go with an easeful grace when it's your time. While this book offers many helpful suggestions, reflections, and meditations to bring you "there," the experience and expression of your liberation will always be uniquely and exquisitely yours, and forever unfolding anew. It might not mean you become an ardent meditator. It might just mean loving more deeply what you already have, honoring more fully who you already are. It might mean rediscovering the beauty right in front of you from the vantage point of an open, loving heart.

In the process, many things will be asked of you: You'll be asked to stretch to love your pain as much as your joy. You'll be asked to learn an unconditional care that your family or culture rarely, if ever, could provide. You'll be asked to stop and simply allow yourself to relax and surrender into a deeper trust in life. Every day, you'll be asked to break down the barriers between the spiritual and the mundane and to make your life your practice and your practice your life.

But before we start our journey there together, please remember one thing: *be easy and gentle on yourself throughout the process.* Whether we know it or not, we are each precious beyond measure. Whatever troubles you likely, in some way, troubles others, too. There is undoubtedly someone else out there right now going through something very similar.

The unfolding of our lives is part of much larger processes at work, of which we are just a tiny part. Our suffering is intertwined with the suffering of all humans before us and all life on Earth. What we've gone through is not our fault, nor is it an obstacle. It's actually the pathway home.

This means that we can relax. Healing and spirituality don't have to be a struggle. We are always just one pause away from a deeper breath and clearer sight. Indeed, the simplest of compassionate means applied in small, thoughtful doses can keep guiding us back home—even when it's hard.

You might have many reservations about trying a new practice or understanding a new process. That makes perfect sense. I totally get it. I simply encourage you to take in what feels helpful to you and leave behind the rest. Part 1 is devoted to the theory of how we suffer and how we heal. If it feels overly intellectual for you, know that part 2 offers a series of experiential practices that will bring you back into your body. If it, in its turn, feels insular or inapplicable, know that part 3 explores how we can incorporate these understandings and practices back into our lives.

Thank you for joining me on this journey. May each of us rediscover our heart's deeply sweet and rich capacities for the sake of all sentient beings.

Part One

THE THEORY

1

THE AGE OF COMPASSION

This first chapter explores the root causes of our global challenges and how we each often unwittingly perpetuate them. Then, we'll examine a simple but profound solution that can help us reverse and uproot the suffering on an individual and, eventually, collective level. Admittedly, it's painful to reflect on the world at this tumultuous time, but it's also essential to ascertain what the world most deeply needs from us. When we see that the global crisis is, at its core, a spiritual one, our inner lives become an intimate part of the solution. In simple and immediate ways, we can each reclaim a vital role in shaping our collective future.

. .

Looking around, we find ourselves together in a new and unprecedented age. Perhaps it was only fifty years ago when we realized that our collective human impact could alter the course of all life on Earth. Maybe only in the last twenty-five years have many of us admitted that we are on a crash course for total ecological and societal collapse. Only in the last few years have many of us had to consider we may have crossed a point of no return—where it will get a lot worse before, or if, it gets better. We face a poly-crisis of mass proportions, from climate chaos and mass displacement to environmental degradation, pollution, and scarcity to spiraling social inequality and unrest—to name only a key few.[1]

Naturally, it's hard not to feel deep in our being the uncertainty and insecurity of these global circumstances. We may very well be the people to witness the unraveling of global civilization at a scale never before seen.

Even if we wanted to, we certainly aren't returning to "normal" anytime soon. No matter where we find ourselves in the world and no matter how privileged we may be, we can no longer escape this reality.

As challenging as that is to face for all of us—myself included—it's also an unprecedented opportunity for human growth. When we can't escape something, it transforms from a practical problem into a spiritual one. For those of us on the healing and spiritual journey already, we know firsthand that when we can't avoid the pain any longer, that's precisely when the real transformational work begins. And to be honest, this is actually when it gets simpler: we have no choice but to answer the call.

Indeed, while crises can scare us into our worst habits, they can also encourage spiritual growth like nothing else. When everything is falling apart around us, it makes sense to search for a deeper refuge that's less dependent on changing circumstances. With some guidance, we can discover a lasting safety and resilience sourced within ourselves, empowering us to weather and respond wisely to the coming storms. This wisdom may be the most valuable legacy we can pass along to our youth, for it's the place from which clear and compassionate leadership can reemerge in the future.

We have no shortage of practical solutions for the ailments we see. Collectively, we know enough about how to reverse climate change, live in harmony with nature and each other, and create equity in our societies. We have ample access to traditional wisdom and modern science regarding happiness and well-being. Our problem lies in enacting and embodying these solutions in our lives; it's a limitation of heart and mind. It's sensible to place responsibility on those with the greatest wealth and influence who control the conditions of so many others. However, it's also up to you and me. What we each fail to heal and transform within ourselves in one way or another ends up as the world's burden to hold. And that burden is simply becoming too great.

Thus, cultivating insight and healing are not just wholesome activities but a necessity of this age. Our hearts must come alive amid the struggle and tragedy, right within the chaos of our world. Our lives must become our crucibles of growth. Few of us can retreat to a monastery anymore, but we can all return to the center of ourselves. When we do, we can retrieve the gifts we and the world need to evolve and transform together.

••

The human heart is a mysterious miracle of evolution. It not only keeps our bodies nourished with rich and healing blood but is also an organ of feeling and wisdom. Only in the last two decades have researchers discovered that the physical heart is not controlled by the brain but is a center of intelligence all its own. With a network of over forty thousand neurons,[2] it processes information and communicates with all parts of us, altering our perception, attention, emotions, behavior, and more. It even learns, remembers, and has its own unique intuition.[3]

As someone with two congenital heart defects that can cause heart pain and palpitations, I've had to study various aspects of the physical heart. However, in the process, I became most compelled by the way this "heart-brain" cocreates the magic of our emotional lives—our capacity to feel and connect deeply. As we'll explore in later chapters, each emotion we experience—even the painful ones—is part of an intelligent system that has evolved to help us. Amazingly, we even have a set of emotions specifically suited for self-healing and liberation such as joy, gratitude, and curiosity. But compassion is the most powerful of all.

Compassion emerges from a deeply wired biological instinct we have as social animals:[4] the undeniable impulse to respond to another being who is suffering. This makes sense. When we hear genuine cries for help, we often find ourselves compelled to run toward them even if danger could be present. This response likely arises from the evolutionary importance of the integrity of our human relationships and communities over millions of years.

A light bulb went off for me, though, when I realized compassion can respond with the same courage to the cries of suffering *within* us. When it does, it provides the safety and connection we need to heal and transform and restores the integrity and well-being of our psyches. When our self-compassion matures, it becomes more than a momentary response. It evolves into a lasting refuge within us that can withstand the depths of suffering while soothing and nourishing us. From this place, we can listen and respond wisely to not just our own cries but the cries of the world—without becoming overburdened.

The brilliance of compassion is in its capacity to meet suffering in a healthy way—a competence that is so crucial in our lives today. I know for me, if it weren't for discovering the wisdom of the heart, I would have fallen into addiction and depression long ago, crushed under the weight of the world around me. Indeed, regaining fluency in the art of compassion isn't just a feel-good exercise or a social nicety. It's not a side practice for when we have time. It's a mental health necessity for each of us.

A Wounded World

The deeper I went on my healing and spiritual journey, the more I realized that my view of the world was incomplete. A typical survey of the state of the world describes the dynamic movements of people and nations, energy and money, goods and services. We see what people are doing or saying and the decisions they're making. However, this is just a tiny fraction of what's happening—each of us has a deep and rich psychic world within us, and lurking in these depths is a potent substance, perhaps the most powerful on the planet: the personal and collective wounding we hold.

When I use the word *wounding*, I'm pointing to the impact of a hurtful event or interaction on the psyche(s) of an individual or group *that continues in some form into the present*. When I say that we hold it, I'm referring to the myriad ways this suffering endures, whether as an active emotional process, a behavioral pattern, or an outlook. It may even show up in our physical health.[5] Recognizing this dimension of ourselves means acknowledging that we are deeply affected by life, and those effects are not dead and gone but often live on within us.

All these painful impacts and the wounds they engender exist on spectrums of intensity and frequency.[6] The more intense and frequent, the deeper they burrow into our nervous systems and condition our perception and behavior from a subtle personality quirk to a debilitating mental illness. Healing exists on parallel spectrums, unfolding in accordance with the intensity and frequency of compassionate attention our wounds receive. For example, a wound can be fully healed and the conditioning it created transformed. It can be partially healed leaving behind a tender scar. Or it can remain open and actively painful, deeply affecting the way we navigate our lives.

According to a World Mental Health Survey, over 70 percent of adults worldwide have experienced intense traumatic events in their lifetime.[7] In addition, everyone naturally experiences a multitude of less severe wounds that condition them. There are wounds I've received from others, like someone maligning or abandoning me. There are wounds I've received from the culture, like messages about my body image or fitting into social roles. There are wounds I've inflicted on myself, like those of self-criticism and self-neglect. Underneath them all is the spiritual wound of feeling separate from life itself (as I'll speak to in the next section).

When I discovered the extent of my own wounding, I felt discouraged at first. I can assure you, though, it's a foundational aspect of healing and spiritual growth. In insight meditation, looking suffering square in the eye is explicitly where the path starts. Without seeing it, we are not only destined to perpetuate it, but we'll never have the chance to cultivate the self-compassion that heals and liberates us. As hard as life can be, we have the capacity for a richness and depth of heart that only pain can ripen within us.

· ·

It can be relieving to realize that our wounding is not just about us. It has a profound historical and collective dimension. We receive painful conditioning from our ancestors and our shared past[8] as well as from the societal and global systems in the present. We can imagine multiplying the wounds in our lifetime seven billion times for the people of the planet and then again by the thousands of generations of accumulated struggles before us. Then we can organize this suffering into institutions, corporations, governments, and other power structures with immense global influence. With all that, we begin to understand the vast and ancient echo chamber of pain and resulting confusion that reverberates throughout the globe.[9]

This cumulative suffering shows itself everywhere. We can see the prevalence of addictive behaviors and mental health disorders, the overconsumption and overmedication, and the constant conflict and polarization between groups. We witness the greedy actions of corporations or politicians, the wars for power and resources, and the destruction of the environment. All of these things, and more, speak to a deeply distressed collective trying to cope with their pain.[10] In fact, we could say that much of our collective modern culture is simply a manifestation of the suffering we carry.

From this perspective, the state of the world is no mystery. It is unfolding according to the laws of human nature, a sort of psychological physics that governs our evolution. The accumulation of pain and its results have occurred because the cycle of wounding has largely remained unbroken. Without the intervention of mindfulness and compassion, one wound leads to the next in quick succession, and the patterns of our conditioning play out as predictably as a computer program. With them, we can not only stop the progression but also reverse it. In the same way, the application of mindfulness and compassion leads lawfully to our own healing and, eventually, healing for all beings.

Realizing this, my own path took on new meaning and focus. There weren't "bad" or "evil" people out there, just those that were deeply hurt— and I was one of them. Scooping out the suffering from my own heart was also bailing water from our collective sinking ship. I figured that with each bucket I dumped, it was more likely our ship would stay afloat amid the waves of change to come. I might have even inspired others to do the same.

However, eventually I noticed that if I didn't also work to repair the root cause of my own suffering—my unique crack in the hull, so to speak— both myself and the world would just keep filling back up with wounding. I couldn't just soothe my symptoms. I had to address the underlying disease.

The Hidden Illness

Even in today's world, I've learned there's always a silver lining. While our wounding can be deeply painful, it also reveals a redeeming principle of nature: *we're affected because life is interconnected.* If it weren't, we couldn't be hurt at all. Recognizing this truth offers a profound advantage and inspiration on healing and spiritual paths. Not only can we leverage the nourishment of our supportive connections—to healthy parts of ourselves, others who love us, the magic of the natural world, etc.—but we're reminded that, no matter where we are, we are never alone or separate. Our innate bond with life itself is fundamentally fortifying.

What's more, our unique wounding actually marks the inner trail back to a place of safety and supportive connection inside each of us. By tracking the scent of suffering within us and tending skillfully to our wounds, we can each come to recover what I call our *original heart*. This is the unscathed, tender innocence we're born with, buried at our center. This is the place where our individual heart meets the shared heart of all things—a space of profound and unparalleled belonging that is our birthright.

At this time, however, this original inheritance remains hidden away for most of us. And because of this, we often feel profoundly alone. A recent study showed that 58 percent of all Americans—and as many as 79 percent of young people—suffer from loneliness.[11] Doctors, social workers, academics, and scientists have all been sounding the alarm on this epidemic for decades, pointing to the mounting evidence linking loneliness to mental and physical illness.[12]

This is in no small part due to the conditions we are living in: we inhabit an atomized society, distanced from nature and filled with social polarization, individualism, and addiction to devices and screens. However, there's an even more fundamental and widespread source of loneliness than any of this: our disconnection from ourselves and the spiritual dimension of life. This disconnection creates an insecurity and sense of lack that permeate our lives and our culture as a whole. We can attempt to remedy it by seeking out new people, places, things, or even spiritual practices—as most do. While such strategies may help for a time, they can't actually make us feel like we are enough or are whole. Healing this wound of separation is an inside job, as it arises from a deeper self-protective mechanism that is buried in the basic formation of our psychological selves—one we unwittingly sustain.

· ·

When I was born, the doctors told my mother my heart was on the wrong side of my body. It took a moment for them to realize that my lung had been punctured and my organs had shifted dramatically. I was taken immediately to an incubator and kept there for seven days. On the last night before I would undergo a risky operation, my lung miraculously healed, and I could return to my family. I was lucky, but the experience shattered my sense of security for decades.

That was my story. But for almost all of us, it was in the early moments or years of our lives that we received the first wounds we couldn't heal. They could have been any number of things for each of us, from a traumatic injury to an early illness, from an unkind caregiver to an early divorce. It doesn't have to be big: even a simple lack of attention or touch can significantly affect us.[13]

For some of us, it was an intergenerational wound unconsciously imparted to us by our parents or close family. This is perhaps most clear in the cases of historical oppression or violence in a lineage (i.e., holocaust, slavery, war, etc.). The field of epigenetics presents convincing evidence that traumatic life experiences can be passed down through changes in our DNA.[14] We remember in the cells of our bodies.

These are what I call our *original wounds*. They are the first times that we experienced substantial physical or emotional pain *in the absence of a felt sense of supportive connection and safety*. At the moment of impact, and perhaps long afterward, we felt alone and scared in our pain. For whatever reason, we didn't feel the presence of a loving and reliable caregiver or a nurturing environment. This meant we couldn't transform, release, or ground the emotional energy from our systems like we are wired to do. Instead, we initiated a protective internal process that sequestered our pain, fractured our psyches, and left us chronically anxious. The more traumatic and earlier our wound was, and the more insecure the relationships and environment it happened within, the more deeply we tended to suppress and disconnect.[15]

In fairness, we did the only thing we knew to do. We stowed the pain deep in our bodies and constructed a protective psychic barrier over it. The instinct was perfect and genius in its infantile way. It protected us both from our own pain we couldn't integrate and from future impacts that would now never again touch the most tender and precious place within us.

Absent the arrival of a profoundly safe connection—to a caregiver, the environment, or the essence of life—our protective barrier stayed firm, and the fracture remained. Seeing no other recourse, we did it again and again with each subsequent wound. We couldn't see this approach had a fatal flaw: the barriers we crafted and the pain we stored obscured our original heart. We began feeling separate from others, nature, and life itself. The instinct was to protect ourselves, but tragically it blocked our access to true belonging. It solidified the idea that pain couldn't be safe, and therefore, the world could never be either.

Without the influence of a countervailing force, once this process begins, it can snowball. As we age, we can separate our minds from our bodies and retreat to distant, rational, materialistic worldviews. We can detach from the immediacy of our experience and construct a sense of self like a fortress. We can shift all our focus to potential outside threats and desires and leave our inner lives behind. And we can readily distance ourselves from the raw, organic realities of nature such as sickness, old age, and death and miss the important messages they have for our lives.

Even though these strategies are *intended* to help, they only trigger us more profoundly and lock our nervous systems into activation. The classic triggered responses of fight, flight, or freeze can actually become our default, creating any number of chronic mental/emotional conditions from light free-floating anxiety to deep destabilizing turmoil. Needless to say, the effects on all our internal systems and our external relationships are profound and lasting.

In this way, all our suffering today can be seen as deriving from those original wounds and our runaway responses to them. In a painful instant, we lost trust and turned away from life. We left behind our ancient belonging to all things. We unwittingly traded a lasting refuge for a limited, temporary, and isolating one. If only someone or something had been there to embrace our pain unconditionally, perhaps we could have grown and healed without ever leaving our original hearts. But there wasn't, and we did.

Of course, we were innocent and overwhelmed. We were surrounded by those who had long ago made the same bargain. However, there is part of us that remembers what we lost and hopes we'll return to rediscover it, to heal what we didn't have the means to then. Indeed, this moment now is not so different than the first moment we turned away so long ago. We can courageously choose anew to forgo the limited protection of separation for the deepest protection of interconnection.

• •

Just like with wounding, these self-protection mechanisms are not uniquely ours. They're just as much historical and collective, amplified over thousands of years and multiplied across the human community. When we haven't been able to integrate a traumatic event as a people—wars, genocides, famines, and so on—we've found ways to stow the pain in our lineages and communities, as well as throw it back on our enemies in revenge. We've tried to form protective barriers through countless means, from defense and weapon systems to technologies of comfort, convenience, and distraction. We've constructed dogmas and moral hierarchies, concocted elaborate mythologies of difference, and persecuted others over and again.

By doing so, we may regain a marginal sense of protection but only reinforce our community's isolation, further fracturing human society and distancing it from the natural world. We gain the temporary protection of getting the upper hand but lose the lasting safety of collaboration. We find ourselves farther and farther from the harmonizing recognition of interconnection that, if collectively realized, could finally liberate us.

I trust that such great confusion, however, could have only happened from an equal amount of pain. I can imagine the original wounds of our species echoing through our collective heritage. Humanity has undergone unimaginable hardships, from cataclysms to ice ages to countless other natural disasters. We've suffered the innumerable small cuts of survival, sickness, old age, death, and the constant loss of what we love. Life as a human being on this planet has always been tumultuous, and the resulting trauma still exists as a memory in our bones.

I find it quite encouraging, however, that there's something more potent than any past conditioning we might hold. It is the presence we wield in this moment. When we turn our compassionate attention inward and heal ourselves individually, we realize just how close the whole world is to healing, too. We may not need to apply complex, herculean measures to undo our old collective confusion. We may simply need to soothe the ancient impulse that keeps each of us restless and reactive in this very moment.

An Ancient Drive

Our evolutionary past has given us a blessing and cast upon us a curse. It has wired deep into our bones an aversion to what is unpleasant.[16] This drive to distance ourselves from pain has been critical in our evolution. It has helped us flee danger, defend ourselves, and innovate new tools for survival. However, when this aversion remains the primary force driving our daily pursuits, it can create significant psychological challenges. This becomes especially apparent in healing and spirituality.

In Buddhism and the practice of insight meditation, aversion is one of the three unwholesome roots of action that are seen to perpetuate suffering—the other two being desire and delusion. In the broadest sense, aversion is simply a "moving away from" or creating distance from the unpleasant aspects of life. Its goal is to protect us from pain of any type in any way it can. On an emotional level, aversion is what gives rise to the protective mechanisms described in the last section, as well as the common fight, flight, and freeze responses. It generates the typical emotions of anger, anxiety, and longing—even indifference. It even motivates the search for pleasure and fuels our addictions.

While some of these responses to life can be very useful, when they are running on autopilot, they perpetually keep us restless and anxious. We compulsively control our circumstances and fixate on how to prevent future pain. This hypervigilance can burden our nervous systems, relationships, and work in the world, making it harder to relax, open up, and experience wholesome emotions like curiosity, gratitude, or joy.[17] All this is what I call the first-order effects of aversion, based on the impulse to protect ourselves from *outside* threats.

Curiously, at some point in our evolution, we acquired the ability to direct aversive energy against internal threats as well. We became able to push away, or even attack, our own emotional pain through self-criticism, suppression, and other means. This unique evolution may explain our species' ubiquitous capacity to hold wounding in our bodies—not letting it shake free as many other animals do.[18]

. .

Self-aversion is a second-order effect of aversion: one that is actively directed toward parts of our sense of self. Here we are not just defending against outside threats or distracting ourselves from a painful feeling. We effectively try to expel whole parts of ourselves or attack our worth or validity. It's akin to a psychological autoimmune response that can be subtle or very pronounced.

Self-aversion may arise as individual thought patterns of self-criticism, self-judgment, or even self-hatred. Or it may permeate our sense of self, as in low self-esteem, low self-confidence, or beliefs of inadequacy. Like many of us, I've tried desperately to hide and change aspects of my appearance, suppress my sensitive emotional heart, and forfeit what I loved just to feel loved by another.

Like loneliness, this debilitating habit of self-aversion is another pandemic of massive proportions today. In fact, they are related, since when we feel alone, we often end up turning on ourselves, and when we turn on ourselves, we often end up feeling alone.[19] Naturally, both have been linked to the development of various mental health challenges[20] and tend to make healing much harder[21] and spiritual insight much more elusive.

If we watch our hearts and minds closely, virtually all of us will likely notice some form of self-aversion. In one recent study conducted by a clothing company, respondents reported thinking an average of three to four negative things about their bodies daily.[22] In another series of surveys by professors at the University of Texas, up to 70 percent of students' thoughts were found to be negative, and one-third of those were concerned with their own inferiority.[23]

This prevalence is due to many factors. Of course, the messages of caregivers, friends, and the culture have a significant influence. From less-than-kind parenting to bullying at school to the inundation of advertising messages and social media to marginalization and oppression,[24] we are provided with various reasons to feel down about ourselves. However, whether we take it in and perpetuate it internally depends upon our makeup. To the degree we've suppressed early wounds and thus fractured ourselves, we've primed ourselves for insecurity, a contentious inner relationship, and an acute vulnerability to others' perceptions of us.

In addition, in early childhood or any relationship where we are vulnerable or dependent, we often find it safer to blame ourselves over anyone else.[25] Blaming or attacking the other person could result in us losing them or what they provide for us or in punishment. We can do the same with the natural losses in our lives. We don't know who else to blame, so we end up taking personal responsibility for unfortunate circumstances well out of our control. When we do, we burden natural pain with self-blame, making things even heavier.

Once patterns of suppression and self-blame are established, a positive feedback loop begins. We have progressively more motivation to keep our wounds hidden as they become more intimidating *and* we must apply more effort to keep them under wraps. Mounting a resistance of resentment, fear, and ill will toward those feelings or parts of ourselves is a logical solution, but it leads to the third-order effects of aversion.

We attack our own aversive habits. We argue with the voices that criticize us. We spiral into greater and greater degrees of self-conflict, but since we can't escape ourselves, there's no way out. Each layer of reactive distance further separates us from our original heart and its essential goodness. This can even happen in spiritual circles, as people mistakenly try to "conquer their inner demons" instead of seeing them as innocent wounds that need a loving embrace. (I'm certainly guilty of this, as I'll recount in the next chapter.)

In summary, self-aversion can first solidify and amplify our existing wounding, ensuring it stays with us. Second, it can suppress parts of ourselves or behaviors that were perceived to create the pain—stunting our curiosity, creativity, and authenticity. Third, it can ever-widen the felt sense of separation we experience inside, as well as between ourselves and others and life itself. In a societal context, this creates a culture of extreme emotional insecurity and, in turn, volatility. We constantly seek the approval of others while simultaneously tearing others down—both in a hopeless effort to restore wholeness to ourselves.

• •

In my mind, the most glaring problem with the strategy of aversion is simple: I might win a battle, but I always lose the war. I can fight the pain, run from it, or try to ignore it—but I can't escape it. If I'm lucky, I might succeed in evading it for a time. However, my fixation on that goal takes a tremendous toll on every aspect of my life. There have been times it's consumed every part of my life, but nowhere did I see its impacts more clearly than in my journey of healing and spiritual growth.

On its own, pain is just an unpleasant sensation, feeling, or thought in the present moment. When we resist it, however, it evolves into suffering. When we can't heal that suffering, it becomes wounding we hold. Pain is inevitable, but whether it becomes a wound is ultimately up to us.

If we let aversion drive our responses, it unwittingly moves us further away from the very things we seek: a felt sense of safety and connection.

When aversion turns against us, it sabotages the exact vehicle we depend on for our liberation: *us*. It's through our sense of self that we open to the process of healing and insight. It's also through our sense of self that we integrate profound spiritual truths into our daily lives. By distorting our relationship to self, we significantly inhibit our access to the spiritual dimension and its embodied expression in our lives.

In these ways, our aversion to pain is the primary force that sustains suffering and wounding in our consciousness. Self-aversion, in particular—in the way it locks us into painful solitary confinement—is the linchpin of the wounded psychology that prevents healthy transformation. This ripples out from the individual to the collective where, according to the World Health Organization (WHO), one out of every eight people today worldwide struggles with debilitating mental disorders.[26]

The good news is our most essential state is not aversive, but instead, an easeful and loving repose. Saints and spiritual adepts across time and traditions have taught us this in text after text. I personally didn't fully believe this until I could see beneath my own wounds. To reveal this hidden nature, however, I had to radically shift my orientation to pain. I had to learn to make each challenge a catalyst for the maturation of my heart, each wound a teacher and a guide on my way back home.

A Pathway Back Home

For me, the most reassuring message of the spiritual life is that, although we've strayed into confusion, there is a home we can return to. I say "return" because it's a place we all belong to but have forgotten. That's why we long for it. Of course, I'm not speaking of a physical home but instead a home within ourselves and life itself. Now that we have some ideas about what caused us to abandon this inner refuge, we can apply the appropriate remedy and cure this existential estrangement.

To review, pain readily devolves into suffering and wounding when we experience it in the absence of a felt sense of connection and safety. This is because, when we feel disconnected, we feel inherently insecure. This naturally initiates the aversion and self-protection that end up tying us in knots. Conversely, when we feel a supportive connection to ourselves, others, or something greater than us, it engenders a feeling of emotional safety inside, helping our systems to intuitively discharge our present-moment pain and past wounding. This process is an ancient part of our evolution as social animals.[27]

When we were children, we relied heavily on our external environment to sustain our connection and safety. As adults, we now must consciously cultivate it for ourselves—even amid adverse conditions—if we want to heal and feel free. We can connect to people, places, and things in beneficial ways, but there is no connection more potentially liberating than the one with ourselves—and life itself—in the present moment. This self-connection is enhanced through the cultivation and application of the natural healing emotions of our own hearts. The more wholeheartedly we invest in this relationship with ourselves and life, the deeper our sense of safety and connection, and thus our capacity for healing and insight.

In this process, self-compassion is without comparison, as it is the opposite of aversion in our consciousness. By welcoming instead of pushing away our pain, our defenses are disarmed, including all our self-aversion. Piece by piece, this softens our protective strategies, transforms the wounding underneath, and melts the feelings of insecurity and separation. We apply the process to every layer of our psyche—including all the parts that don't feel compassionate or safe—all the way back to the first time we turned away (i.e., our original wounds). Eventually, all parts of us are reintegrated, first into our psyches and then into the fabric of life itself.

To approach ourselves this way, however, we must first draw on the miracle of our self-reflective consciousness. Counterintuitively, the first step toward inner connection is actually a step back. We "unfuse" from our present-moment experience, witnessing it without interfering. This is called mindfulness, and it is the foundational act of conscious reconnection to our bodies, hearts, and minds—as well as the first potential glimpse of inner safety.

Amazingly, this simple act of mindfulness alone has been shown to bring myriad emotional, mental, and physical health benefits.[28] In healing, it's essential because it allows us to finally step out of the cycles of wounding for a moment. We begin to see what we've been doing, and true choice in what we think, say, and do becomes possible again. Most importantly, we can decide how we *respond* to what's within and around us—with aversion or with compassion.

For example, we might simply stop. We might breathe out long and slow. We might give ourselves a break and stop trying to keep it all together for a moment. Life can be hard, but our habitual hypervigilance makes it harder. Even in that little pause, we might naturally feel more connected to everything around us *by doing less instead of more*. We might feel a spark of gratitude to realize our systems intuitively incline toward well-being, healing, and insight—if we let them.

As the journey continues, mindfulness keeps revealing more suffering while compassion deepens our intimacy with it, creating safety and connection inside. Eventually, instead of staying a distant observer of our experience, we warmly and wholeheartedly embrace it until no separation remains. From here, our wounds begin to reveal their deeper, spacious, and radiant nature.

The effects of these simple but profound acts reverberate through our whole interconnected system. Our internal world begins to relax and clarify. The doors and the windows open up and the fresh air rushes in. We feel at home in ourselves again, but this time without any limitations. A renewed energy of authentic creativity and joy animates our lives.

· ·

It's wonderful that compassion has become a popular topic today. However, it's a concept that can be easily misunderstood. All too often, compassion is equated with what we *do*, as in "doing the right thing," or with who we *are*, as in "being a good or virtuous person." It often becomes a moral judgment of character and action tied to our self-image and social esteem. We habitually fuse it to an agenda or an outcome, using it to fix or right something in the world. In other words, compassion often manifests as an idea and an ideal and escapes us as an *embodied experience*.

At its core, compassion is much purer and simpler than we think. It's the spontaneous alchemy of two ingredients, care and suffering, comingling in an open human heart. This care is not an anxious worry. It's an attentiveness toward wellness—a mixture of mindfulness, goodwill, and empathy, to be exact. When it notices suffering, the result is a trembling resonance of sincere warmth that emanates through the emotional field.

Like observing a rare animal in nature, we must slow down to see and appreciate it. When we witness it in its raw and natural state, with all preconceptions set aside, it's nothing short of exquisite. While it certainly may inspire thought and deed, it precedes both. It lives in the present moment as an embodied feeling. True compassion is not preoccupied with who, why, or even how, but with intimacy itself.

This intimacy with pain appears in *compassion*'s Latin linguistic roots. The two parts of the word mean to "suffer with." In the world today, however, "suffering with" is not adequate to fully heal and liberate us. There are simply too many cries for help from every direction. Without additional support, our compassion can eventually turn to anxiety, overwhelm, and eventually burnout or compassion fatigue. We need the assistance of wisdom.

For example, buttressed by mindfulness, compassion doesn't collapse into distraction or sentimentality. Imbued with nonclinging, it doesn't tighten into forcing things to be a certain way. Braced by equanimity, it doesn't avoid empathetic pain by escaping into pity. Suffused with the resilience of interconnection, it remains vulnerable but doesn't succumb to pressure or manipulation. With supports like these, our compassion can remain strong, balanced, and focused. The synergy of wisdom and compassion within us can create what I call *true compassion*, a concept we'll explore further in chapter 5.

We are all born with the capacity to care. However, the wounds we carry and the protective coverings we grow over them often curtail this natural feeling. Therefore, just because we have the capacity doesn't mean it will necessarily be easy to feel or access our compassion. To bring it forth into its truest expression requires devoted attention. The good news is that our natural capacity resurfaces and strengthens with each wound we heal. So things get easier and easier as we go. All this being said, it will be hard to fully appreciate the real jewel of the compassionate heart until we've become students of it within the laboratory of our own hearts and minds. And this is precisely what we'll do together in this book.

• •

The opportunity to heal and discover ourselves is an immense privilege. In our world today, billions are consumed by simply maintaining the very necessities of life. Many are stuck in circumstances too unsafe or unstable to open to their wounds. If we have even a few minutes a day to devote to ourselves, if we have even a semblance of safety and stability in our lives, we don't want to miss the chance of a liberated life. Every bit we help ourselves, we are that much more able to help others do the same.

Many of my students are baffled at how quickly patterns they've struggled with for decades can transform by changing how they relate to them. For example, a struggling meditation practice can often become an easeful refuge by simply welcoming instead of pushing away our thoughts. A nagging pattern of self-doubt can transform into a courageous companion by realizing that it was always just trying to help us. A lifelong anxiety or depression can shift from an untreatable illness to a doorway into our deepest freedom by seeing it as our guide and teacher. One of my students—a mother of four—went from feeling spirituality was always out of reach to finally integrating it in her everyday life. These transformations—and many more—are always *so* close, yet we can't recognize that until we take those first steps.

I know I struggled with cultural messages that compassion was too soft or too sensitive. For years, I also believed the spiritual messages that compassion was too preoccupied with the illusory concerns of the self. I had doubts about my capacity or whether I needed it. Naturally, our illness rejects the medicine at first. We're afraid to feel what's there and face what it might mean for our lives. We feel awkward; the practice seems forced. But it soon softens and opens. So notice what you feel *right now*, and welcome that as normal and expected.

The theory and practices in this book are designed to transform us, but in our own way and at our own pace. No matter where we're at on our path—whether just stepping on or many decades in—the nature of mindfulness and self-compassion is to meet us there and then guide us to the next steps as we're ready. We can use them as a topical treatment for the scrapes of life or a powerful tonic for the deepest ailments. When turned to in conjunction with a larger spiritual path and understanding as described in this book, they can ferry us into the most liberating spiritual insights. Join the process wherever you are and take it however far you'd like to go.

Our wounding isn't our fault, but it is our responsibility. No one else can do the healing for us. In the end, we'll be indescribably grateful that we put in the work. Each of us has a perfectly unique configuration of conditioning—unique circumstances, perspectives, wounds, aspirations, and fears all layered one upon the other just so. When our exquisite uniqueness is finally met with true compassion—when it's fully seen, understood, cared for, and supported—we all respond in very similar ways. It's like a key in a lock. Our hearts fall open. And no one is more suited to offer that to yourself than you.

Summary, Practices, and Prompts

CHAPTER SUMMARY

- The world is in crisis because we are all wounded and act from it unknowingly.
- We exacerbate and perpetuate this wounding through our aversion to it, which further amplifies the conflict and disconnection within us.
- Mindfulness can instead reveal the pain we hold, while self-compassion can embrace it, restoring safety and connection and initiating the process of healing and insight.
- This process, when sincere, not only restores wholeness and harmony to our psyches but can eventually do the same for others and the world at large.

JOURNAL PROMPTS

In the journal prompt exercises throughout this book, the instruction is to write freely without overthinking. In this way, it is a potent opportunity for self-discovery, often revealing aspects of ourselves we wouldn't otherwise see. There's no right or wrong answer here; leaving a question blank is fine if you don't know. Just keep your pen moving for a few minutes with each question. Take a short pause and a mindful breath between each.

This process is designed to help you digest and integrate the content of the book in a more personal way. Some of the insights will be immediately applicable in your life. Others will inform how you engage with the guided practices introduced in part 2. Still, others may become a valuable reference at some future point in your journey. I recommend dedicating a small journal to this pursuit and keeping it with this book.

- What are the primary emotions you feel as you consider the state of the world? How do you often react to those emotions when they arise? What is one habitual behavior these feelings can lead to?
- What are one or two core wounds that you know you still hold? How do they still affect and condition you today? What primary emotions do

they engender? *Alternative query: What is your original wound—the first time you turned away from life?*

- Do you feel disconnected or alone somewhere inside? Do you sometimes feel you don't belong or have a true sense of home inside? If so, how do you experience that feeling in your body? What is one habitual behavior that feeling can lead to?
- What parts of yourself do you not like, blame for their inadequacy, or wish would go away? What do you fear might happen if those parts or patterns were allowed to be? Do these fears stem from a past wound, and if so, what might that be?
- How do you feel about trying self-compassion? Are there any hesitations, judgments, or forms of resistance that arise for you? If so, what do you fear might happen if you dived into the practice?

GUIDED PRACTICE

The end-of-chapter practices in this book are of two types. The first is *mindful self-reflection,* an intentional and conscious engagement with important reflective questions related to healing and spiritual life—a technique further described in chapter 5. In particular, these brief practices are designed to help you further understand and explore that chapter's journal prompts through a guided process. The second type are *experiential practices,* which are short guided meditations designed to help you embody key pieces of wisdom from each chapter in a direct and nonconceptual way.

The information and experience gathered through these end-of-chapter practices can support a deeper integration of the book's content to better prepare us to wholeheartedly engage in the core progression of Dharma of Healing practices described part 2 of the book. To get the most out of them, create a quiet and undistracted place in your home to explore this process. It's best not to write during the meditations but to have your journal close by for written reflection afterward.

• •

You can listen to both the end-of-chapter practices and the core practices at www.justinmichelsondharma.com/thedharmaofhealing/practices and at www.shambhala.com/dharmaofhealingpractices.

2

MINDFULNESS ALONE
IS NOT ENOUGH

In the last chapter, we covered the foundational causes of our suffering as well as basic tools for personal and collective liberation. Now, we'll explore in depth why emotional healing is essential on the spiritual path. We'll examine a series of traditional spiritual teachings and instructions and consider how each can conspire with our wounding to actually create more suffering instead of less. Then we'll learn how the addition of self-compassion can transform these approaches into effective and efficient agents of healing and insight.

· ·

Mindfulness has always been a foundational aspect of Buddhist practice and philosophy. As described in the last chapter, it helps us direct and focus our attention so that we can discover what's happening in our own heart-minds. However, as Buddhism has grown in popularity in the West, mindfulness has been extracted from the tradition and taught as a secular technique. It has been incorporated into countless areas from medicine to sports to business boardrooms to military training programs.

For many of us on the healing and spiritual paths, mindfulness has become a central technique in our practices. It's often the first tool people learn in various styles of meditation, as well as in yoga and other healing arts. Even in insight meditation, it often takes a dominant role in teaching and practice. This makes sense, as it adapts easily to Western culture and has numerous immediate benefits. However, in the long term, mindfulness alone is rarely enough to transform us—and in its traditional Buddhist context, it isn't meant to; it's just one tool in the toolbox.

For example, the nonjudgmental nature of mindfulness allows it to easily coexist alongside unexamined beliefs, unhelpful habits, and even unethical behavior. It also readily partners with the strongly intellectual approach to self-improvement and spirituality common in the West. Moreover, while it can be clear-seeing, it can also be cold, impartial, distant. It doesn't require a warmth of heart to operate.

For these reasons and many more we'll explore, mindfulness is best returned to its original place within a family of techniques and qualities. Compassion and other heart qualities have always been essential to grounding mindfulness in intimacy and integrity. Without the heart engaged, we more easily confuse the spiritual teachings and instructions we hear. This can not only impede our healing and insight but, in some cases, cause us and others direct harm.

It's important to note that, thus far, I've used the word *heart* primarily to reference the emotional aspect of human experience. However, I've also used it to point toward the essential goodness at our core. With the word *mind*, I've been alluding to our powerful, cognitive gift of thought. The two, however, are inexorably intertwined. Hence, as is traditional in the Buddhist teachings that insight meditation draws from,[1] when I'm referring to the psyche as a whole encompassing both emotions and thoughts, I'll begin to use the hyphenated word *heart-mind*.

A Rude Awakening

My personal journey with meditation began when I was fifteen. My mother invited me to a six-week class just for teens. The timing was perfect for me. Without hesitation, I gathered up my high school friends and we went. I still vividly remember that first session. It was a revelation for my high school mind: *I can be satisfied by just watching my breath? I don't have to try to fit in, do everything "right," or become what others want me to be?? I can discover who I actually am. Wow,* I thought, *this is great!*

Enamored, I stuck with it, and the next seven or so years of practice was what I might call the honeymoon phase or beginner's mind phase of my journey. All I wanted to do was meditate. I could barely stay in college. I explored various Buddhist traditions, longer and longer silent retreats, and living/working at retreat centers. My main practice was just to sit still and watch my breath, and despite its simplicity, it was showing me powerful truths of interconnection, impermanence, and peace. Meditation felt like the golden tool that could solve everything—endless in richness and depth.

Gradually, though, the newness of the practice and its grand results began to shift. I had burned through the first tank of my youthful, masculine energy. I was entering a new phase of my path—what I might call the revealing phase. Unbeknownst to me, the practice had been peeling back the layers of my heart-mind, and deeper, more painful emotional and mental patterns and experiences started to emerge.

For example, underneath my curiosity and passion for the practice emerged anxious, impatient, and self-judgmental parts of myself that started to get in the driver's seat. Meditation was so valuable and important to me as well as to helping the world, and I had devoted all this time . . . so I felt it had to go well. Even though I was tired, I had to keep trying to become my ideal self or else I somehow wouldn't be OK any longer.

Meanwhile, unexplainable emotional experiences such as deep fear and anxiety were beginning to arise in my experience without invitation. From my vantage point at the time, they usually felt like tenacious pockets of body tension—a relentless tangle in my gut or a claustrophobic tightness in my chest. Then my own fear and resistance to those sensations would pile on with force, and my nervous system would seize up. I would feel trapped.

My mindfulness merged with a hypervigilance, and I tracked the tension intensely. I knew its every movement and my reactions to it. I applied all the wisdom teachings I could remember. My strategies could manage it, but as the months and years went on, I became more exhausted. Even when I tried to do the opposite and practice effortless or choiceless attention, my system would gradually end up freezing in fear or gently dissociating. I didn't realize my anxiety wasn't just the object of my attention but had commandeered my mindful observation itself. In trying to help, it was actually reactivating and amplifying my core wounds that *the world isn't safe*; *I'm trapped*; *I'm going to get in trouble*; *I'm alone . . .*

In the Dharma communities I was in at the time, no teacher seemed to be able to say anything meaningful to help me with my struggle. Instead,

I was often applauded for my "good mindfulness." The techniques would relieve some tension but only temporarily. Underneath I suffered silently, feeling defeated, stuck, alone, and scared. Then on a monthlong silent retreat, after weeks of managing this body tension, a newer, younger teacher said, "Maybe you should see a somatic therapist."

Admittedly, I didn't act on the suggestion at the time, since it seemed to be a way of conceding failure or defeat, of admitting the practice didn't work. It would end up taking a dual crisis of a debilitating illness and an explosive intimate relationship to bring me to my knees. Only then was I humble enough to ask for support in a new way. But that was just the beginning.

The first years of therapy were still quite awkward and disjointed. The therapist would guide me into a personal dialogue with the tension in my body, even encouraging visualization of the pain. I would emerge from each session moved in a powerful way but also not quite believing in it. Was I just imagining the voices I heard or images I saw from my childhood— even from my birth? From my meditation background, I had picked up that thoughts and images were just mental fabrications of an illusory self that I could let go of. Now, in order to move through my crisis, I was being asked to take my stories and memories personally and seriously. Naturally, I had great doubts and, on several occasions, almost didn't go back.

However, like a hidden image emerging from a Magic Eye picture or a high-powered microscope coming into focus, the tension I had been holding slowly revealed a whole subconscious world. It wasn't just a passing phenomenon but a series of living, breathing, personal experiences seared into my body that had been trying to get my attention. These wounded parts of me weren't concerned with the fulfillment of my spiritual path; they were still in the heat of a decades-old, life-or-death battle for the safety and protection of my psychological self. They didn't need my rational assessment; they needed the sincerest and most unconditionally loving presence I could muster.

This became the aspect of the therapy I could begin to fully trust. I knew there couldn't be anything wrong with compassion for my terror. In fact, it seemed to allow me to feel a depth of my own pain I never could from mindful observation alone. The internal dialogues and visualizations ended up not being a distraction but instead a conduit for both deep feeling and sincere self-compassion. I realized I had only dismissed thoughts in my practice because I was afraid of their cunning and quick power over me. In Buddhist terms, I had been so averse to my own delusions, I had never been eager to explore them, let alone heal them. Now, I began to trust my intuition in the healing process.

Merging my Buddhist practice with somatic therapy and Internal Family Systems brought me slowly into a third phase of my practice: the integration phase. I needed to make sense of the spiritual truths I'd experienced *along with* the painful wounds I had discovered and the messiness of my everyday life. But the process wasn't easy. I had to surrender many of the transcendent spiritual ideas and monastic ideals I had clung to. I had to learn to heal as I built a new business and committed to a new relationship. I had to learn to honor the insights that come from living within the world and realize they could be as powerful as any long silent retreat if I let them. And, in time, they were.

The very suffering that had frozen my spiritual practice and brought me to therapy began to ripen the capacities of my heart-mind to love and showed me the essential companion to mindfulness: *compassion.* As this personal and engaged approach to healing gradually restored my internal safety and connection, I was relieved to discover older spiritual insights returning. A natural radiance started to reemerge, but this time right in the middle of my life, shining through my work and relationships. Without the preoccupation of feeling unsafe and alone, my heart's capacity for joy, gratitude, playfulness, wonder, and love awoke. There was the essential awareness, the luminous nature I had sought after, only now it included the whole of the mind and body and emanated through the unified field of the heart. This marked an important shift in my ongoing journey.

• •

A key purpose of spiritual practice is to humble us. One insight after another reveals the confusion we have built our life on without even knowing it. In my case, I thought I had had a "good childhood" and an uneventful ancestry—nothing to see there. Instead, I held a complex world of hurt recorded in the cells of my body and through my lineage. I didn't realize that, from the moment of my traumatic birth, I had never felt safe in my body or in this world. I didn't realize that after my early childhood, I had never felt safe with people again. I didn't realize that every influence and every wound I had left an imprint on my heart—creating patterns that tried to protect me but actually hijacked my authentic responses to life. I had spent my life unconsciously trying to restore a safety and connection I had lost at the beginning, but in all the wrong ways. That is, until I met the Dharma and then, finally, devoted myself to true compassion.

Today, as I teach the Dharma, I try to help others avoid the mistakes I made and see the things I couldn't a little sooner. I know my healing process didn't have to be as confusing, painful, and prolonged as it was. However, fulfilling this task as a teacher has proved more difficult than I imagined. We are all masters at obfuscation. Depending on our personality, how we practice, and our historical makeup, it can be many decades before we truly see the wounds we hold—if we ever do.

This isn't our fault. It's just the nature of things. Wounding is the water we swim in. Thus, we naturally transfer the coping mechanisms we use for our lives to our spiritual practices or the idea of spirituality itself. For example, even though I initially relished meditation as a refuge from the ideas of "doing it right," only a handful of years later they resurfaced right in the middle of my practice. In judging and evaluating myself, I became both the perpetrator and victim of my past pain, taking on the actions of those that hurt me. Only when the maladaptive strategies finally and completely wore me out—exacerbating many other wounds along the way—could I finally consider the deeper pain underneath.

Many people come to me thinking they're not "good" at meditation, but being "good" at meditation—like being able to focus for long periods—doesn't necessarily give you any advantage. You can become attached to elevated spiritual experiences and self-images and use the practice as an escape. In fact, it's often better to be a "terrible" meditator. Then, you come into direct intimate contact with the healing work that needs to be done. You have to address your low self-esteem, your anxious and distracted mind, and meet your longing to be free. You can't use meditation as a way to get over yourself.

We have to understand that mindfulness, in its essence, isn't a vehicle that takes us somewhere or makes us become someone. It's just a mirror. In its deepest clarity, mindfulness can show us the radiant nature of consciousness. But it often more strongly reflects back exactly what we bring to it: the conditioned habits we constantly employ that make our lives heavier and harder. Sitting with the reflection of our own messy heart-minds, we then have to cultivate the inner capacities to grow with them.

• •

Whatever it looks like for each of us, when aversion to pain combines with spirituality, we are likely to create our own unique flavor of spiritual suffering. If we don't actively incorporate emotional healing into spirituality, we are likely to use our practice to avoid or resist our own wounding somehow. To put it another way: if we don't see the psychological and spiritual dimensions of ourselves as deeply interdependent, then we are likely to miss something important.

This tendency to use spiritual ideas, teachings, or practices to skirt around our emotional pain is a well-known phenomenon. It's called *spiritual bypassing*. When we use such teachings to bolster our self-image or status, it's called *spiritual materialism*. As spiritual ideas such as mindfulness proliferate in Western culture, we can witness some particularly flagrant examples of bypassing and materialism. However, if we look with humility, we can see the same patterns appear more subtly in our own minds: We underestimate or deny the effects of our wounds on our present-day reality. We devalue or dispute their relevance in our spiritual life. We don't admit our human shortcomings or allow others to support us. We think we should be able to meditate away our needs. We easily see ourselves as different than others, knowing more than them, because we've devoted ourselves to healing or spirituality. While these strategies are attempts to protect ourselves, they, of course, only make us more vulnerable to harming ourselves and others. We don't need to be ashamed of them. Instead, they are opportunities for compassion and beneficial connection.

In the next section, we'll explore how certain spiritual teachings and instructions can contribute to this habit of avoiding our wounding. To start, we might ask ourselves: *Why do we meditate or do any healing practice in the first place? Is it because we want to get rid of the pain or the person we are or hope it makes the world a less painful place? Or is it because we care about that pain, person, and world regardless? What if we woke up tomorrow and couldn't practice or heal any further: could we still be OK as we are?* The answers to these questions can help us begin to discover the roles healing and spirituality are playing in our psyche and how we can mature our approach.

The Trauma of Dharma

The search for deeper happiness in our lives is natural and necessary. Engaging in it is paramount to not just our well-being but that of the world. While all spiritual traditions speak to this, insight meditation occupies a special place in my heart, as it so thoroughly details the beauty and pain of the human predicament. It also boldly declares that the end of unnecessary suffering—a true and lasting inner peace—is possible for all of us.

Rooted in Theravada Buddhism, the teachings describe the mechanics of our suffering and the art of liberating ourselves from it in various ways. The cause of our suffering is often explained as arising from craving, which can be broken down into desire, aversion, and delusion. Simply put, desire is the wanting of things we don't have; aversion is the not-wanting of things we do have; and delusion is not knowing what we have—or a lack of attentiveness. In this book, I argue that, especially when exploring the meeting place of healing and spirituality, aversion is the most important form of craving we must heal. The act of resisting our pain (aversion) naturally prevents us from knowing our pain (delusion) and, in turn, we easily get lost seeking solutions outside of ourselves (desire).

While these ways of relating to life are very natural, they are declared not to be inevitable. Instead, the tradition offers a series of practices and perspectives to transform these patterns and thereby end unnecessary suffering. Most often, the core teachings invite us to see the impermanence, the impersonal nature, and/or the limited satisfaction of the experiences of each present moment. In doing so, the heart-mind becomes more able to release its preoccupations, experience a deeper spiritual refuge, and find peace amid life's challenges—even sickness, old age, and death. Essentially, true happiness comes through "nonclinging" or letting go.

These core teachings are deeply profound and timeless in nature. However, when interpreted through the wounded minds of modern practitioners, we can overlook the emotional dynamics that underlie and perpetuate the craving—creating unintended results. In this section, I speak to the theoretical concepts and practice instructions we can receive in the

Dharma or in other spiritual paths and why they can lead to further confusion or imbalance within us. Then, through the lens of compassion, I evolve a more heart-based vernacular for the modern spiritual seeker.

THE END OF SUFFERING

The most basic place we can get confused in the healing journey or spiritual path is within the fundamental emphasis on *ending suffering*—a priority that is particularly strong within Buddhism. This teaching speaks to our universal longing for freedom, reaffirming that it's possible for us and motivating us to discover it. However, it also speaks to the parts of us that desperately want to avoid or escape any additional pain. Ironically, we often use the goal of ending suffering to justify overlooking the suffering that's already embedded within us.

Personally, I find a better place to start is with *understanding* suffering, intimately and personally. To do so, we have to walk with curiosity through the heart of it. *What gives rise to this thought or emotion? What unmet need is it expressing? What are the effects of various ways of responding to it?*

Paradoxically, what we'll discover is that as long as we're trying to get rid of suffering, it will never end. Hence to "end suffering," we have to first come to terms with it thoroughly. Then we are free to relate to it in heartfelt ways that can actually heal and transform it.

AWAKENING AND ENLIGHTENMENT

On the spiritual journey, we hear about awakening and enlightenment. We also hear about elevated states of bliss and ecstasy. From my own experience, I know these positive potentials can be very inspiring at times, but I also know how they can lead to additional harm and suffering. Just as we can run from what pains us, we can run toward relief in a goal-oriented way, attached to a particular imagined outcome. But awakening or enlightenment will never be what we imagine—that's guaranteed.

When we're in a goal-oriented mode, all it can take is to experience a deeply sublime state once or twice or even just read about it. Then our spiritual journey can become an endless attempt to get it back or replicate an idea. Likewise, in any meditation, we can habitually judge how "good" we did compared to our past meditations or to someone else. For example, if we felt happy or relaxed, it was a success. If not, it wasn't. We remain caught up in the simple duality of pleasure and pain, but awakening isn't defined by pleasure and pain at all.

When we're constantly assessing our progress, we hold an idea of who we should be or become. Perhaps we should be calm and wise and patient and so on. But of course, trying to be a particular person or express a preset range of qualities is always going to lead to suppression and stress. When we look/act the part, we may get congratulated by ourself or others, but when the inevitable trigger or chaos arises, we are set up for self-judgment and self-doubt. Believe me, I speak from extensive personal experience here.

If our motivation for practice is based in a perception that we're not enough or complete, we may never change that mindset. I remember a seventy-year-old spiritual seeker of fifty years who joined one of my self-compassion retreats and was humbled to discover that her spiritual journey had devolved into berating herself for *still* not figuring it out. That is our inevitable fate if we let this mindset continue; it compounds as we grow older. In other words, running toward a better version of ourselves is always reckless. At some point, we'll have to turn back to the parts we abandoned and clean up the mess with patience and kindness. Only then can we become who we're authentically meant to be.

In this way, letting go of awakening and enlightenment isn't giving up. In fact, by embracing the way things actually are now, we liberate the qualities of heart that are most effective at taking us deeper on the journey. We can now approach our spiritual inquiries with true curiosity, wonder, and even playfulness—instead of from a fear that we wouldn't be OK otherwise.

IMPERMANENCE AND NONATTACHMENT

Spiritual teachings often instruct practitioners to maintain nonattachment in regard to our experiences. In insight meditation, we are often instructed to see our thoughts and emotions as impermanent or as "passing phenomena." While these approaches can sometimes yield deep insight and letting go, especially in certain long-term retreat environments, they don't necessarily *transform* the confusion and distress we carry. In fact, without care, they can actually help us bypass our wounding altogether.

For example, we might mindfully notice the changing or insignificant nature of a thought or emotion in meditation. In focusing less on the content and more on the characteristic, the thought or emotion is often de-powered or dissipates completely. We might think to ourselves, *It's just a story*, or *This too shall pass*. We might even experience our thoughts and emotions like impersonal clouds floating across the empty sky of our mind. However, unless we sustain impeccable mindfulness when we get off the cushion, the pattern inevitably returns and continues to condition our perception and behavior. I've known this all too well, finding myself frustrated at the constant and convincing return of impermanent mental patterns.

Moreover, focusing too deeply on impermanence, in particular, has overwhelmed many of us. When we truly glimpse that nothing and no one is stable, we can also lose the inner stability we need to attend to our experience in skillful ways. If this happens before we've established ourselves within a deeper inner refuge in compassion or awareness, it can activate immense fear without a way to return to safety. I know I spent years inadvertently in a trauma response to the perception of this deeply unstable nature of reality. This is yet another reason to lead with practices that establish first a felt sense of safety and connection.

NONSELF

The teaching of nonself is one of the most provocative and oft-cited in the Buddhist tradition. It states that nothing in our experience is "me" or "mine." Profoundly, our conception of lasting selfhood, and the identification we have with our experience, can be a core cause of the suffering in our lives. (We'll discuss this topic further in chapter 8.) However, when we try to apply this teaching before healing or without nuanced understanding, it can easily have detrimental effects.

One of the first things it can do is reinforce any existing aversion we might have to ourselves or any one of our identities, usually via suppression or self-criticism. Now armed with a spiritual justification, our aversion amplifies any tendencies toward inner conflict and low self-worth. In particular, if we have been wounded from being neglected or abandoned in our lives, even subtly dismissing our sense of self can directly mimic those past painful experiences and unintentionally re-wound us. This was one of my many humbling discoveries. Sadly, in this self-dismissal, I only inflamed the wounded sense of self that I erroneously thought was the problem.

Like reflections on impermanence, common reflections on nonself like thinking, *I am not my thoughts*, or *This thought is empty* may lighten or dissipate that thought in *that* moment but are unlikely to make a lasting change to our patterns of mental fixation. This is, in part, because the attempt at disidentification so often comes from an aversive, distancing impulse, which again reinforces inner division. The sense of "me" remains pervasive but can just split in two, as it's still glued to the lens of the meditative self managing the spiritual process. Now we have a spiritual self and an illusory one—but think we have none—which risks making us both blind to our spiritual ideas as well as the potential wisdom present in our passing thoughts. For many, a much safer and more effective approach is to use intimacy instead of distance, heart instead of mind, and love one's sense of self into an easeful dissolution.

HINDRANCES, DEFILEMENTS, AND ILLUSIONS

In Buddhism and Hinduism (which share common origins), troubling emotions and thoughts are sometimes labeled as "hindrances," "defilements," or are implied to be illusory in some way. Likewise, they are sometimes described as entities intending to deceive us (i.e., Mara or Maya). It's true that there are patterns that can limit us. There are wounds that can distort our good intentions. Likewise, when we identify fully with the painful stories we hold, we can live in a sort of alternate reality.

However, we have to be *very* careful here. Any aversion we have in us is ever ready to adopt a new reason to judge, shame, or bypass. Labels are quick, catchy, and effective. When our anxiety is labeled a hindrance to a peaceful mind or our ill will is judged as a defilement of a pure heart or our distracted thoughts are perceived as being lost in an illusion, we are liable to suppress or dismiss these natural mind states or, at the least, not see them clearly for what they are. This risk is amplified when we add a moralistic layer to what we perceive (right vs. wrong) or ascribe malevolent intentions to emotions or thoughts (e.g., evil forces trying to seduce or manipulate us).

I can certainly understand the tendency. Judgmental labels are a way we seek to distance ourselves from what we perceive to be a threat. But for me, falling back on them is just a sign of my laziness, an unwillingness to open my heart to the discomfort within me. Indeed, it's possible to cultivate a resilient ease *in the presence of anxiety*, not just in its absence.

Moreover, in distancing ourselves, we often make an enemy out of a friend. Surprising as it may be, instead of defiling us, even the unruly forces within us are just trying their best to help. Let's take, for example, the sensual desire, ill will, distractedness, worry, and doubt that make up the "five hindrances" in Theravada Buddhist thought. They are not pathologies. They are all coping mechanisms for responding to a lack of safety and connection, especially in the face of discomfort or threat. By understanding and treating them as helpers, we realize they show us where and why we are out of balance and what responses are needed to restore it. So, in practice, the actual hindrance isn't the mind state itself but instead our aversive view and response to it.

QUIETING THE MIND

If we've ever practiced mindfulness, we've heard the instruction to quiet the mind. This simple phrase is one of the more detrimental instructions people can get hung up on in meditation.

Don't get me wrong: I can attest that having a quiet mind is pleasant. Silence can feel deeply peaceful and profound. However, I had to learn the hard way that a quiet mind for any sustained period is actually a *by-product* of various other factors, not a goal to adopt or a technique to employ. Attempting to make our minds quiet often just adds more noise through over-efforting, frustration, and self-judgment. Countless have quit the practice because of it, believing they "just couldn't meditate."

A quiet mind is best seen as an occasional side effect of wise practice. For example, when we practice in a way that helps us feel deeply safe, trusting, connected, or wholeheartedly engaged, the mind naturally begins to settle and clear. The opposite is also true. If we have any contention with our thoughts, we will only have more of them, and they will be even more unpleasant.

Just like the nose smells, the tongue tastes, the eyes see, and the ears hear, the mind thinks. Trying to stop thinking is like trying to make your eyes stop seeing! Sometimes people spend decades in practice before realizing this simple fact. And beyond that, if we adopt a spiritual idea that says quietude is an experience we *should* have, then we won't give ourselves the opportunity to find peace *amid* thought. We will artificially confine our contentment to a small window of "quiet" spiritual experience.

FACING YOUR TRAUMA

Practicing intensely and pushing one's limits have their place, but these strategies never apply all the time or to everyone in a room. Teachings that emphasize urgency or warrior-like practice risk creating pressure, tension, and self-judgment that reinforce certain types of wounding and close us down to new insight. Moreover, such directives can overlook the fact that we're not all wounded equally. For people and populations that have experienced intense traumas or for those in the middle of a deep healing crisis, even "normal" instructions can feel very tricky.

For example, there are times when the common direction to close one's eyes can feel too unsafe for some. The instruction to "sit still" (let alone sit long silent retreats) can trigger past patterns of feeling trapped, shut down, or even dissociated from one's present-moment experience—a psychological detachment that, in meditation, can sometimes be confused with peace or ease. Hearing directions to "sit with your pain" can feel oppressive or overwhelm the system. Even the invitation to "focus on the body" can re-trigger body-based traumas that are too much to integrate. There are times when any instruction can feel threatening.

While they may sound extreme, these are natural and normal responses from the complex wounding that affects more people than we think. To be honest, I've experienced all of them at one time or another although I didn't understand this till years later. It's humbling—and sometimes quite upsetting—to discover that the ways we've tried to or been told to help ourselves are actually creating more harm. However, to one degree or another, this type of discovery is inevitable for all of us as we learn and grow.

While the teacher and teachings are important, it is ultimately up to each of us to be discerning, to watch what's happening in our meditation practice. As a general rule, it's best not to push or force ourselves into discomfort, especially when we're already at our edge of tolerance. Instead, we relax within the circumstances or practices that already feel safe and let our courage and curiosity grow naturally from there.

PEACE BEYOND CIRCUMSTANCES

It's easy to think that if we just practiced harder or better, we'd be free—even when we're in extremely adverse conditions. Teachings that emphasize the accessibility and universality of awakening are beautiful and important, but sometimes miss the fact that we are not all handed the same conditions. People and groups that experience more hardship (BIPOC, LGBTQIA, those in the lowest income brackets, and so on) often hold more wounding. Hence, the burden of healing can be much greater for them, while access to supportive resources is often more limited.

It's good to remember the historical Buddha grew up within cloistered castle walls as a prince. He likely felt very safe, securely attached to his caretakers. This stable beginning likely formed an extremely supportive foundation from which he eventually enacted the deep spiritual courage for which he is known. Today, most of our lives are very different.

When we come from a personal baseline of feeling unsafe in our lives, teachings to "accept the way things are" can feel like being asked to resign ourselves to constant threat and anxiety rather than an invitation into peace. Likewise, when we're trapped in the middle of adverse circumstances or systemic inequality, teachings about "inner peace" are often immaterial. Instead, we need to actively respond in a way that works to restore safety and connection inside and out—which can in turn lead to acceptance and peace in the future. In other words, if we don't honor our complex histories of wounding and the circumstances that keep reinforcing them, the teachings will feel two-dimensional at best and retraumatizing at worst.

Without an appropriate caveat, even the first noble truth of Buddhism that suggests everyone suffers can feel like it overlooks the disproportionate burden that some people carry. If we skip over honoring how societal disparities affect the way we walk the healing and spiritual paths, we can apply impractical standards to ourselves and others, comparing and judging for not achieving the same results. Moreover, in many situations, the traditional tools and techniques like mindfulness meditation or silent retreat practice may not be adequate, appropriate, or timely. In the face of adversity or in marginalized communities with a history of oppression, many tools *and practical actions* are needed to restore a foundation of safety from which true spiritual well-being can arise.

While we should never release the possibility of peace even in the worst of moments or circumstances, it's also true that our lived realities have a huge influence on us. They affect our ability to feel safe, to have time for practice or study, to access support, and so much more. By leading with compassion, we can remember that spirituality is not only about changing the inside. We can't meditate away poverty or racism or the like. Sometimes it's the outer conditions that actually need to change before or alongside the inner ones.

CROSSING THE BRIDGE OF THE HEART

The sections we've just explored are just a few prime examples of spiritual lenses that can unconsciously color our mindfulness practice, rendering it less effective or even harmful. We can resist suffering, reach for salvation, overlook wounding, push and pressure ourselves, or deny the reality of our circumstances. The confusion arises both from the language of teaching and instruction offered (which has its own sordid past) *and* from the wounded perspective we bring to it. It is a powerful cocreation and one that can cost us immensely on our path if we're not careful. The potential loss is nothing less than the promise of the journey: the very actualization of inner freedom itself.

To reiterate, the traditional insight meditation teaching asserts that freedom arises through letting go, through releasing craving or clinging in our lives. That letting go is said to come primarily through *seeing*. We use mindfulness to see ourselves, which gives way to insight, which eventually becomes wisdom. Gaining wisdom about the nature of our suffering and the true nature of life, we let go.

While it's possible for mindfulness and the resulting insights to cut through all our wounded conditioning amid our complex lives, it's a tall order. Moreover, to integrate a significant letting go, we must actually transform the patterns, not just release them. To do that, we must address their most basic needs directly—namely, a deep internal sense of safety and connection.

Most of the time, mindfulness alone will simply be overpowered by our insecurities and unmet needs. It will be employed as a strategy for protection, predicated on liberation from suffering but controlled by anxiety and aversion underneath. In other words, if we don't come to feel that it's *safer* to let go, we will undermine our own mindful intentions toward doing so.

Thus, the journey between the seeing and the embodiment requires crossing the bridge of the emotional heart. A sustained and sincere engagement with ourselves soothes our anxious strategies and dissolves our fearful distortions. Then we have a chance to release and let go without preoccupation. This has been true for myself and for countless of my students: restoring internal safety and connection is often a prerequisite for release.

For these reasons, I believe it's well past time to reemphasize and reprioritize the sometimes sidelined heart-based practices of insight meditation and reactivate the powerful spiritual capacities of our own amazing heart-minds.

The Missing Wing

There is a metaphor for the Dharma in the Mahayana Buddhist tradition: it's like a great bird in flight, and its two wings are wisdom and compassion.

We can all visualize what would happen to a bird if it only had one wing. It would spiral downward in circles. Likewise, if one wing were shorter or weaker than the other, the bird would veer to one side and go round and round, never getting where it is going. It's only when both wings beat together with equal strength that progress can be made on the path.

Wisdom is the clear knowing or understanding of the nature of things, both in a moment and in general. Naturally, it arises from careful observation through practices like mindfulness and the insight they can bring. Mindfulness, insight, and wisdom all share a tendency toward a cognitive emphasis on the path. In secular mindfulness, they are often associated with the science or analytic study of the mind. In Western and Buddhist culture, they are associated with qualities of the masculine. However, while wisdom sees clearly, it is not necessarily heart-full or embodied.

The dominance of the wing of wisdom in Theravada Buddhism and insight meditation is apparent in various ways. The Pali Canon, which is the scriptural basis of Theravada Buddhism, contains many more passages related to the development of wisdom, concentration, and insight than those related to heart qualities like compassion. Moreover, the former are much more often linked to liberation, while the latter are often linked to lesser outcomes, such as better worldly conditions or a good rebirth.[2] Likewise, surveying a catalog of Theravada Buddhist books or commentaries shows the same imbalance—and many who have practiced in insight meditation communities, myself included, have noticed this. Teachers like Sharon Salzberg, Tara Brach, and others have helped to rebalance this, but there is more work to be done. Lastly, such a disparity shouldn't be mentioned without also pointing to the long and painful history of patriarchy in Buddhist and Western culture,[3] which likely bears some responsibility here.

If you're like me, you've seen this imbalance in your own heart-mind as well. For most of my practice, I found myself retreating to and inhabiting a small region of my experience: the space behind my eyes—my thinking mind. I habitually stepped out of the moment to think *about* my spiritual challenges, trying to analyze or strategize or evaluate. I preconceived countless conclusions about myself and the path instead of opening into simple, heartfelt curiosity. I regularly overlooked the direct feeling already present in my body to get where I thought I needed to go.

After flying in circles on the wing of wisdom for so long, many of us need to overcompensate in our spiritual practice so we can fly straight again. In my opinion, erring on the side of compassion tends to be a much safer bet anyway. This is because while wisdom can lack heart, compassion can't ever shut its eyes to what it's caring for. The sincere heart is more inclusive, naturally encompassing the mind.

In Theravada Buddhism, there is one teaching, in particular, that best illuminates our heart's capacity. It's called the *brahmaviharas*—translated as the "divine abodes." Traditionally, they are fourfold: *loving-kindness, compassion, sympathetic joy,* and *equanimity.* According to certain suttas, they can support concentration, tranquility, and liberating insight, as well as protect from various sorts of physical and mental harm.[4]

In addition, there are now modern secular practices that work to cultivate our natural capacities to care, and some, such as those taught by the well-known psychologist Kristin Neff, are directly inspired by the brahmaviharas.[5] In particular, the results of "compassion science" are quite encouraging. They show that practicing compassion has measurable positive effects on virtually every part of us, from the physical to the emotional to the mental. A few of the benefits documented in Neff's research include lowered anxiety and/or depression, greater resilience and motivation, and better health and relationships.[6] It has even been shown to boost physical health outcomes.[7] Other wholesome emotions like joy or gratitude can act similarly.

For meditators specifically, the intervention of self-compassion in our practice has specific observable effects. It works to increase calm and ease within the heart-mind, thus stabilizing our mindfulness. Then, it slowly draws our hidden wounds into view and applies the appropriate attention-medicine for transformation. As we heal, our path is cleared for liberating insight to bloom and for its wisdom to integrate into our lives. In other words, it calms the push and pull of aversion and desire and clarifies the muddy waters of delusion. Various students of mine have confirmed that, until the addition of self-compassion, they couldn't integrate the deeper teachings of insight meditation into either their bodies or their daily lives.

To be more specific, I'll use the spiritual adages from the last section and show how self-compassion can transform the process and lived experience of each. While these transformations might sound magical, they unfold very lawfully according to simple psychological principles (which we'll discuss in greater detail in chapter 3).

BEFRIENDING SUFFERING

If we can notice our longing for suffering to end, we can then apply self-compassion, and a healing process can begin. For example, we might first notice an anxious energy that is monitoring, evaluating, and correcting our spiritual course or perhaps a self-imposed pressure to perform or achieve. The idea of "getting to the end" may have activated tension in our bodies or even desperation in our minds.

When we offer compassion to these various forms of stress, we often begin to feel the exhaustion underneath. We feel how much effort it has taken to embark on this endless pursuit of ending suffering. We also feel the aching pain of lack embedded within the longing itself.

When we then hold the aching exhaustion with compassion, we might notice shame arise in its wake. Having not arrived at the end, part of us may feel we have failed. If we couldn't complete the task, it must have been our shortcoming, we think. Caring for this shame, a deeper layer of grief, hopelessness, or defeat might reveal itself. We are facing the hard truth that life is inevitably tragic at times.

Consoling ourselves with compassion around the human condition, our essential vulnerability and tenderness may begin to reveal itself. As we relax and open with these feelings, we sense their universality. Even though it's painful, it feels nourishing to be connected to something larger than us, something that is undeniably real and true.

Breathing gently with this, before long we might find ourselves sitting in a clear and expansive space within—a space of equanimity. We sense, *This is just the way it is for me and us right now. This is just the nature of things, and it can be OK for now.* In the mourning of our not-arriving, we have arrived again at the beginning, the foundation of peace. Suffering isn't ending, and yet our practice and life feel distinctly sweet, rich, and accessible again. We can act now with clarity and courage.

This is an example of how self-compassion, when it's thorough, can take a seemingly trivial assumption and melt its composite layers down into a warm wisdom experienced as a felt sense of safety and connection. While this process will look different for each of us depending on our makeup, a truly compassionate orientation is always adept at untangling us. Instead of grasping after an idealized outcome for our path, it helps us refocus on the much simpler and truer reality of this very moment. As we release the demands on our own liberation, paradoxically, the end of suffering draws nearer.

WHOLEHEARTED INTIMACY

A similar process can unfold in relation to awakening and enlightenment. Through self-compassion, we can discover how much tension we hold around trying to attain and sustain blissful, peaceful, or even just relaxed states in our practice or lives. We realize, ironically, that we can make ourselves miserable by chasing after happiness or doggedly trying to keep it when it comes.

As we care for the various layers of this stress and exhaustion, we discover a softer approach. Instead of making enlightenment, or even relaxation, the goal—which often puts us in conflict with our lived reality—we can make *caring for whatever is arising* the purpose of the path. This is a wholehearted intimacy or humble devotion to what is: even if that's anger or fear or something not "spiritual" at all. If, in the process, we happen to experience relaxation, that's just a welcome side effect. If someday we happen to get "there" (i.e., enlightenment), that's just the gravy on top. As the well-known spiritual saying goes, "Enlightenment is an accident. But we can make ourselves more accident-prone." The application of wise self-compassion does just that.

In the process, we may happen to discover that our own inner warmth is more fulfilling and reliable than any fleeting moment of attainment alone could be. Our own devotion to what's real might be richer than any moment of bliss. It could even dawn on us that true contentment isn't the absence of pain at all; it's something that blooms right within it. Oddly, we might not even have to feel happy to be truly at peace.

WISE AND PRECIOUS VISITORS

When we take the impermanent phenomena that we practiced nonattachment with and apply self-compassion directly to them, our thoughts and emotions come alive in a new way. They transform into living, breathing parts of ourselves with real wants and fears. By listening to the content of our heart-mind, we begin to realize many passing experiences hold vital information that can actually help untangle us.

Old patterns we've seen a thousand times may be returning simply to let us know they still don't feel safe or connected, perhaps longing for a truly sincere care. Hence, instead of being "in the way" of our meditation, our thoughts and emotions can become *wise and precious visitors*. Each guest becomes an opportunity to learn and grow our heart's capacity to listen and respond with care.

While mindfulness can identify and sometimes see through the phenomena, applying compassion works to alchemize the pain as it passes through us. Our heart-minds pick up on the scent of the suffering in our thoughts and emotions and begin to track them with care. Every time a pattern passes through, the magic of compassion alters it, so when it returns, it is often softer, lighter, and less sticky. Feeling safer, the patterns settle. Over time, they may reveal their deeper layers. Eventually, their core needs being met, they might not feel the need to return at all.

In effect, practicing this way shifts our focus from the characteristic of impermanence in our experience to the characteristic of *interconnection*.

Noticing and acting on our connection through compassion is a deeply stabilizing and strengthening force in our psyche, supporting us in journeying further into our inner unknown. Change will take every person, place, and thing in our lives, but it can't ever take our fundamental connection to everything. That's a birthright that compassion helps us remember.

In addition, a self-compassionate approach shifts our focus from nonattachment to nourishment, yet has similarly profound results. Through the self-fulfillment of our own embrace, we naturally loosen our grip on the more transient and limited forms of happiness over time (e.g., wealth, status, power, or even social approval or sensual pleasure). This renunciation, however, happens naturally without the haughty distance or transcendence that can characterize trying to be "unattached." Instead, we are increasingly drawn to prioritizing the deepest nourishment within us that, in turn, allows the rest of our lives to unfold with an uncanny grace.

INTERCONNECTED SELF

When we approach the teaching of nonself with compassion, it can transform into an experience of interconnection. Instead of searching for the absence or emptiness of self, we discover a vast fullness and warmth. Indeed, in its deepest expression, the realization of interconnection is analogous to the teaching of nonself. If we are not a separate or permanent self, then we must be intimately connected to the flow of everything. Compassion can show us this not only because it creates a sense of safety within us but also because, by its nature, it naturally moves us toward greater connection and expansion.

Amazingly, we begin to notice the more compassion and kindness we can shower ourselves with, the softer and lighter our being becomes. The softer and lighter, the more translucent and porous we are. The protective walls of the self and identity, as well as the process of identification with our experience, are fundamentally anxious or restless strategies. They can naturally relax when our inner warmth brings the feeling of deep safety we crave. We discover we don't have to destroy anything; we can love the self into dissolution. As a student once put it to me, "When I was always trying to protect myself, I didn't understand and couldn't imagine letting go of the self. But with self-compassion, I no longer needed the protection, so I could finally find moments of relaxing any sense of separation back into life."

In this way, applying self-compassion helps us prevent multiple unintended effects of the nonself teaching. First, it prevents or addresses the common perversion that there is a spiritual problem with the self that needs to be fixed—undercutting any self-reinforcing judgment. Second, compassion can initiate the often-surprising dissolving of internal boundaries *and* also help regulate us as we learn to integrate the experience back into our lives. Third, it can prevent clinging to this teaching as a spiritual idea or a new spiritual identity, as that clinging involves a subtle but painful separation that can't be sustained in the face of sincere compassion.

HELPERS, PURIFIERS, AND TRUTH-TELLERS

By applying true compassion to our "hindrances" and "defilements," our view of them can transform. The emotional and mental patterns that disturb us reveal themselves to be quite well-intentioned, as is being discovered by the emerging fields of evolutionary psychology and psychiatry.[8] They are like a child, who, wanting to help accidentally makes a mess instead. When we scold instead of love them, they eventually lash out in resentment. If we're loving, they become allies and teach us in the process. With a compassionate approach, our challenging thoughts and emotions don't defile us. They instead help us purify, polish, and mature our heart-minds—for which we become forever grateful.

As for the illusions that haunt us, with a warm welcome, they become honored guests who always have a seat at the table. They are here to tell their truth; their experience is real to them. We can serve them tea and hear them out, even if we don't end up taking their advice. Approaching humbly, sometimes we'll actually learn surprising things that are crucial for our healing journey.

At a recent self-compassion retreat, a student shared that sincerely saying thank you to his decades-long anger problem was finally the simple medicine it needed to soften and be workable. It had tried to protect his precious heart for decades; it just needed acknowledgment. He was so relieved. Sometimes just changing our view of what disturbs us inside is the catalyst for true healing and transformation.

Compassion helps us befriend our experience, preventing judgment and dismissal. It helps us understand the needs of our patterns instead of seeing through or past them because we know better. It helps us honor and respect our wounded nature alongside our transcendent nature, so we can walk through life with conscious humility and care.

REVEAL THE MIND

Instead of trying to quiet the mind, applying compassion helps us reveal and understand it. For example, we might notice there are different types of thoughts. There are those that come from wanting what we don't have (e.g., fantasizing, wishing, planning). There are thoughts that come from *not* wanting what we do have or worrying about what could happen (e.g., judging, worry, blame). There are thoughts that are just bored and drifting through our minds (e.g., daydreams, random images).

Understanding our essential human struggles, the compassionate heart naturally wants to help—not quiet—our thinking. It does so through the emanation of care and connection, soothing the wanting and nonwanting and making the present pleasant and nourishing to be in. Feeling the support, our thoughts will often be happy to rest and our heart-minds can finally relax and enjoy the moment. This joy then further stabilizes the mind and opens us to deeper concentration and insight.

One of my students spent over two decades practicing ardently in the insight tradition before learning this. She felt stuck and frustrated when no technique she'd learned allowed her to "clear her mind" for any length of time from worries or fears. It all changed when she turned toward her thoughts and emotions with compassion. Now, she tells me she has a reliably calm and joyful place within her when she meditates, even if thoughts still sometimes naturally take her away.

UNCONDITIONAL PATIENCE

When we operate from self-compassion, we don't amp ourselves up to "face our trauma" or try to conquer our demons. We will never win a direct fight against our conditioning; it's far too strong and cunning. Like flowing water over rock, only the gentle power of the compassionate heart can melt the mountain of hardened pain within. We can actually hurt ourselves by forcing things. I still remember one of my teachers warning me in my early twenties against "pulling the petals of our heart-mind open too quickly."

For several of my students with a history of intense trauma, the most important medicine was permission to rest and be easy with themselves.

Their healing and spiritual path had become yet another crisis to manage, like so many in the past. Naturally then, it was driven by the most desperate and anxious parts of themselves, keeping them locked in that aversive and stressful mode of being. They "had to heal" to escape the pain. It was only when they realized, paradoxically, that unconditional patience and kindness *were* the fastest way to relief that relief surely came.

We don't need to pressure ourselves into anything. We can stay simple and kind. Our compassionate energy will gently invite our wounding to emerge in its own time as it's ready. If, instead, our wounding has already surfaced in full force, we don't pressure ourselves to feel it all. We might not even sit in meditation at all for a time but instead engage in the most soothing and nourishing activities we know. We may have to release the techniques or teachings we read about and listen to the guidance of our own pain.

COLLABORATING WITH LIFE

When self-compassion meets challenging circumstances, it doesn't look for peace beyond them. It meets our lives where they are and cocreates from there. We first honor the pain of what is and what has been, offering ourselves or others ample understanding. Then, we put in the work to make things better. We do so because compassion reminds us how precious we are.

This may not look spiritual. It may not bring any ease at first. Instead, we may spark into unbridled rage as our self-worth and strength return. Others might even tell us we're not doing the practice right. If we sustain our self-compassion, however, our energy can eventually evolve into measured strength and heartfelt resilience. We may have to learn to heal *as* we work to improve our conditions.

Thus, in many situations, self-compassion may not look like silent sitting but instead energetic action to improve one's life or that of one's community. In healing or spiritual communities, this is often the work of increasing understanding and inclusion for all people, especially those with a history of marginalization. For those occupying privileged identities and social positions, in particular, we work toward learning how we perpetuate harm even when we're trying to help so we may create safer spaces for the healing of all people.

True compassion doesn't stop there, though. As we grow and heal, we may realize that our challenging conditions are not just a burden. With compassion, they can actually mature us quicker and more deeply. We may have had less privilege, but we may have also had more access to the raw reality of life and its essential truths. Healing through adversity can build a deep wisdom and resiliency of heart that can't come through spiritual practice alone.

Eventually, we can realize that no matter what happens, no matter the social location we inhabit, we can never fundamentally lose our access to spiritual fulfillment. People, places, and things will hopefully change for the better, and we can have a role in that, but along the way, our home in life remains. That is our birthright.

A NEW SPIRITUAL VOCABULARY

In all the ways just described and more, applying self-compassion is a direct antidote to what confuses us on the spiritual journey. In its bold engagement with pain, it is the cure for aversion and apathy. In its intimacy with all of ourselves, it is the remedy to separation and aloneness. In its caring embrace, it is the panacea to a lack of safety and connection. As one of my students said to me, compassion created enough safety to help her shift from "a model of spiritual transcendence [i.e., escape] to a model of radical inclusivity." Instead of struggling against being a mother to fulfill her spiritual longing, she realized she could make motherhood a complete spiritual path.

In other words, compassion can help us fully let go, and when we do, *we fall together* into wholeness instead of falling apart into conflict. We fall into our lives *as they are* instead of falling out of touch with our lived reality. We are greatly supported by mindfulness, insight, and wisdom, but the letting go ultimately happens through the alchemy of the heart. The Buddha himself may be hinting at this in the Majjhima Nikaya, when he states, "The purpose of the holy life does not consist . . . [of] states of concentration nor insight and the eye of knowledge. The unshakable deliverance of heart, the sure heart's release; this and this alone is the object of the holy life, its essence, its true goal."[9]

However, in practice, the path of compassion is a humbling one. We meet the pain in our hearts and in our communities again and again. The instructions we receive and the language we use can either support us in alchemizing our wounds into insights or keep us stuck. This also includes the speech we employ in our spiritual friendships and communities: compassionate and inclusive or the opposite.

To that end, I'll summarize some of the linguistic changes we've explored in this discussion. To start, our hindrances can be helpers; passing phenomena can be wise visitors; our mental quietude can be a by-product of inner safety; and unconditional patience can be the fastest way through intense trauma. The absence of the self can instead be a deeply interconnected self that embraces the totality of what we are, including our identities and circumstances. Likewise, emptiness can instead be a fullness or wholeness.

Enlightenment could best be a reunion with the unconditional safety and connection already within us—not an identity or state to attain. Finally, the path to the "end of suffering" could be a path of always embracing suffering, no matter what. In the end, welcoming all of what is—including all of the strife and struggle of life—may be the only way to find the goodness and wisdom at our center, the place within that is already and forever whole and complete.

The Four Noble Truths of Healing

The four noble truths are a fundamental teaching in Buddhism and insight meditation.[10] They are said to have been the first teaching of the Buddha after his awakening over 2,600 years ago. As such, they outline the basic logic and component parts of the Buddhist path. However, in the spirit of what I've presented thus far, I want to consider an alternative articulation that hybridizes the four noble truths with an understanding of the value of emotional healing.

The alternative phrases appear below, followed by the original teachings in parentheses. The four noble truths correlate with the four aspects of compassion that I will describe in detail in chapter 5.

1. **Everyone Is Wounded . . . (There Is Suffering.)** Due to our innate interconnection, our tender hearts are vulnerable to the conditions of life. We are painfully impacted by the people, circumstances, and

messages around us, as well as our own inherited and learned conditioning.

2. **Because We Don't Feel Safe and Connected. (There Is a Cause of Suffering.)** Wounding occurs when (a) we experience pain in a state of insecurity and disconnection from ourselves, others, or life; (b) we employ various forms of aversion to protect and distance ourselves from that and future pain; and (c) we reinforce those protective strategies over time, leading to chronically suppressed emotions and harmful habits.

3. **Liberation Comes through Caring. (There Is an End of Suffering.)** A wholehearted, caring embrace of our wounding gradually reverses the effects of aversion and restores inner safety and connection, thus facilitating healing and creating the conditions for liberating insight and letting go.

4. **We Have the Support We Need Within. (There Is a Path to the End of Suffering.)** We already contain the goodness and wisdom, as well as the core capacities of mindfulness and compassion we need to be free. In addition, we have access to spiritual support from our interconnected nature and life itself. Traditionally, this is articulated as an eightfold noble path (see below). *Note: this doesn't mean we don't also benefit from the support of others.*

This alternative articulation of the four noble truths serves to (a) connect us in humility through our shared human condition, (b) identify the core unmet needs that perpetuate it, (c) encourage us to move courageously into intimacy with ourselves (and our lives), and (d) assuage the habit of searching outside of ourselves for the fulfillment we seek or the tools to cultivate it. In other words, we feel unsafe and disconnected amid our challenges, but by devoting ourselves to true compassion, any of us can heal, awaken, and help others do the same.

A WISE AND COMPASSIONATE PATH

Mindfulness alone was never meant to be enough. In the traditional eightfold noble path, it's part of an interconnected family of eight factors:

wise view
wise intention

wise speech

wise action

wise livelihood

wise effort

wise mindfulness

wise concentration

These eight factors can be viewed as a linear progression of steps, a group-ing of three interrelated sections (wisdom, ethics, meditation), and/or as an interdependent web or system. As a progression, the journey starts with wise view and wise intention, suggesting that the perspectives we hold and our attitudes dictate our speech, action, and so on. Part 1 of this book starts the same way, offering an alternative *view* of the spiritual path and then detailing the wisest *intention* we can employ: compassion.

The traditional ordering of these steps is insightful. Wise intention's position at number two on the list suggests that compassion is a precursor to or prerequisite for everything that follows, including wise mindfulness (the seventh step). The way we speak, act, and live also precedes mindful-ness practice. Without the steps before, we are increasingly likely to expe-rience the limitations of mindfulness alone—as described in this chapter.

When we look at these eight steps as an interdependent web or sys-tem, we can imagine how the quality of each factor affects everything else. For example, applying a wise intention like compassion can help us relax our effort, concentrate more easily, speak and act kindlier to ourselves or others. It can even help us view ourselves and life in a more forgiving and understanding way. Conversely, the way we practice everything else, in-cluding mindfulness, affects the quality of our care. In this interconnected view, none of the factors can operate optimally when they function alone. We can't skim the first and then skip to the seventh and eighth, trying to shortcut the process.

There isn't space for a full explanation of the eightfold noble path here, but I've woven its various factors throughout the book. For example, part 2 of this book offers a series of practices utilizing wise effort, mindfulness, and concentration. Part 3 delves into wise speech, action, and livelihood in relationships and the world. Keep your eye out for them. They can be helpful reflections at any moment: *How am I viewing myself? What is my intention right now? How am I speaking or acting toward myself? What type of effort am I using?* Etc.

To conclude let's set aside this eightfold teaching and return to the simpler metaphor of the great bird once more. One wing is wisdom, and the other is compassion (which we could also see as wise view and wise intention). We can trust that when wisdom and compassion are balanced, we will learn everything else we need to.

Summary, Prompts, and Practices

CHAPTER SUMMARY

- In my spiritual path, I struggled for many years with wounding that I couldn't understand or address through traditional Dharma teachings alone.
- For many of us on the path, our wounding conspires with spiritual teachings to actually create more, instead of less, suffering.
- Self-compassion is critical to rebalancing Western approaches to spirituality, allowing modern-day practitioners to truly integrate and embody the liberation they seek.
- Mindfulness and compassion are part of a larger path called the eightfold noble path that reminds us connect inner freedom with our everyday lives.

JOURNAL PROMPTS

In the journal prompt exercises, the instruction is simply to write what comes without overthinking it. The intention is to provide an opportunity to reveal what's there, not to have the right answer. Just keep your pen moving.

- Reflect on how your spiritual or healing path has unfolded. It's never a straight line, but perhaps you might name some of the phases of your practice over the months, years, or decades. What phase are you in now, what are your current challenges, and what support do you need to keep moving?
- Reflect on the ways you've been or are confused by spiritual teachings you've heard along the way. How might the addition of compassion clarify those teachings?

- Reflect on the ways you've allowed your wounding or unhealthy conditioning to co-opt your spiritual path. How might the addition of compassion help you restore clarity?
- Write down the four noble truths of healing as "I" statements (e.g., "I am hurting," "because I don't feel safe and connected," etc.). Beneath each, write ways that each statement could be true for you. You can focus on a particular circumstance that's troubling you or speak generally.

GUIDED PRACTICE

This guided practice invites us to recondition our spiritual ideas and techniques from a compassionate viewpoint. It moves through the teachings above with a combination of mindful reflection and self-compassion. You can access the guided meditation at www.justinmichelsondharma .com/thedharmaofhealing/practices or www.shambhala.com/dharmaof healingpractices.

THE ART OF HEALING

Now that we've explored the importance of compassion on the spiritual path, we'll shift focus to the domain of psychological healing. This chapter illuminates the unique structure of our heart-minds and the compassionate principles that unlock easeful and effective healing. The often-untold secret is that healing is entirely natural and innate to us. When care and connection guide the process, we can intuitively find our way home. Moreover, learning this art is an essential part of cocreating a healthy and peaceful world.

· ·

If you're like me, you weren't ever taught about healing. You weren't told about how your heart and mind worked and what maintenance or repair they might require. Most of us weren't even told that our habits or patterns were malleable, not to mention that they contained important information. Mostly, they were just who we were. We just thought, *I'm depressed, I'm happy, I'm afraid. . . . I'm someone who believes this or that.* Even years into healing, we can cling to this two-dimensional view of ourselves.

Likewise, if you're like me, when you experienced intense emotions (or saw them in others), it was often a "problem" in the eyes of family or school or work—something to fix so you could get along better. The primary wound was not even noticed. Instead, the symptoms were pathologized and became static—monolithic even—divorced from their past origins. In that world, it was safer to be "fine," even though we really weren't.

Fortunately, today, more and more people are actively engaged in self-discovery, courageously exploring the hidden pain that robs the richness of our lives. It's even becoming accepted that wounding is not just in the deeply traumatized or in the violent and unruly, but that it's actually part and parcel of *everyone*.[1] This is a steady, positive trend toward normalizing what can be a lonely, isolating experience. As a result, countless people are slowly retrieving their joy from the depths of themselves.

Indeed, everyone could use a therapist, a friend, or a healing practice—not just the "messed-up ones." I'm personally grateful to have and have had many support people on the path. Perhaps counterintuitively, healing is just as needed in spiritual communities and among spiritual teachers—if not sometimes more so—as it is for any of us. Healing creates the opening for our spiritual discoveries to find a foothold amid the messiness of our daily lives and relationships.

The overarching psychological principle is simple: because we were conditioned, we can be unconditioned. The spiritual corollary is that because we can observe our conditioning, there must be a part of us that is outside of it and, therefore, not controlled by it. This is a hopeful place to begin, reminding us that our emotional and mental patterns aren't set in stone, nor do we need to be limited by any diagnosis or identity. In fact, when looked at in a wise way, our patterns can actually teach us.

Rediscovering the Heart-Mind

The way we understand ourselves has a large impact on how our healing process unfolds. If we don't know the structure and function of our heart-minds, when we look inside, we will just see a disorganized cacophony of thought, emotion, and sensation. We won't notice the deeper patterns at play and how to resolve them.

Observations in the biological sciences offer us a starting point to marvel at the complex creatures we are. We are made of an intricate web of nested systems. There are muscular, skeletal, cardiovascular, digestive, endocrine, and nervous systems—to name a few. Emotional wounding and healing are connected to all of these, perhaps especially the last two.[2]

All these systems synergize to cocreate our realities. They process thousands of pieces of information at once from our internal and external environment, filtering it into both simple understandings (e.g., *I am sitting here reading a book*) and more complex perceptions about ourselves and our lives like the stories of our wounding (e.g., *I can never do things right* or *Partners always leave because I'm inadequate*). Within an instant, we react to stimuli based on the previous perceptual pathways we've established.

Knowing just this much can help us deepen our appreciation and wonder for who we are, as well as foster forgiveness for the multitude of inner processes that inevitably go unnoticed. Even though we're complex, we are also equipped with the amazing tool of our own attention. Wielded with humility and curiosity, it can reveal a surprising amount about our heart-minds.

In ancient Buddhist texts like the Abhidhamma, there are extremely accurate and detailed depictions of how our brains create our reality at the snap of a finger in each moment, as well as how dozens of different mental states arise or cease. Amazingly, these ancient understandings mirror the latest neuroscience.[3] This is a reminder that we don't have to study psychology, attend medical school, or train as a therapist to discover enough to heal ourselves. Once we have a basic understanding of how our heart-minds work, each of us can be a curious scientist in our own inner laboratory.

In the sections that follow, I use science and metaphor to describe seven characteristics of our heart-minds that, taken together, hint toward the most effective healing strategies.

BEING UNKNOWN TO OURSELVES

This is the first condition of the human experience—and it's quite an odd one. It's not just the people that seem to act unconsciously that don't know themselves; it's all of us. As we begin to look at our heart-minds, we discover we've largely been driving this vehicle of self on autopilot without understanding much about its mechanics. Neuroscience confirms this perspective, revealing the vast ocean of subconscious experience that we never see: 95 percent of our brain activity may be unconscious,[4] and we humans have around six thousand thoughts a day.[5] How many of them do you even notice?

From an evolutionary perspective, it was likely much more efficient for survival to allow the impulses within us to run cycles of habitual behavior unhindered by self-reflection. Said differently, our ignorance may actually be a compassionate strategy our organism employs to protect us. In terms of the healing, if we can't see the pain we hold, we don't have to feel it and risk it dysregulating our system. In the language of insight meditation, even our "delusion" is only there to try to help us.

On a subjective, experiential level, this opaqueness of mind is maintained by the process of *fusion*. Moment by moment, our attention fuses or merges with our experience. We become our thoughts, emotions, and sensations, often completely. This function, often called *identification* in insight meditation, is also just trying to help or protect us. However, it's only when the flow of conditioning is interrupted and the bonds of this force are broken that we can finally see what's happening within ourselves.

Sometimes, great challenge or change in our lives will interrupt this fusion process naturally—albeit often painfully. We'll suddenly have insight into our previous emotional and mental patterns and be able to choose to do something different. However, we can also interrupt fusion in any moment in an easier way: through the application of mindfulness and compassion.

Overall, the first thing to know in healing is that *there's a lot we don't know*. That's OK because learning to be comfortable with not-knowing is actually an essential skill in healing. We're not trying to accumulate new knowledge, adopt novel views, achieve new states, or have profound transformations. We're just gently and curiously uncovering what's been waiting for us inside and welcoming it into the light.

THE LAYERED SELF

Everything you've ever experienced has left a mark on you somewhere. Some effects are infinitesimally small; some are life-shattering—and then there's everything in between. The effect depends on many things beyond the intensity of the event, including our vulnerability at the time, how much agency we had, our inner resources, and our external support. Regardless, each impact alters us in known and unknown ways, and often forever.

Developmentally, this creates what I might call a *layered* structure of self. I like to imagine that from conception we are constructed brick by brick from the bottom up. Each new experience is layered on top of the old to create a unique and complex architecture of body, heart, and mind. Today, we look out from the top of a teetering skyscraper of experience we colloquially call our "self."

In this image, the top layers of this building are like our heads, filled with recent thoughts to navigate the surface of our lives. The middle layers are like our hearts, teeming with deeper emotional urges—loves and longings. The bottom layers are like our bodies, operating with the ingrained impulses of physical survival. Indeed, neuroscience has revealed that there is not just one but three brains within us. There is the brain within our skulls, but there is also the brain in the heart and the brain in the gut— each with a massive bundle of its own interconnected neurons.[6]

As we go through the healing journey, we can imagine descending from the head, down into the heart, and deeper into the body. To do so, we do our best to pause the construction process on our skyscraper of self. Powered by mindfulness and compassion, we take the elevator down through the interior to reveal and repair. We don't need to dismantle the entire building for liberating healing and insight to occur, nor do we need to clearly understand each impact; we just infuse the structure of ourselves with our compassionate presence all the way to the ground floor.

In doing so, a fourth layer of self is revealed: our interconnected nature and the universal awareness that runs through it. Scientists still can't locate or understand awareness or consciousness.[7] They can't find a central control center in the body, heart, or mind because it's not located there. Miraculously, our three brains cooperate within a larger field of nonlocal knowing that we can't isolate or cognitively apprehend. This larger field doesn't hold wounding; it transforms it. Its immense healing energy and the deep sense of fulfillment it engenders are essential additions to the healing journey.

THE TIMELESS MIND

The layered nature of self reveals something else of great importance: *all of us is always present.* Our experience of the past is still very much here with us now.

We tend to think of ourselves as moving horizontally through time, from the past through the present and into the future. But to the degree we're moving at all, it's more along a vertical axis. In this sense, the past is beneath us. The future we grow up into. The larger interconnected field surrounds us on all sides.

In the context of healing, that means discovering our conditioning or old wounds isn't a process of "going back in time" but rather of seeing the past within the present moment of your mind. Likewise discovering interconnection is seeing the influence of everything else on what's already within us. If we look closely enough, every reaction we have holds the traces of so many other moments. Indeed, any emotional process can be a portal into the deeper and wider layers within. Follow any fear to its source and you might find the fear of death hiding underneath; drill down into any desire and perhaps discover the longing for liberation at its core.

Meditators often worry that if they get lost in thought, they'll leave the present and go into the past or future. In reality, that's impossible. We are *always* in the present, interconnected moment; we just aren't always aware of it. For me, this realization greatly stabilized my attention and righted my relationship to thought and emotion, as I realized they held much less of a threat than I had previously imagined. The arisings of the heart-mind might be bewildering at times, but they couldn't actually remove me from my essential home.

This is all quite good news. Knowing that we don't have to struggle to become present, we can practice allowing presence to reveal itself, bubbling up to the surface of our consciousness. Knowing that we don't have to go searching through our history for wounds, we can just attend wholeheartedly to what is now. Practicing in this way, the opaqueness of the mind becomes transparent with greater ease and, in time, reveals what it needs to reveal.

THE MULTICENTRIC PSYCHE

If you're like most of us, you've unconsciously adopted a monolithic model of mind. In this model, each of us is a more or less solid, static, and isolated self. Of course, we know we contain many moving parts, but we quite readily glue them together with a name and story, with an identity and self-image, and think little of it. However, when we look closer—as many meditators and neuroscientists have—we find we're a whole lot more complex. In fact, we have a multiplicity of drives and motivations operating simultaneously and independently within us.

In mindfulness practice, we start by taking advantage of this multi-centric capacity of mind by adding yet another axis: a mindful or meditative self, sometimes called *witness consciousness*. "I am here watching while my thoughts and emotions pass by," we might say. This vantage point gives us a more objective view of our heart-mind. We realize our conditioned patterns have a life of their own, often operating something like subselves with their own agendas and motives.

Having a multicentric mind is not a new idea. In the West, it was articulated in varying ways by founding psychologists like Sigmund Freud and Carl Jung[8] but has taken more modern forms, first with Voice Dialogue and then more recently with Internal Family Systems and other cognitive-behavioral approaches. Multicentricity is also foundational in the ancient tradition of Theravada Buddhism, which identifies dozens of mental factors that cocreate our internal reality.

It's not uncommon for us to think and speak in ways that acknowledge this nature of mind. We might think, *Part of me wants to commit to this relationship forever, and another part would like to leave tomorrow and experience something new.* What we mean is that the part wanting to commit operates within its own constellation of desires and fears that includes its own history of experiences with going out—good and bad. The part wanting to leave is the same way.

These aren't literally different people within us, of course, but they are distinct and palpable patterns of conditioning that now have their own momentum within us. They arose in response to different life conditions or past relationships, often from different time periods in our lives. All we needed was a stimulus, like getting in an argument or meeting someone new, and they were activated. Taken together, these discrete patterns within us interact in a system of psychological relationships not unlike other bodily systems that affects our overall well-being.

In neuroscience, the rough equivalent of psychological parts is the concept of neuropathways. We receive impressions from life; we form a pathway in response; we deepen the groove over time. Any new stimulus that looks like the old one reinitiates the neural pathway and the associated habitual behavior.[9] The behavior can be beneficial, maladaptive, or (most often) some of both depending on the context.

Having a multicentric mind provides us with amazing flexibility, but it can also lead to inner conflict. Not only do parts of ourselves "disagree," but instead of entering the conversation as a mediator, we usually inflame the situation. We may take sides and argue; we may freeze in overwhelm as the voices attack us; we may fall into indecision and anxiety about what to do. Rarely do we respond in a way that truly harmonizes our psychological system and allows a deeper wisdom to emerge.

It's only when there's harmony inside that we can learn to value this unique nature of mind. When we embrace our multiplicity with an open heart, a doorway opens to a more fluid and connected experience of being. We can feel more flexible and understanding, soften our rigid identities and beliefs, and initiate an embodied understanding of our interconnected selves. Speaking for myself, seeing in this way was a pivotal shift that unlocked my capacity to observe new layers of my mind and care for them more skillfully.

PROTECTIVE AND WOUNDED PARTS

So far, I've used both the words *parts* and *patterns* when speaking of different habits of thought and emotion within our psychological systems. The concept of psychological parts is often a more generic reference to a thought or emotion, yet it can also have a more intimate and personified feel (e.g., a young and scared part of me), which can be useful in cultivating compassion. The concept of patterns, instead, can often feel more specific (e.g., a particular habit of procrastination) yet also more impersonal (i.e., it's an inherited pattern; it's not me or mine), which can be useful in supporting wisdom reflections, as described in later chapters. In this book, I use the terms interchangeably.

What's important is that we learn to identify the different types of parts or patterns within us. Various people and traditions have categorized our inner lives in different ways—from Freud's id to Jung's archetypes to the primary and disowned selves of Voice Dialogue[10] to the managers, exiles, and firefighters of the Internal Family Systems (IFS).[11] In the insight tradition, dozens of *mental formations* are identified, but we can generally boil them down to *unwholesome* and *wholesome*—those that create unnecessary suffering and those that help liberate us.

In healing, it's particularly important to notice the patterns that carry or create psychological pain because, by working with them directly, we can alleviate the suffering. To describe these, I find it most helpful to borrow the common designations from IFS: *protective patterns* and *wounded patterns*. Considered in a somatic way, we might describe these categories as (a) mental-emotional experiences that feel tense or hard in our bodies (i.e., protective) and (b) those that feel tender or vulnerable (i.e., wounded).

Using the metaphor of the building of the self offered earlier, these patterns are layered through every level of the psyche like alternating bricks. We are wounded, we form a protective strategy to protect it, and then we repeat. However, our wounded and protective patterns are also wired together across time via association. The older the wound and associated strategy, the more powerful (and hidden) it can be within us.

For example, even though we may be fifty years old when our partner yells at us, it can hit the same tender spot (wounded pattern) that it did when our dad yelled at us when we were five. We can quickly freeze up (protective pattern) and look at the floor in submission (protective strategy), just like we did back then. At least, this is what can happen without any intervention from mindfulness and compassion. When we learn healing skills, we find out how to relate with and rewire these wounded and protective patterns to bring benefit to our lives.

Our protective patterns are most easily recognizable, as they use some variation of the well-known fight, flight, or freeze responses. They are visible as our surface-level reactions, neuroses, and personality traits. While they are trying to help, they often create more harm. Yet we actually gave them their jobs long ago. By leading with gratitude for their tireless work protecting our tender hearts, we can artfully help them let go, take on a new and more helpful role, or at least reflect to them their essential goodness.

For me, this basic understanding—that the parts of myself have a benevolent and innocent nature (i.e., protective and wounded)—was essential to growing sincere care and gratitude for myself. When my sentiments became truly heartfelt, they went deeper into me, soothed me more effectively, and facilitated greater transformation. (See chapter 4 for more in-depth explorations of protective and wounded parts.)

OUR RELATIONAL HEART

Science has shown beyond a doubt that everything is interconnected, both in nature and in the human mind.[12] Subjectively, we recognize this truth as relationship. Indeed, for the psyche, everything has always been about relationships. From day one, every single touch, word, and moment of eye contact mattered immensely. Every interaction with our environment taught us something essential.

Due to our nature as vulnerable biological beings, the organizing principle of our relationships is safety. This gives rise to what in psychological theory are called *attachment styles*. These are ways we related to our primary caregivers as we grew and explored the world. These early patterns set the habits that we carry into adulthood.

A key message from this theory is that feeling secure in our relationships creates a liberating sense of freedom. When we know we are supported—especially lovingly and unconditionally—we can find the courage and confidence to grow into our best selves. Most of us, however, didn't have caregivers that could always be there for us physically, emotionally, or spiritually. But we can still recover safety and security today through our own journey of healing and insight.

It starts by realizing (often the long and hard way) that the most important relationship in our lives is with ourselves. In a powerful turn of focus, we consciously apply our innate relational wisdom and capacity to care *onto itself.* We unfuse with ourselves so we can see the patterns within us, only to then come back into an even more intimate relationship with ourselves. We learn to become the unconditional support for ourselves that we've always needed but never had. We eventually develop an internally regulated sense of safety and security. This, in turn, helps to heal the conditioning from every other human relationship we've had.

My own realization of this innate relational nature helped me to feel comfortable employing compassionate self-talk—the verbal aspect of self-compassion described in chapter 5—in my budding healing practice. I could trust infusing my meditation with thinking (which I had previously perceived as "more noise") when I realized that my wounding was constructed from less-than-compassionate relational experiences that, at this point, only I could resolve by enacting a new relational approach. Moreover, I realized that the parts of myself in pain were enmeshed within the paradigm of a separate monolithic self and, paradoxically, only interacting with them through their paradigm would allow them to awaken into interconnection. In the process, I realized words were a more powerful thing than I ever imagined.

THE NARRATIVE BEING

Language plays a central and fundamental role in our development as individuals[13] and as a species. From the first years of our life, we come to perceive and understand ourselves and everything in the world through it. This means all our emotional and mental patterns, as well as our capacity to regulate emotionally, are entangled within its modes of expression: *stories and narratives.*[14] That includes all our past wounds and trauma that are embedded in our subconscious and in our bodies.

Said differently: the language of stories is spread like mortar through the building of our being. Each past experience stores a perception of its world within us, written in our flesh. Even if we aren't speaking, we're not silent; we already contain volumes. Every part or pattern has a story to tell if we let it. We can't escape the systems of meaning embedded within us.

Whether we like to admit it or not, we all hear voices in our heads. It's not something we can or should shut off. What's more, we can use the same power of words to heal and transform existing stories and, if we'd like, live by simpler and healthier ones. Honoring our storied nature allows us to curiously engage with language, image, and metaphor in ways that can speak to our deepest human experiences and help them return home.

PRIMED FOR MINDFULNESS AND COMPASSION

In sum, we have multilayered and multicentric heart-minds that are organized around relationship, programmed by language, and in a constant search for safety and connection. Being this way, they are exquisitely vulnerable to the systemic medicines of mindfulness and compassion—especially when they're used with compassionate self-inquiry and self-talk. Mindfulness and self-inquiry reveal the layers within while self-compassion and self-talk heal our relational heart-mind—allowing our mammalian brains to finally release and transform. Along the way, we discover what our patterns are trying to do for us—to protect us or show us something—and custom tailor our compassion to our own unique manifestations of pain.

When we practice healing, we're not just doing it for us; we're participating in a critical frontier of scientific research. Like exploring the bottom of the ocean or the far reaches of the solar system, the vast depths of our own individual and collective consciousness is a largely unknown terrain, and it's one that has perhaps the most relevance to the future of life on Earth. With high-powered microscopes, we've peered down into the subatomic level of life; now we need to learn to do the same with our own subjective psychological selves, for what we fail to see and care for in ourselves, we end up unconsciously spilling into the world, and the result is the chaos we see around us.

Principles of Healing

The activity of healing, in its most basic and discrete sense, is simply when a painful emotional experience undergoes the process of releasing and/or transforming. Subjectively, this can feel like a relaxing, a softening, and an opening—among other things. In the moment or over time, more spaciousness, ease, and well-being arise in place of the wound or alongside it. Often, this is accompanied by a deeper understanding of oneself.

There are many methods and models of healing worth exploring, each with its own principles. However, most share a common core in that in one way or another they employ the two most powerful tools we each have at our disposal: *our attention* and *our intention*. We decide where to place our attention and how to use it once it's there. This is also the foundation of all meditative practices and paths.

As such, this is the first and core principle to reiterate: *wise* attention and intention lead to healing. This is what mindfulness and compassion do, as we've discussed. We (a) direct our attention to the contents of our heart-mind and (b) care for them sincerely. That's it! However, while this sounds simple, when we're in the grip of old patterns, we will find ourselves quickly confused again. Therefore, it can be helpful to consider several additional principles that help us to avoid the most common missteps. Alone or together, they can serve as supportive additions to any heart-based healing approach.

CARE VS. AVERSION

There's a simple equation that explains the presence or absence of healing within us. When our care is *equal to or stronger than* our aversion, healing happens. Whether in relation to a specific pattern in the moment or as an overall balance through our journey, if our care for our pain equals or outweighs our resistance to it, healing is the eventual assured outcome.

Fundamentally, it's that simple. It's the physics of the heart-mind system. When care for an aspect of our experience outweighs our aversion, it starts to provide the internal safety and connection for healing to begin. The greater the influence of care for our pain in relation to aversion, then the greater the strength and speed of our healing. The longer care is sustained, the deeper the patterns it can resolve.

The type of emotional pattern doesn't really matter. Often neither does the circumstance. It might be fear, jealousy, sadness, etc., from a fight, a loss, or an abuse. If our care is applied and sustained, it will inevitably eventually work its magic. Amazingly, this is even true when our care is only equal to our aversion because everything within us already longs to heal; it just needs to not be held back by aversion.

Being cared for is perhaps the deepest human need, on par with—if not greater than—physical safety. Indeed, most of us would choose a life where we feel deeply connected in love—even if we're physically unsafe—over a physically safe life where we are anxious and alone. Of course, achieving this level of care for our internal experience is not easy in the face of pain. It can feel like rolling a rock up a hill as we're cultivating this capacity, but, in time, the rock starts to roll down the other side on its own.

CATHARTIC AND TRANSFORMATIVE HEALING

The deepest intention in healing and spirituality is to *uproot* the suffering we experience. However, we can easily get caught in types of inner work that don't address the deeper cause. In this regard, it's important to consider two related approaches to healing: *cathartic* and *transformative*.

Cathartic healing refers to healing that releases or clears emotional/mental energy from the body or mind, usually all at once, through specific techniques. It is often practiced through methods like breathwork, sounding, shaking, and movement therapy, but can also happen naturally through crying or laughing. Sometimes, energy release can even happen spontaneously through meditation or yoga practice. This approach of healing can be very helpful in clearing stuck or trapped emotions from our bodies. However, by itself, it doesn't necessarily transform the root cause of the pain. The disturbed emotional pattern readily regenerates and must be cleared again and again.

Transformative healing may release or clear energy, but its main focus is on (a) rewiring our painful patterns into supportive forms and (b) liberating their true nature (e.g., goodness and wisdom) through insight. The intention here is not to remove the pain but to transform its character, usually gradually, so it becomes softer, more open, and eventually a force for healing itself. Such transformations can happen with a single thought/emotion within a single session of practice or over the course of longer periods with more complex internal patterns.

While there are many examples of each approach, the key differences lie within our attention and intention. In catharsis, we often act from aversion to pain, wanting it "out" so we can feel better again or move on. We're also often fused or identified with the mental-emotional process we're releasing, which reinforces the message that part of us isn't wanted. Underneath the stuck emotion, the various formative narratives and beliefs—including the perception of separation itself—are left untouched. In this way, catharsis alone can be like putting a fan next to a hot burner. The heat is wicked away, but more will soon be generated as the deeper cause is left intact.

In transformative healing, I like to remember the first law of thermodynamics: energy within a system cannot be created or destroyed but only transformed. This is the same as realizing there is no "away" when we throw our trash away. We can try to destroy or throw away our negative energy, but we ultimately fail. We'd be better off recycling it into beneficial forms so we can reuse that precious life force for living.

Admittedly, this took me a while to understand. For many years, I would do breathwork, shaking, or energy work to expressly get rid of the unpleasant experiences, and it sort of worked. It was only after revisiting the same patterns hundreds of times that I realized my aversive mentality was not truly healing but instead reinforcing the very pain I wanted to clear. So I devoted myself to a more compassionate approach. I didn't necessarily stop helping my body loosen frozen energies (as in the guided somatic meditation in part 2), but only did so after establishing a foundation of unconditional care *first*.

To this end, in transformative healing, we unfuse with our internal process and maintain a compassionate presence as the energy moves through at its own pace and in its own way. For example, we might feel angry with ourselves or another for a mistake or transgression. Instead of trying to release the anger temporarily only to have it build back again, we provide the compassionate touch needed to transform it into the sadness that lives beneath it, and then further into forgiveness and kindness, and yet further still into awakened action. The energy of anger, then, is not destroyed but instead transformed into its most beneficial expression.

CONNECTION OVER RESOLUTION

To enact transformative healing, we need to reflect critically on our view. As we know, it's all too easy to overly fixate on the resolution or ending of our pain and miss what's really needed right now. Unfortunately, impatience doesn't heal. No amount of pushing, negotiating, or clever technique can surpass the power of unconditional companionship with one's pain.

When a child falls and scrapes their knee, they don't need to feel pressured or baited into getting over it quicker. They don't need to hear how they could have done something different. For the first while, they often don't even need a Band-Aid. *They just need to be held.* A wise and compassionate parent intuitively knows this. When this is enacted, soon enough the child is back out, playfully pushing their edges again.

It's no different for us as adults. Ninety percent of what our wounds need is just our sincere, caring presence. Through this, our patterns learn that our bodies, hearts, and minds—and, by extension, life—can actually be a safe place, even though it's very painful sometimes. We don't need the pain to end because that's not how life works; we just need a healing refuge to return to when it happens.

Unlike a scraped knee, however, some of our deeper traumas require significant time to heal. In fact, they might need all the time in the world, and only you can give them that permission. Paradoxically, the healing journey can only be successfully sustained to its conclusion if we shift our focus from the destination to a timeless heartfelt embrace, from the ends we seek to the means themselves. In this way, we commit to being a compassionate presence no matter what happens—even if a wound or pattern stays just as it is forever.

This is the principle of focusing on connection over resolution.

SURRENDER, THEN CHANGE

Fully surrendering to our moment-by-moment process of healing, without knowing if or when it will end, is challenging for us for a number of reasons. One of the key sticking points is the worry that if we fully feel our wounding, we might be stuck inside it forever. We might not only be trapped within ourselves but have to resign ourselves to situations or relationships that are hurting us.

These protective anxieties are valid. We certainly don't want to make things worse. However, tragically, that's often exactly what our habitual, aversive approach does. By fearing the pain, we amplify it and lock it in place, effectively locking ourselves in the very situations that created it. Conversely, surrendering to our pain can actually allow it to move and shift and free us to take action.

When we surrender as an act of compassion instead of resignation, we end up caring for ourselves even more deeply. We stand up for ourselves and the authentic needs and desires we carry. Knowing our preciousness, we aren't afraid to take necessary action to ensure our safety. This type of surrender also unlocks beneficial qualities of heart that can further support our courage like curiosity, creativity, joy, etc.

Hence, surrender and change don't need to be at odds with one another. One way to practice them is to simply *do one before the other*. By honoring and caring for our pain first as it is, we can then respond appropriately instead of reacting impulsively. Our actions to change then can come from a calm, clear, and connected space. This can prevent us from causing even more harm, often saving us and others an immense amount of grief. In fact, sometimes we realize that the best action is actually to do less or nothing at all.

Of course, there will be situations when this sequential approach is not possible, especially when we are in imminent physical or emotional danger. In these instances, we accept that we must take action and do what we need with the most clarity we can. When conditions permit, we can then refocus on surrendering to healing.

THE WINDOW OF CARE

Trying to heal can actually be harmful if we don't practice in a balanced way. As I can attest, it's easy to become excited, take on too much, and get in over our heads.

When the level of internal challenge exceeds a certain threshold unique to each of us, the emergency protection systems of our psyche are activated. The alarm bells go off, and we are flooded with our fight/flight/freeze responses. When this happens, our conscious intentions for healing are often overpowered, and our growth process stops—or worse, even reverses. If we're pushed far enough, this can lead to retraumatization.

With mindfulness, we learn to notice the signs and symptoms of this activation and come back into balance in skillful ways (which we will talk more about in later chapters). The common instruction in psychological circles is to learn to first stay within your *window of tolerance* and then eventually expand. This is a helpful concept, protecting us from potentially damaging overwhelm. However, while "tolerating" may be better than panicking, it is limited in its healing capacity. Our pain really needs our full embrace. So I'd suggest we practice working within a *window of care* instead.

The principle of the window of care is that if we *can't* be with something in a caring or compassionate way within ourselves, then we should shift our attention to a part of our experience for which we can. As an instruction for meditation or therapy, this prevents us from stalling our progress through internal resistance. Instead, this approach effectively prioritizes the internal cultivation of care *first*, creating a refuge of well-being within us that we then use to expand to greater challenges.

Staying within the window of care ensures that our heart capacities actually develop before we try to address deeper pain or more challenging circumstances. By starting with what's easy and growing our confidence, we naturally find the window expanding. Our sense of inner safety becomes more resilient, eventually growing into the realization that our external circumstances don't have to dictate our internal well-being.

Of course, many of us, myself included, only come to this by trying it every other way first. Personally, I would push into the edge of my tolerance, seeking expansion at the expense of intimacy. I would stubbornly avoid the window of care, because I knew that when I did soften, I would have to eventually open to all my pain. Looking back, I hold a compassionate respect for my stubbornness, my fierce and stalwart protector that worked for years to guard me from what I wasn't yet prepared to heal—until I finally was. We're still good friends to this day.

The concept of the window of care can be supportive no matter where we are in the journey. It creates a heart-based foundation for sustainable healing over the long term. While it may seem like it will make us go slower, it's likely the fastest and surest way to heal and keep healing throughout our lives. Instead of the backtracks and sidetracks of the overzealous "spiritual warrior," we become steadily stronger and clearer in accordance with our authentic expression and never stop.

BLAME AND RESPONSIBILITY

When we get hurt emotionally, one of our first instincts is to assign blame. Like all protective strategies, this is intended to help us. We think that by determining fault, we might be able to protect ourselves from future harm. Or we think it might help by providing a temporary diversion from the immediacy of the present pain. In the context of healing, however, blame is not mandatory. In fact, it only hampers our progress.

Many of us may have directed our blame back at ourselves for what happened to us. This adds a heavy, personal weight to our wounds, freezing them in place and preventing transformation. To access healing, we must first acknowledge that we were doing the best we could at the time with the understanding that we had. In some cases, as with childhood and ancestral trauma, it barely had anything to do with us at all. Thus, while it's valuable to assess what we can learn from a past event, we can't hold on to self-blame and expect to heal. We must offer ourselves understanding and, eventually, forgiveness.

However, when we relieve ourselves of blame for the past, it can be tempting also to abdicate any further responsibility in the present. This conclusion, as well, leaves us handicapped in healing. Painful past incidents live on within our perception and behavior in the present, and if we don't take responsibility for their residual effects, we are likely to perpetuate the harm. Hence, taking responsibility means recommitting to our own healing process, which can include accountability for harm we caused.

Until we learn from the past, reclaim the agency we lost, and create the inner safety we were missing, many of our patterns will persist. It's hard to do this if we keep blaming and judging the *other* person(s) involved. Waiting for others to do, say, or learn something will likely just prolong— or forfeit altogether—our internal resolution. While it can be valuable to communicate how we felt to another who hurt us, we can't cling to blame toward others and expect to heal fully. In fact, doing so can actually communicate to our subconscious that the other person still has power over our well-being. Therefore, to reclaim our full sense of agency in our lives, we must work to give others understanding, and eventually forgiveness, for their harmful actions.

In healing, we are often best served by holding a paradoxical view. What happened to us in the past was not our fault. Or, at least, we did the best we could and are thus forgivable. At the same time, the pain and conditioning that we carry now *are* our responsibility to address. While we can, and often should, request support in our healing, in the end only we can see it through. This is the principle of blame and responsibility: *What happened in the past wasn't our fault, but it is our responsibility to heal it now.*

CALLING ON DEEPER SUPPORT

There isn't a person among us—even the spiritual masters of the ages— who hasn't needed support on their journey. We can be very wise and skillful inside, but if we don't also learn to ask for and receive help, we're missing half of the equation. Especially on the deeper levels, healing and insight simply don't happen from our effort alone.

Miraculously, there *is* support available to each of us if we just reach out. Of course, there are books and podcasts, friends and therapists. More fundamentally, though, there is nature, the elements, memories of joy or images of those we love, inspiring spiritual figures, and even the ineffable essence of life itself. Just like we have a constellation of patterns inside, we are also part of a larger constellation of life in this universe. By opening ourselves to receive—from something that feels supportive, of course—we affirm the basic spiritual and physical reality that we are interconnected. This beneficial vulnerability further strengthens our sense of safety and trust in the healing process and allows additional growth to happen.

Moreover, when we practice calling on deeper support, the equation of healing changes. It's not just our care that has to be stronger than our aversion for healing to happen. It's our self-generated care *plus* the care and support we can open to *from* the beneficial forces in the world around us. This is powerful, and why I often love to practice in nature where the support and resultant safety pours into me.

At many times on the path, I've reached a point where I simply can't do it. Trying to push through only makes things worse. When I remember to pause and reach out to the benevolence in myself and the world, I'm always pleasantly surprised to be met with grace. In the practices in part 2, we will have an opportunity to practice this calling on deeper support as a meditative technique.

HEART-BASED HEALING

The list of principles we've just gone through is not exhaustive, but it offers basic guidelines for an effective, heart-based orientation toward healing. By attending with care and connection, we are more likely to transform wounds instead of just releasing them, grow our capacity and resilience instead of becoming overwhelmed, and intuitively open to deeper supports that can help us. By taking responsibility but not blaming ourselves, we can surrender to the needs of our pain while still having the courage to change our circumstances. By utilizing these principles, we prevent ourselves from slipping into various forms of resistance, helplessness, and, ultimately, ineffectiveness in our healing journey.

The last principle—calling on deeper support—is particularly important. Just as it's our interconnection that allows us to be wounded in the first place, that same interconnection allows us to heal. We were never meant to do it alone, and we don't have to. In fact, we don't even necessarily have to ask to receive. We only need to come into alignment with the support that's already here.

The Five Natural Forces

There's a little-known but very important secret about healing: when we commit to a healing or spiritual journey, we come into alignment with the entire universe. This may sound romantic or dramatic, I know, but it can be described quite logically.

Biological sciences have long acknowledged that the evolution of an organism occurs for its own benefit. All species enact strategies or undergo adaptations to try to survive and thrive (i.e., to improve their fitness for their environment). If they didn't, no creature would have persisted, including humans. However, we notice much more hesitance to acknowledge this in the psychological sciences, not to mention various spiritual traditions. Instead, many of our thoughts, feelings, and behaviors are seen as ill-intentioned—maladaptive at best and pathological at worst.

A key aspect of our adaptive evolutionary process as humans is our capacity to repair and restore our systems from the harm—including psychological harm—that we have endured. This means we've evolved to be able to heal. It's built into us as a process that's always trying to happen, a balance that's always trying to be restored. When we align with this programmed impulse for healing, we become much more powerful than the patterns that create harm for ourselves and others. This is because healing is deeply aligned not only with our psychological and biological nature but with nature itself.

As we've covered, interconnection is the fundamental reality of our world. Healing is essentially a multilayered, psychic process of returning every part of us to this embodied understanding. We can imagine this force of interconnection always pulling under the surface on the heart-mind like a magnet, drawing us back home. This pull back to the default mode of nature is built into our nervous systems and our DNA. This is why we all contain a deep longing for reunion and why healing and insight feel so good (at least afterward!). It's also why when we relax and let go we feel *more* connected, and why when we welcome our pain it transforms us in beneficial ways.

When we see healing this way, we can then recognize one reason why our capacity to care may have evolved: it helps our own heart-minds return to the natural state of wholeness. By leveraging our psyches' evolutionary design to care and connect,[15] we will always have a natural advantage over aversion and separation. This is good news! When we devote ourselves to the beneficial forces inside of us, they will always prevail.

If you're skeptical, that's good. I know I was. It makes sense: such ideas are easy to dismiss in what can sometimes feel like a cold and meaningless world where "bad guys" seem to get ahead. However, remember that you don't need to believe anything or figure out the Truth with a capital *T*.

Just try these perspectives on for a moment and see how they *feel for you.* That's what's most important. For many folks, these perspectives become very practical. Seeing themselves this way does *a lot* of the heavy lifting on the healing path.

GOODNESS

Everything within us is trying to help.

This perspective is perhaps the most practically important mantra for healing work. Just as we generally accept for our bodily systems, our thoughts and emotions are also trying to help us. When we look at ourselves with this lens, we can notice our distressed patterns are either trying to protect us somehow or show us something important, maybe both. Consequently, we soften and lean in. We get curious and grateful and relate with kindness.

Eventually, we begin to really *feel* the goodness within ourselves. We realize that everything we (and others) do is based in care at some level. It may not be the wise care that creates compassion. It may be an exclusive care (perhaps limited to oneself), a protective care (perhaps pushing something away), or a confused care (manipulating instead of honoring). However, each of these is a form of care nonetheless. These forms of care may objectively be unhelpful in a given moment, but they're *trying* to help in the only way they know. Even the most maladaptive patterns within us are made of good intentions. Their expressions just become twisted through our own disconnection and insecurity.

This perspective is powerful because it has the capacity to uproot and transform all the latent self-aversion in us. When applied to our troubled emotions or thoughts, we start to say, *Thank you for trying to help* or *Thank you for caring so much,* instead of *Why are you here?* or *Why are you doing that?* Our inner lives immediately feel different. Our pain is offered the grace to transform.

COHERENCE

Everything within us wants to work together.

If the cells in our bodies didn't orchestrate themselves like a masterful symphony the vast majority of the time, none of us would be here to read this. They clearly evolved to work together much more than the opposite. Our thoughts and emotions, too, long to return to the same coherence that our lungs and beating heart embody. The relationships have just broken down temporarily.

When we observe with this lens, we notice that all the various parts of us are actually on the same team. We see even the thoughts and emotions that seem actively opposed to us, or our best interests, would rather not struggle and fight. Instead, the contentious patterns within us are likely quite exhausted from constant conflict. Once they're truly heard and understood, they can remember their deeper desire to work together as one unit—which is immeasurably easier.

Over time, each of our patterns has developed its own insular momentum. It forgets not only why it started but also its effect on the whole. Through mindfulness and compassion, we remind ourselves of our wholeness and our intention for healing. Our steady compassionate presence acts as a catalyst for renewed internal coherence.

This perspective has the capacity to effectively resolve conflicts within us. We stop saying, *Why are you doing this to me?* and start to ask, *How are you doing?* We listen, and then inquire, *I know you're hurting, but is there a way I can help facilitate your deeper intention to connect?* Eventually, we begin to witness the harmony unfolding naturally within us. In time, our outer relationships may follow suit.

LONGING

Every wound within us longs to be healed.

Just like a cut on our skin activates a predictable healing process, a cut on our hearts also naturally longs to heal. We are taught to clean and stitch a wound on our body, but with our hearts, we don't always know how to support the healing trying to happen. Often, we even assume that our thoughts and emotions are stubbornly determined to hurt us or others.

Instead of recoiling or reacting, we have to learn to hear the longing of our pain. For example, if we hear a familiar voice in our head say, *You're not good enough*, we don't believe it or argue with it, but realize it's actually a distraught call for help. We can then approach with compassion, find out what it might need, and support its natural longing to be free.

Processing things this way helps us relax into the healing journey. We realize we don't have to do all the work. We can stop saying, *Why are you still hurting?* and start saying, *I trust you want to heal, and I'm here to support that when you're ready.* This is similar to the last force of coherence, where we see beneath the surface to support our pain's deeper purpose.

If this force weren't real, we'd constantly have to fight against our wounds to heal. Compassion or kindness would never work. But, amazingly, as I and countless others can attest, it does. The longing to be free is not only natural, but it's part of a much bigger longing. It's the calling of life to return to itself, and nothing could be more powerfully supportive than that.

WISDOM

Everything within us knows how (and when) to be free.

Just like a seed that sprouts when the conditions are just right, healing happens when we sustain the conditions that germinate wisdom within. A seed is wise not because it is studied or practiced but because it's encoded with the connective wisdom of life. Everything in us, too, knows how to free itself. Deep cellular wisdom is bestowed on each of us just by virtue of our birth.

It's all too easy to struggle and strive on the spiritual journey, forgetting what we already know. In pursuit of our goal of liberation, we step over the very parts of ourselves that know the way. When we finally notice what we've missed, we often apply top-down techniques that re-wound us instead of listening to what's actually needed.

When we see the wisdom in our pain, we can loosen our control over our healing process even further. We give the power back to the patterns themselves and imbue them with our trust. Instead of saying, *This is the right thought or emotion to have*, we might say kindly, *You know how to heal. I trust your wisdom.* Just like a child, when our pain receives our faith in it, it often opens like a flower or flows like a river, going through the natural healing process embedded in our bones.

This perspective allows us to set down the desperation and anxious concern for ourselves and instead follow the lead of our wise wounds.

Eventually, we release any personal agenda for our pain, and a great weight is lifted. We stay with our pain yet trust that our healing and awakening unfold in their perfect timing, and lo and behold, they do.

WHOLENESS

Everything within us is already whole.

The body is still whole even if part of it is very sick. And the same goes for the heart-mind. No matter the size of the fractures or the intensity of the conflict within us, we are still fundamentally whole. Likewise, no matter where we are in the healing process, we are enough and we are complete. We can loosen our fixation on achievement and outcome.

When we look through this lens, we discover the judgment, impatience, and resulting pressure we've been putting on ourselves. We see that although our inner process is messy and troubled at times, it is no less perfect than any other part of nature. It's the most natural thing. When we view our wounds this way, but still stay present with them, the burden of healing is lightened even further.

Instead of saying to ourselves, *You're not finished until you feel or act in this ideal way,* we might say, *You're absolutely whole and perfect as you are* as well as *There will always be ways we can heal and grow together.* This helps us learn to hold a paradox whereby we can have permission to be happy even while healing unfolds and life is tough. This, of course, only increases our healing capacity.

In this way, all parts of ourselves can retain their dignity throughout our path and practice. They are inherently worthy, not only when they perform according to our ideals. There wasn't and won't be anything wrong with them. There may still be hurt, but in this wholeness, everything is somehow also OK.

MAKING HEALING INEVITABLE

These forces of healing were gradual realizations I extracted from my own intimate healing process over many years. They were the gracious attitudes that became a prerequisite for my deepest wounds to heal but that also harmonized with my spiritual insights from the Dharma. They aren't always easy to feel, but they've been like guideposts that bring me back to alignment again and again. Each time I move through them, they stretch me to embody a growing trust in my own heart-mind that helps me return fully to the present without an agenda. They reliably unlock my innate heart-wisdom and capacity for magnanimous care.

Seeing the heart-mind in this way as being organized *for our benefit* can greatly increase the effectiveness, ease, and enjoyability of the healing process. I've never had someone sincerely try them on who didn't feel their benefit. Through the simple recognition of our goodness, coherence, longing, wisdom, and innate wholeness, we align with the natural healing capacity of our psyche. It doesn't have to be as arduous as we often think.

Our restlessness and struggle lessen. Our wholesome capacities expand. We stop doing all the heavy lifting and instead hold space for a process larger than ourselves. We stop maintaining our separation through our own hidden assumptions and trust that the interconnection from which we were built is working to bring us back home. We realize we always have the upper hand in healing because nature itself is on our side.

If goodness, coherence, wisdom, etc., are more fundamental to our psyches than their opposites, and if we choose to align with them, they will eventually transform all the pain within us. If we feel them deeply within us as forces of nature, our healing becomes not only inevitable but is greatly accelerated toward its fruition. If we combine these healing forces with deep spiritual insight, as we do in the practices in this book, full freedom becomes assured at some point down the causal line.

Likewise, when we feel these perspectives as forces of nature, we realize they are not limited to us. They are part of the collective consciousness of living beings, arising from the organizing truth of interconnection. Hence, we realize how close everyone around us is to healing and sense that the conflict and strife dominating our world can't last forever. It simply takes too much energy to sustain patterns inimical to nature. Someday, from one series of causes or another, there won't be the means to maintain it. Whether we're here to see it or not, at some point these forces of healing will return to prominence again—especially if enough of us align ourselves now with the path.

Summary, Prompts, and Practices

CHAPTER SUMMARY

- When we understand how our hearts and minds work, we can then understand why mindfulness and compassion are so effective in healing and take the steps to apply them wisely.
- When we align our healing process with practical principles based on care, connection, and responsibility, it unfolds with greater ease and effectiveness.
- Our healing journey is profoundly enriched and supported when we see all parts of ourselves as inherently good and wise.

JOURNAL PROMPTS

1. Do you believe healing is possible for you? Do you believe you can transform your thoughts and emotions in ways that will better support your life, including your spiritual growth? If you answer no, or you have resistance to the healing methods presented, consider where that might be coming from.
2. Which of the seven characteristics of the heart-mind felt the truest or more relevant for you? Which felt the least true or relevant? What might that reveal about your healing journey and what you might benefit from most at this time?
3. Which of the seven principles of healing is the most valuable for you to remember right now? In what ways would it support your current healing journey or life situation? Imagine using this principle in action.
4. What forms of deeper, beneficial support beyond yourself can you connect with when you need to? Nature? Spiritual figures? The essence of life? List a few of them and be as specific as possible. Then, practice opening to receive them.
5. Which natural force of healing do you most resonate with? In what ways would it support your current healing journey or life situation? Imagine aligning with this force in a particular situation, and feel what that would be like.

GUIDED PRACTICES

There are two guided practices for chapter 3. The first is a meditation on the key principles of healing. The second is a meditation exploring the five natural forces of healing. They are both a combination of mindful reflection and mindfulness of emotions in the body and are intended to help to align ourselves with the healing path more deeply. The guided practices are online at www.justinmichelsondharma.com/thedharmaofhealing/practices or www.shambhala.com/dharmaofhealingpractices.

4

THE HEART OF THE MATTER

In the first three chapters, we explored the overarching principles of compassion-based healing and insight. Now, we're ready to zoom in on the mechanics of the process. To do so, we'll focus on a central component of both our psychological and spiritual experience, one that is often de-emphasized: *our emotions.* We'll examine the psychological origins, benevolent purposes, and assorted types of emotional experiences and—most importantly—exactly how we can use them for healing.

· ·

Our heart is a finely crafted instrument perfected over many millennia. Emotions are its native language. As such, they have each been tuned with specific functions and wisdom—even the unpleasant ones. However, if you were like me, you grew up believing the opposite: that emotions are weak and misguided; that if our will is strong enough, we can override and master them. But it's from this very lack of honor and respect that emotions become deeply imbalanced and distorted within us.

In our relational lives, the biggest consequence of this emotional illiteracy is a lack of intimacy with ourselves and others. In our physical bodies, it's the tension we hold or even the illness we can develop. In our spiritual lives, it's no less than the loss of *embodied* connection to the essence of life. Without our emotions on board, we'll struggle to feel balanced, connected, and tuned in in many aspects of our lives.

We often think that we're the ones driving our experience, but when we investigate inside, we realize there are a lot of other hands on the steering wheel—and the gas pedal and the brakes—sometimes all at the same time. These hands are our buried emotional patterns acting for us without us knowing it. Until we're ready to befriend them, they will keep taking us back to the same places again and again.

.. .

There are countless spiritual techniques that try to help us discover greater truths about ourselves. In traditional insight meditation alone, there are dozens of approaches to meditation. For us modern laypeople, it's my view that the most effective avenue to develop a healing and insightful meditation practice is through the gateway of our emotions—in particular, our *emotional body*. This is the energetic realm of emotions felt as sensations in the body, as we'll explore shortly.

For me, practice began with focusing on my breath, as I was instructed at the time. Over time, however, I noticed areas of my body would become tense when I was upset or stressed, and my attention was drawn there out of curiosity. I realized that in being with these emotions in my body, I could stay present through challenging experiences without getting lost in thought. As the years progressed, I discovered just how powerful this organic tendency was.

Emotions are an especially effective focal point for several reasons. First, they are situated uniquely at a midpoint of our being. They are the engine of our thoughts "above" and intimately embedded within the physiology of the body "below." In addition, used skillfully, they are a conduit to something greater than us through our heart center. Hence, they are the energetic connective tissue between our body, mind, and spirit. The effects of healing our emotions therefore extend throughout our being—including to the limiting beliefs and narratives we hold. This is why self-compassion can create systemwide healing and coherence.[1]

Second, using emotions as a focal point prevents bypassing. When we focus our attention solely on the body, as is common in meditation, we can find ourselves sinking beneath thought and emotion, missing the patterns that ail us. A similar result can occur when we focus our practice solely on interconnection or awareness. Centering our attention on thinking would be an option, but the stickiness, speed, and complexity of thoughts easily outdo us and often distract from the emotions that fuel them. Indeed, attending to emotion *as it's felt in the body* is an inclusive centerpoint of focus, keeping us grounded and engaged in the present moment.

Third, practicing with emotions leads us eventually to our deepest subconscious drives and distress—like our existential angst, dread, and terror—which we otherwise may never touch in normal meditation (or if we do, we aren't prepared). These powerful primal forces limit our liberation much more than our restless thoughts or body pains ever could. Indeed, they are embedded in the ancient recesses of our brains and easily overpower our rational minds.[2] This is why when we're really emotional, we can't think straight or sometimes even feel physically sick. Emotions take control of our physiology and behavior when the threat or attraction is great enough.[3]

Finally, skillful meditation practice with emotion eventually leads to deep healing for body, heart, and mind, restoring fundamental safety and connection throughout our entire being. In turn, this becomes the fertile soil within which wholesome heart capacities can take root and liberating spiritual truths can grow and mature.

The Garden of Feeling

Over the centuries, scientists and psychologists have defined and described emotions in many ways. Even though there is no current consensus on the matter, we can broadly state that emotions are the "affective aspect of consciousness," per *Merriam-Webster*'s definition. Or we might say that they are interconnected neurophysiological processes mediated by the brain, heart, and body, as the scientific literature suggests.[4] However, for the purposes of our work together, I'll define emotions as *the aspect of our consciousness that is neither physical nor cognitive but influences our sense of self and behavior and can be felt as sensation in or around the body.*

This definition first distinguishes emotion from physical sensation (i.e., input from the five senses) and thinking (i.e., using internal words or images). Second, it suggests not only its importance but how it can be observed. Emotion is energy moving through our system that can be felt as changing sensations within or around the body. Learning to temporarily isolate and observe emotion in this way, healing becomes simpler and more effective, especially at the beginning.

For example, we can discover that what we thought was just emotion is often emotional energy *plus* a narrative layer *plus* our judgments about it—greatly increasing the density of the experience. By relieving ourselves of the judgment, the felt sense of the emotion changes, often lightening greatly. By untangling ourselves from the narrative, the emotional energy is distilled even further. Then, we can offer compassion directly to the embodied source of pain.

Likewise, with the body, we can discern when there is just pure physical sensation present and when, instead, we are having an emotional experience *within the body*. We discover sometimes that what we thought was just a physical ailment has a vibrant emotional life and is calling out for healing. Or we find that purely physical pain is made exponentially worse by our emotional resistance to it. Hence, by soothing our emotions, our bodies often feel the healing too. Conversely, by sending compassion to our bodies, we often discover and release emotional distress.

Refining our mindfulness to be able to isolate the raw experience of emotion in the body is not inevitable from an average meditation practice. This is partially because spiritual teachings and environments can overlook, or even diminish, this aspect for our experience. It's also because English speakers tend to lack some nuance in their language of emotions. The verb *to feel* can reference physical sensations, emotions, and even thoughts. For example, we might say, "I feel sick to my stomach," "I feel nervous," and "I feel like I need to run and hide"—all in reference to the same experience. However, as I'm defining it, only the *sensations* of nervousness—the heat, vibration, tension, "butterflies," and so on—moving through the body signal the emotion itself.

When we explore our emotions with mindfulness, we might agree they are an amazing creation of nature. It took millions of years of evolution to develop their miraculous design. However, if we haven't been tending to them, our emotional lives might initially feel a bit like an overgrown jungle. Large and dangerous creatures live there; it's tangled and dense. When we tend to ourselves with kindness, we slowly begin to recultivate a rich and nourishing garden of emotion that can support us.

Emotions come in myriad varieties—sadness, playfulness, longing, awe, gratitude, doubt, curiosity, fear, etc. They can coexist in different patterns and connections, like an ecological web. They cross readily into various hybrids. Despite our own ideas to the contrary, our hearts can handle being joyful and sad, fearful and excited, or disgusted and awed at the same time. They can even layer upon each other. I've used the example that anger can sometimes present first but then reveal a sadness beneath it, and then give way to kindness and ease yet further down.

The embodied experience of emotions is a world unto itself. They can be perceived in varying shapes, sizes, even colors—and in different locations. We may grow emotions in our hips, our stomach, or our throats. They come with differing intensities, from very mild to unbearable. They live varying lifespans, passing in a dramatic flash or smoldering for many years. They can be a momentary impulse, a lingering mood throughout the day, or even harden into lifelong personality traits.

Due to this fluid and multifaceted nature of emotions, the total number of emotions that researchers identify varies. Some modern researchers have classified more than twenty-five,[5] while the ancient Buddhist text *Abhidhammattha-sangaha* lists fifty-two distinct mental/emotional states. In addition, our experience can change depending on various biological and cultural conditions such as neurodiversity, gender, culture, language, etc.[6]

Getting to know a broad range of emotional experiences is a critical first step. When we become familiar and comfortable with each flavor of feeling, we can understand how to see and relate to them in beneficial ways.

• •

In the following sections, I offer diagrams that map our diverse emotional states into twelve core energies and list their common attributes and functions. Note, the intention here is not to box in our experience of emotions or assert the correct way to understand them but instead to set out a practical emotional framework through which we can enact the process of healing and insight. For some, this discussion may feel dense and analytical. Don't try to take it all in on the first pass, as there are many layers to the material. Each of us experiences emotions differently, so just take in what resonates with you right now and leave the rest. You may choose to dog-ear the pages with diagrams so you can return when needed.

As you'll see in Diagram 4.1, each circle encompasses a familiar emotional energy or tone. The primary emotion is centered in bold print (e.g., anger, sadness, etc.). Then these are surrounded by two related emotions of lesser or greater intensity. Various others could be included for each emotional tone—you might write in your own.

As you review the diagram, first consider each of the primary emotions. As you do, recall how each tends to feel in your body. Imagine each as a button you can press so that you feel a trace of that energy—just enough to taste it.

While you're feeling, notice the way you perceive each emotion. You might pinpoint the ones you habitually tend toward and the ones you rarely experience. You might reflect on the ones you like and the ones you wish never visited—or that you don't let arise. You might even notice emotions that you don't think belong in spiritual life.

The way we see our emotions is fundamentally important, since it greatly affects the way we relate to and experience them. First, in this practice, we work to see all our emotions as natural, normal, and deserving of our understanding, care, and support. In other words, they all belong here and have value, even if they are painful or confusing at times. Then, in the practices in part 2, we'll also learn to see them impersonally as collective or archetypal energies that are shared among humanity and live on through our lineages.

THE DUALISTIC NATURE OF EMOTIONS

On the next page, Diagram 4.1 is divided into two sections by a horizontal center line. Colloquially, these sections would be termed "positive" and "negative" emotions. I once used these terms as well, but I eventually realized that such labels only reinforce our aversion to what's unpleasant. So we won't use them here. My heart still breaks a bit every time I hear self-help gurus tacitly encourage the age-old crusade to "clear," "control," or "master" negative emotions or inner demons. Likewise, it does the same when I hear teachers cite the early Buddhist texts to proclaim all emotions are born of delusion or ignorance—as our wounded Western minds only use that as more ammunition. There are more insightful causes for and attributes of these two categories that better inform our healing and spiritual journeys.

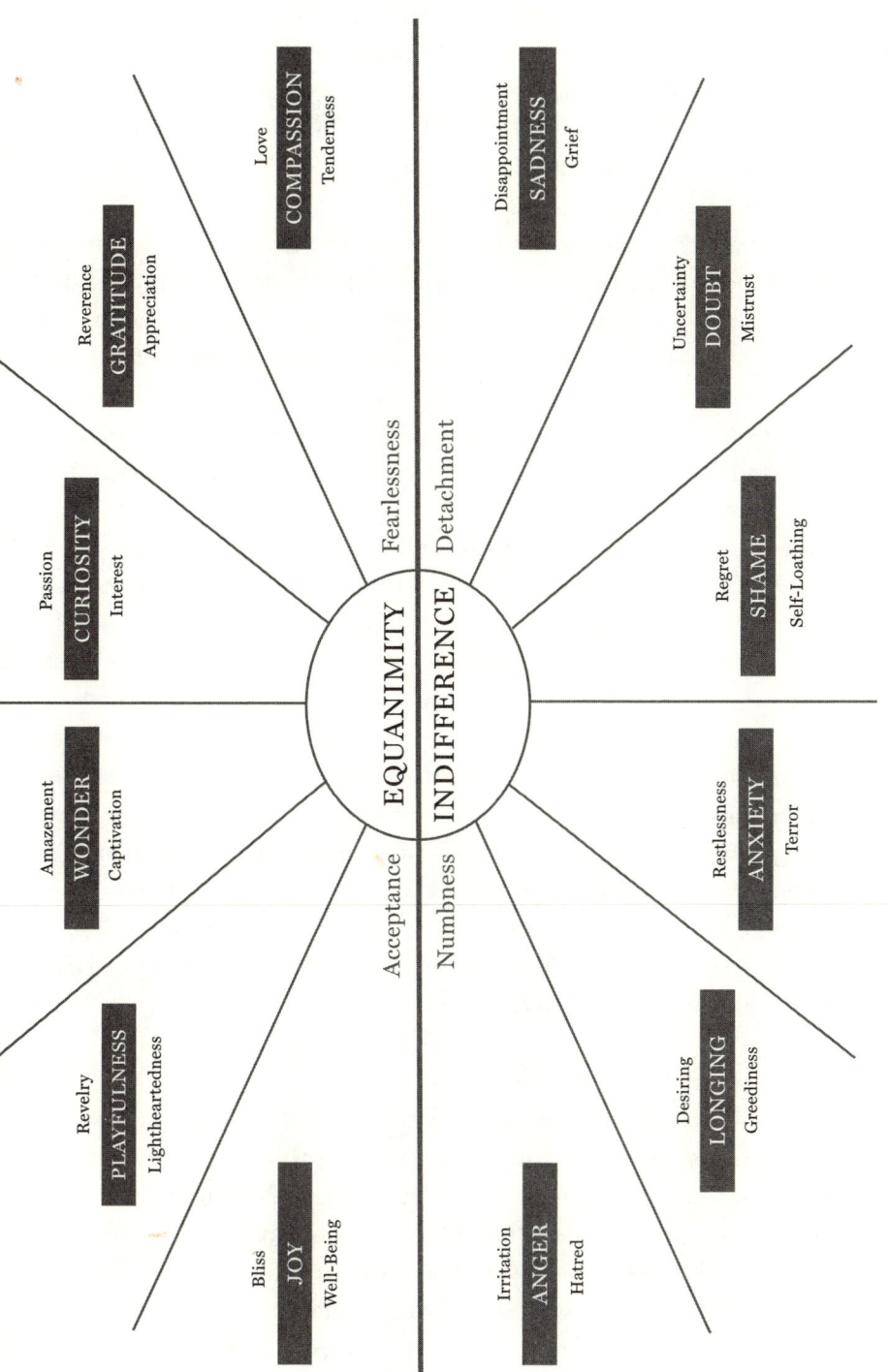

FIGURE 4.1. WHOLESOME AND UNWHOLESOME EMOTIONS

For example, the emotions on the top half of the diagram could simply be called pleasant, as they each tend to arise from pleasant or favorable experiences. Likewise, they could be called safe, as they often arise from a sense of emotional or physical safety. They could even be called fulfilled, as they can arise from having our emotional or physical needs met. We could likely come up with other options.

While each of these labels can be supportive in different contexts, for the purposes of healing and spiritual growth, I prefer to term these two broad categories of emotion as *wholesome* and *unwholesome*. However, I use these words slightly differently from their English connotations and their common Buddhist scriptural translations of "healthy and unhealthy" or "good and bad." Instead, the emotions on the top are wholesome because they tend to *arise from and are sustained by* a felt sense of wholeness. The more connected we feel emotionally and spiritually—all the way to feeling ourselves *as* everything—the more wholesome emotion and natural care emerges. In addition, the more care and connection we cultivate through practice, the more these wholesome emotions are energized. Conversely, the emotions on the bottom tend to *arise from and are sustained by* a felt sense of separation or disconnection and are energized by aversion.

In this way, these two categories could also be thought of as *connected* and *disconnected* emotions. Because the healing and spiritual journeys rely on supportive connection, this is a vital distinction to understand when navigating our emotional lives. If we're unsure which type of emotion we're feeling, we can simply check if it's helping us feel more connected (often softening and opening) or more separate (often tightening and closing).

Note there are several important exceptions to this dualistic model that I'll explain in greater detail below.

OUR EMOTIONAL CENTER

The six wholesome emotions and the six unwholesome emotions (as well as their variations) create a map of our overt emotional expressions. However, there are also times when our hearts seem absent of feeling. These subtler states are shown as a circle in the center of the diagram. The wholesome portion of this circle is equanimity, and the unwholesome portion is indifference.

Equanimity is most easily described as a stable state of calm or ease. In this way, it could be said to be the absence of emotion. However, I prefer to see it as a full and vibrant place at the center of our hearts where all other emotions can rest and from where we act most wisely. We can experience a rudimentary version of this inclusive and responsive state simply from an absence of stimulation or triggering experiences. Or we can experience its full expression as a hard-won result of healing and insight. In the latter, equanimity becomes a refuge for our heart and a place from which wholesome emotions emerge effortlessly into our lives.

Indifference, on the other hand, is a state of emotional distance or disregard, absent of clear feeling or connection. While it can appear calm and unperturbed, it is not the absence of activation but instead a protective cover for pain hidden underneath. Being rooted in separation, it gives rise to all manner of unwholesome emotion. Indifference can develop as a habitual dismissal of our emotional lives or as a response of resignation to repeated wounding we feel we can't control. It can be a subtle disconnection we carry or mature into a debilitating numbness.

Learning to discern equanimity from indifference is important in healing and spiritual growth. If we find ourselves without clear emotion, we can simply inquire into the quality of the state. Namely, do we feel connected and responsive or disconnected and dismissive?

EVERYTHING IS TRYING TO HELP

With the emotional diagram in mind, let's reconsider the five healing forces in relation to unwholesome emotions. They are (1) everything within us is trying to help, (2) wants to work together, (3) wants to be healed, (4) knows how (and when) to be free, and (5) is already whole. Notice that the five healing forces all point to one overarching truth: goodness and wisdom are inherent to all our emotions—even the unwholesome ones.

Perhaps the most important force for us to understand early on is the first—that everything is trying to help and, thus, is based in care. This opens the door to the rest of the forces to flow naturally. However, it requires a significant shift from our normal mode of perception. We'll focus here first.

To start, it helps to acknowledge that while each emotion is *trying* to help, it clearly may not be helping the *best* way it can. However, every emotion can *always* become an ally if we relate skillfully (which we'll explore in the following section). Let's take some time with each unwholesome emotion and consider the ways they try to help us.

- *Anger* exists within a spectrum from subtle irritation to blind rage. As we likely know firsthand, anger tries to help us by creating boundaries and reclaiming power. It can also pull us out of emotional shutdown or indifference. While it's important to honor and experience this emotion fully, care must be taken when expressing it. Held with gratitude and compassion, it often melts into exhaustion and sadness, respectively—and reveals our wounds underneath.

- *Longing* exists within a spectrum from a gentle preference to an absolute demand or a rapacious greed. It tends to be our preferred escape route from pain, trying to help by gathering our energy toward the obtainment of something that might please, protect, relieve, or distract us. When unfulfilled or threatened, it can transform into protective anger. When it's met with gratitude and compassion, it can melt in the same way as anger does into exhaustion and sadness.

- *Anxiety* exists within a spectrum from restlessness to all-out terror. For many, it's one of our deepest-held emotions. It tries to protect us by keeping us on alert, often hypervigilant, scanning our environment for any potential problem. Being inherently unstable and uncomfortable, it often leads to longing and anger. Held with gratitude and compassion, it can reveal the deeper tenderness and vulnerability that it's been trying to protect.

- *Shame* exists within a spectrum from a minor embarrassment to a deep self-loathing and is one of the most self-destructive emotions. It tries to help us by keeping us small, contained, and within a familiar perception of self. This may prevent us from getting into further trouble or making more mistakes while pushing us to "get it together" and "do better." It's often the most powerful link in habitual patterns of distress. Held with compassion, it can transform into ease and even playfulness.

- *Doubt* exists within a spectrum from casual uncertainty to paralyzing inner turmoil and is a subtle but powerful emotion. It tries to help by showing us potential harm and risks, often convincing us to play it safe so we don't get hurt again. It may be especially strong when we are trying new things, making important changes, or solidifying commitments. It works closely with fear and shame. However, when spotted with mindfulness and offered a steady, reassuring presence, it can transform into a grounded confidence.

- *Sadness* exists within a spectrum from minor disappointment to deep depression and anguish. It often resides underneath other unwholesome emotions. It tries to help by showing us what we love and care about—which we don't always acknowledge or remember—and then invites us to let it go. In doing so, it can actually invite us back into wholesome connection. Sadness mixes naturally with compassion, which can help it release and move toward ease and even joy.

As for the pleasant or wholesome emotions, it's more obvious how they help us. Wonder shows us the sacred in life; playfulness allows us to explore without fear; joy gives us energy and fulfillment. Curiosity helps us discover new things. Gratitude makes us feel whole and complete. Compassion helps us transform the suffering we meet. When focused toward our healing and spiritual paths, these emotions provide unparalleled support and insight. By welcoming wholesome emotions when they come, we can assist them in helping us even more.

WHOLESOME DESIRE

While desire is depicted next to longing amid the unwholesome emotions, when used wisely it can also be very supportive. However, if we've been exposed to meditation or Buddhism, we can easily get the impression that desire is all bad. Yet it's the *desire* to heal or liberate that brought us here, and we don't want to lose that. Indeed, we naturally want to live a rich and meaningful life filled with joy, love, and wonder—not just because it's deeply nourishing for us, but because it supports the liberation of all beings.

Wholesome desire arises from wholeness and calls us back to it. When we sense the calling to heal and liberate, we are actually feeling something much larger: our heart's natural pull back into communion with life itself. Tuning in to this ever-present draw breaks us out of complacency and compels us to dig deeper into ourselves.

By conventional standards, we might have a really good life, and yet we may find we still crave a deeper, nonmaterial fulfillment. (This can often be confusing to those around us.) Embracing this deep, intuitive desire and what it asks from us is eventually what brings us all the way home. This may require immense effort or arise as a simple and quiet remembrance.

In this way, we could say that wholesome desire is at the root of all desires. On the surface, we think we lack the right people, places, or things. At the core, however, we actually lack a reunion with life itself. Hence, there's nothing inherently aspiritual about surface-level desires; they are just stray pieces of a deeper longing. When seen in this way, the pain of unmet desires (i.e., lack or dissatisfaction) can be honored as a wise messenger that helps us redirect our attention to the true fulfillment waiting underneath.

In a more practical sense, wholesome desire is desire that arises from and/ or moves toward *care and connection* instead of aversion and separation. In our relational lives, this means a heartfelt intimacy and goodwill toward the people and places around us. In healing and spiritual practice, this means not practicing to be good, right, or even to improve but instead simply because we care about our restless heart-minds. It means letting go of becoming different or special and focusing on restoring our belonging to the community of life.

WHOLESOME GRIEF

We all know the unresolvable type of sadness, the one that is replete with self-pity or loathing, lack or longing, and defeat or hopelessness. It cycles and grows heavier, collecting shame, doubt, and fear, and ending in the dark hole of depression. This is the unwholesome sadness that unfolds from an internal sense of separation and insecurity, a sadness that I used to not let myself feel out of fear that it would cripple me. However, when we feel safe and connected, or when we hold ourselves in compassion, sadness can become a potent transformative emotion.

Wholesome grief is an ancient psychophysiological process that was designed to shake us free of painful states, acting like a drain plug for our nervous systems. As one of our deepest-held emotions, it attracts, aggregates, and then releases the other unwholesome emotions along with itself back into the embrace of interconnection. This delivers us into equanimity again and again and prepares the heart for forgiveness or even joy.

In this way, sadness can have an endpoint in debilitating depression *or* regenerative healing, depending on how it is held. To know which type of sadness we're experiencing, we can ask *Will we be OK in the end?* If the answer is anything but yes, we are likely coming from a place of separation, and our sadness may have hybridized with various other unwholesome emotions. The remedy is to apply compassion to restore safety and connection and alchemize our pain through wholesome grief.

SPIRALING THROUGH THE UNWHOLESOME

Without mindfulness and compassion, we tend to get stuck in cycles of unwholesome emotion. Each emotion tries to help, but instead can accumulate an increasing burden. For many of us, the cycle starts and restarts with anxiety and can collect multiple other unwholesome emotions. Here's an example of one potential cycle that depicts how all six unwholesome emotions can trigger each other.

Not feeling safe or connected (often due to past wounding), *anxiety* tries to warn us something's wrong. Uncomfortable, *longing* tries to help us find something to fix it. When it doesn't work or last, some form of *anger* takes over to use more force to get the job done. Eventually exhausted with that approach, *sadness* helps us to release the tension and calm down. Meanwhile, *doubt* convinces us that it's too risky to keep trying to find safety. *Shame* jumps in to personalize the pain of our failure to make sure we don't try and fail again. Before long, *anxiety* overpowers shame to warn us we're still unsafe, and the cycle starts over. Eventually, after spiraling again and again, we can fall down into the center, first in hopelessness and then *indifference* and numbness.

A summary of this cycle could be understood as the push and pull between anger and sadness, each of which tends to aggregate other unwholesome emotions. For example, our unresolved anxiety and longing gradually build into anger. When we find a way to discharge it (or simply get exhausted), we collapse into sadness that often feeds doubt and shame. Anxiety returns and the cycle repeats.

In the bigger picture, each of these emotions is trying to point to a deeper issue. They're trying to show us that we're disconnected from ourselves, others, or life. To break the cycle, restore supportive connection, and spill over into the liberating side of our hearts, we just need a little help from the "healing emotions" (as we'll speak to in the next section).

Diagram 4.2 shows the full potential unwholesome cycle described above, beginning with anxiety and continuing clockwise with solid arrows (Cycle 1). It also shows the wholesome cycle that can come from a healing emotion like compassion, facilitating the transformation of anger (and its attached emotions) into sadness, and sadness (and its attached emotions) into equanimity and eventually joy (Cycle 2).

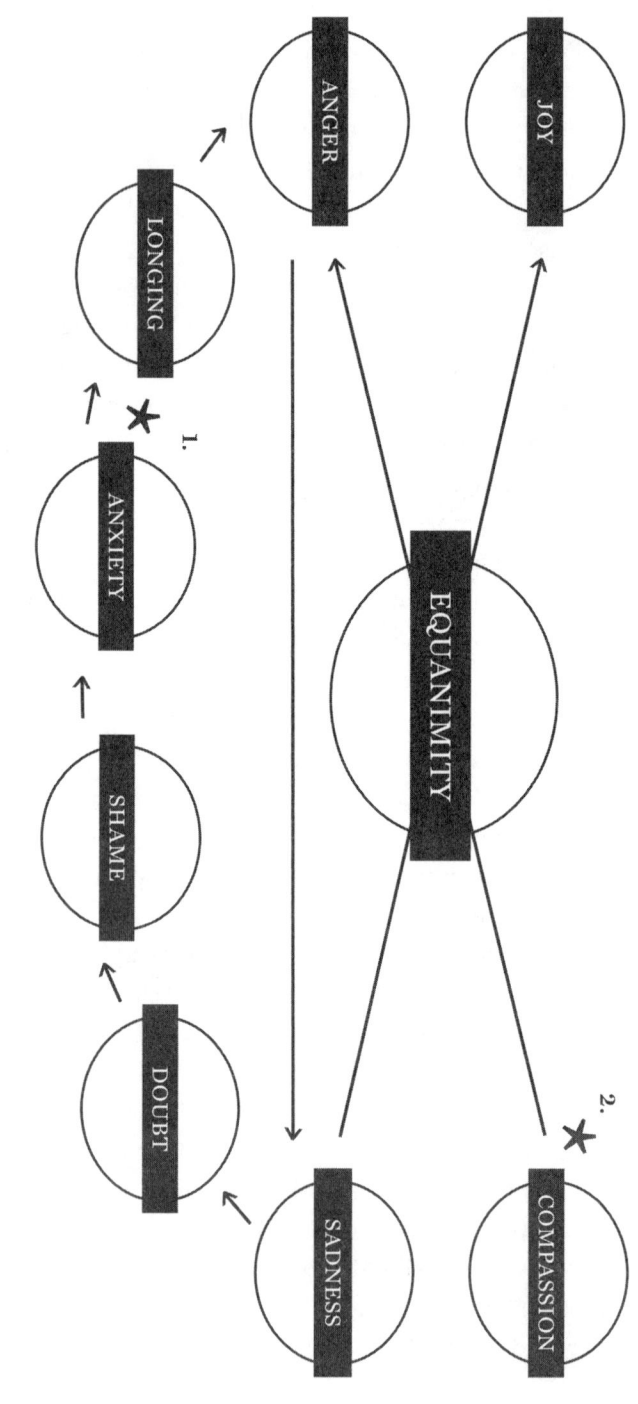

FIGURE 4.2. WHOLESOME AND UNWHOLESOME CYCLES

OTHER SOURCES OF EMOTION

It's important to note that not all emotions arise from psychological or spiritual causes. They may stem from our present-moment bodily health (e.g., nutrition, minerals, hormones, medications, gut flora, chronic pain, or illness). They may be deeply embedded in us from our biological or ancestral past or be products of systemic traumas like racism or classism. There is no hard-and-fast distinction between body, heart, and mind nor self and community, so there are countless potential sources of emotion.

Personally, I remember being surprised to discover emotions emerging—unassociated with narratives or outer circumstances—from digestive dysfunction, viral sicknesses, and, as an empath, even other people. Before I made the connections, I would interpret these experiences as indicating a lack of personal psychological safety or connection, and think I needed to practice "better." In reality, I needed to take care of my body or remove myself from a situation. Over time, I learned not to limit myself to compassion as the only solution.

That being said, regardless of where the emotion might be arising from, a wholesome way of seeing and relating to it will always help us respond to the situation with greater clarity and, when needed, encourage healing. Mindfulness and compassion have even been shown to help with speeding recovery from illness. In the end, however, pain will always be a part of life. True well-being has to be able to exist *alongside* it, not be waiting on its absence. With devotion, we can find a nourishing inner refuge growing from our wholesome response to challenge itself.

Emotions That Liberate Us

Without mindfulness, our brains tend toward unconscious patternmaking. They push the buttons of our emotions to send them traveling in well-worn patterns and essentially act for us. In these unconscious modes, we are completely subject to our circumstances. If things don't go well for us, we feel a familiar pattern of unpleasant emotions. If things do go well for us, we feel a familiar pattern of pleasant emotions. Often, in practice, we experience a complex mixture of both. Regardless, our well-being remains *conditional*.

In insight meditation, the genesis of our emotions is described in simple terms. If something is pleasant, we unconsciously tend toward wanting more of it—desire and its related emotions. If it's unpleasant, we move away—aversion and its related emotions. If it's neutral, we ignore or dismiss it. The unconscious effect is that we are constantly wanting, avoiding, or not seeing clearly. While these instincts can help us in limited and temporary ways, they can't ever bring lasting peace as they are often in direct conflict with reality. Instead, they commonly re-wound us by enacting the same strategies that others inflicted on us and conditioned into us.

The solution here is to see these dynamics with mindfulness and change the way we relate. Ideally, we notice the raw experience of something pleasant, unpleasant, or neutral and choose to relate with gratitude, compassion, and curiosity, respectively. Gratitude neutralizes desire for the pleasant, compassion neutralizes aversion toward the unpleasant; curiosity prevents dismissal of the neutral. This short-circuits unwholesome responses and cultivates the wholesome.

In practice, however, by the time we become mindful, we are often well-entangled in unwholesome emotional reactions—often from triggered stored patterns. Hence, our main work becomes learning to notice this reaction cycle and then relating to each emotion in wholesome ways.

THE FOUR WHOLESOME RESPONSES

When we make our emotional life conscious, we begin to regain choice about how we feel. We don't get to choose a happy and peaceful self overnight, however. We wake up within the existing patterns that we've inherited and humbly realize that, through our lack of attention to date, we have actually been unconsciously cultivating the suffering we've been trying to escape from. Recognizing this, the responsibility becomes ours, for if we're not actively choosing a new and wise approach, we're probably inadvertently engaged in creating more suffering. Our choice, then, lies in how we relate to the emotional patterns already within us. Below are four wise approaches that stop re-wounding us, slow the river of unhelpful conditioning, and over time, reveal the original well-being lying underneath.

- *Allowance.* The first wise approach to our emotional lives is *allowance* and aligns with the traditional insight meditation instruction around working with feelings. We simply bring mindfulness to the feeling of pleasant, unpleasant, and neutral emotions to break the chain of unconscious proliferation. Instead of wanting more pleasant, we simply be with the pleasant while it's here. Instead of avoiding the unpleasant, we remain with the experience of the unpleasant as it is. Instead of ignoring the neutral, we pay intimate attention to it—bringing it to life. It's a valuable approach, as it can short-circuit unhelpful patterns in the present moment, preventing further suffering. It doesn't, however, necessarily *uproot* preexisting patterns and wounds so they heal and transform.

- *Cultivation.* The second wise approach is direct *cultivation* of the wholesome. Most simply, we can mindfully embrace pleasant emotions when they arise in our lives, which naturally deepens their resonance within us. In a joyful moment (due to some success, perhaps), we can stop and go inside, breathing joy throughout our bodies, consciously receiving its medicine. Slightly more complex, we can use internally spoken phrases or visualizations from joyful memories to actively evoke the wholesome and then dwell within it. (This is similar to the traditional practices of the brahmaviharas in insight meditation.) These practices create new neural pathways that shift the balance of our emotional lives toward the wholesome, soothe our nervous systems, and bring resilience and strength to meet our challenges.

- *Application.* The third wise approach, and the one most emphasized in this book, is the *application* of wholesome emotions *to* unwholesome emotions. This is the conscious process of transformative healing. We acknowledge or invoke a wholesome emotion and directly apply it, in a mindful and continuous manner, to a painful emotion via internally spoken phrases or visualization (lots more on this to come). These practices cultivate the wholesome while *simultaneously* transforming the unwholesome into its liberated expression over time. Effectively, this process is simply applying connection to separation, thus restoring our wholeness.

- *Surrender.* The fourth wise approach is *surrender.* When the conditions come together for us to let go, we take the opportunity. This might arise as the result of one of the previous approaches, of direct intentional practice to surrender (as we'll also do together), or just from serendipitous conditions in our practice or lives. When we surrender, something miraculous can happen. We can be carried by the five forces of healing and by life itself. The wholesome emotions arise within us spontaneously because they are natural expressions of a connected heart. If continuous, the act of surrender sustains wholesome expressions by freeing us from aversion.

These four approaches are not in conflict. In fact, they often need each other and can even act as a progressive training. We can first learn to see and allow what is. Then, we can cultivate the wholesome to gain strength and confidence. Then, we can apply it to the pain that we carry to heal and transform. This allows us to surrender, which brings forth even deeper healing and wholesome expressions. Depending on what's arising within us and what we need, we can use any of them alone or sequentially. As a progression, however, they show how using the wholesome for healing is a positive feedback loop with compounding benefits. The more we cultivate, the more deeply we heal; the more we heal, the more we surrender and wholesome emotions emerge naturally. This, in turn, allows us to heal even deeper, and the cycle continues.

THE FOUR CATEGORIES OF EMOTIONS

To deepen the analysis, we can draw a vertical line down the middle of Diagram 4.1 to produce four quadrants of *protective emotions, wounded emotions, healing emotions,* and *liberating emotions.* (See Diagram 4.3.) Dividing our twelve core emotions into these categories can further illuminate their function and wisdom in our spiritual path. In particular, it can help us understand the profound results of the third approach to wise relating described above: *application of the wholesome to the unwholesome.*

In Diagram 4.3, the emotions on the lower left—anger, longing, anxiety— are those that *tend* to be most protective. Said differently, protective patterns or parts express themselves using those emotions. The false peace of indifference fits here, as well. The job of these emotions is to safeguard our wounds from further impacts, as well as shield us from our own pain. Interestingly, many of us discover protective emotions have actually been the primary motivating forces for our healing or spiritual practices. These emotions can be recognized by their signature manifestation: a feeling of tension or tightness in the emotional body.

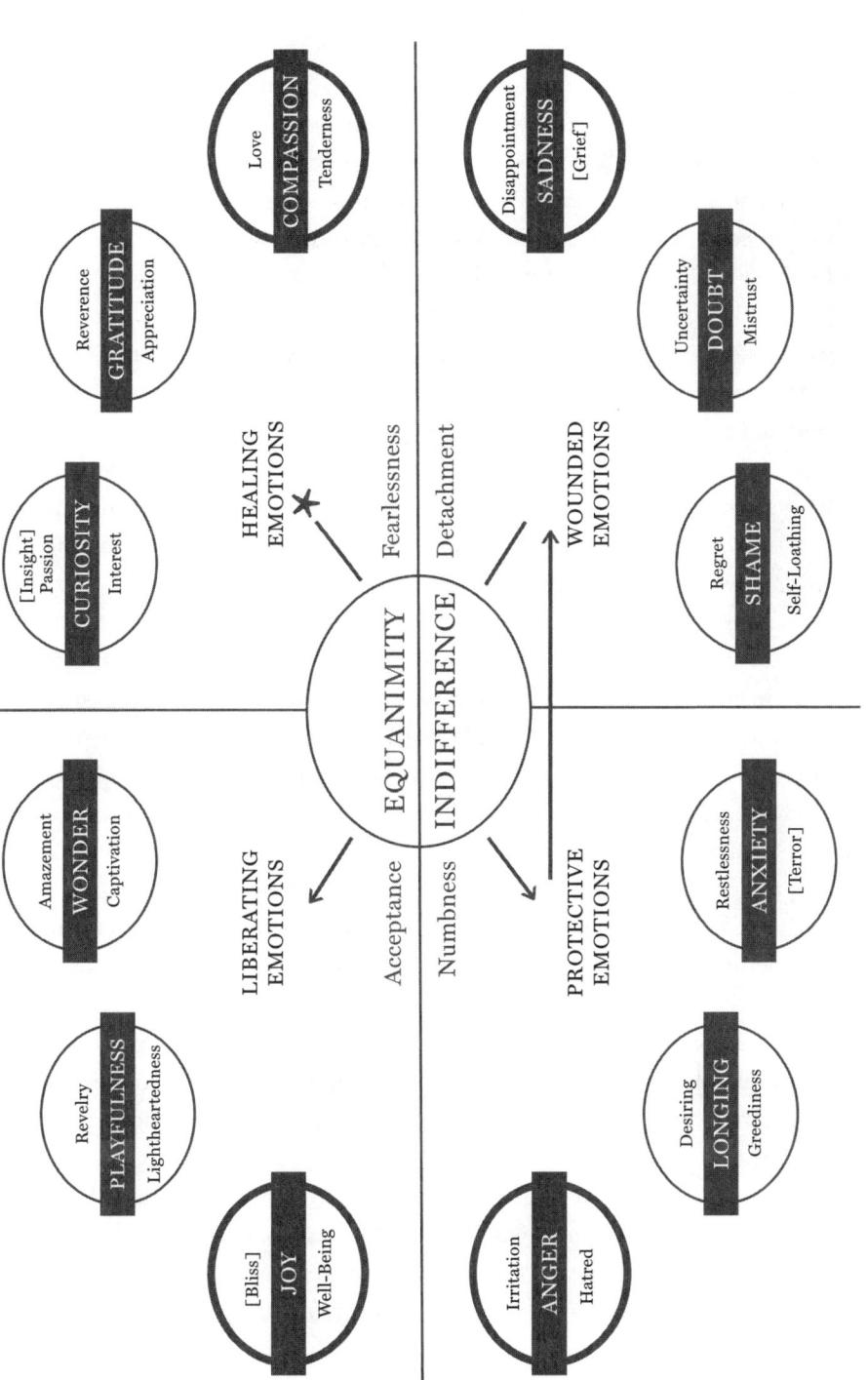

FIGURE 4.3. THE FOUR CATEGORIES OF EMOTIONS

Anger has the darkest outline in the group because it tends to be our strongest protector, often taking the lead in situations perceived to be most threatening. In addition, I see anger as a "transformative emotion," as it tends to gather the energy of other unwholesome emotions and, when held compassionately, can transform them into grief. Note, while worry and anxiety are often employed as regular protective habits, terror can be lodged deep in our bodies from past wounding. Because of that, it tends to fit better in the next category and is bracketed to indicate this.

On the lower right are the emotions that commonly arise from our wounds or wounded patterns—terror, shame, doubt, and sadness. These tend to be the emotions that most deeply need our compassionate attention and are often the most potent doorways to spiritual transformation. Their job is to get our attention so that they can lead us back to our original hearts. They can be recognized by their signature manifestation: a feeling of tenderness and vulnerability in the emotional body when they are not covered by protective emotions.

Sadness has the darkest outline in the group because it is often the deepest expression of our wounds—often more so than even fear and terror. This is particularly apparent as we heal through the grief of our original wound of separation from life itself. As described in the wholesome grief section, grief can be a powerful transformative emotion as well, and thus is bracketed to indicate its connection to the healing emotions.

On the upper right are the healing emotions—compassion, gratitude, and curiosity. They are the most potent emotions for the cultivation of healing and insight. This is their job. Interestingly, in their maturest forms, they actually shield us in stronger ways than the protective emotions ever could. When we cultivate these healing emotions, protective emotions begin to rest back as they realize there's another equal or greater protection now available. Compassion has the darkest outline in the group because it's the most potent healing force. It can do anything anger can do but with less or no harm.

Healing emotions are generally recognized by a feeling of warmth and openness in the emotional body. These emotions are designed for healing, but they are also the natural product of a healed heart, making them quite connected to the next category of liberating emotions. Note that insight is also bracketed here, as it is a heightened and sustained state of curiosity and self-discovery that leads to liberating emotions.

On the upper left are the liberating emotions—joy, playfulness, and wonder. The inclusive and responsive state of equanimity fits here as well. These emotions arise naturally when our needs are met, as in the playfulness and wonder of a healthy child. They can be very supportive in healing to soothe and strengthen our nervous systems, as well as in spiritual growth to deepen our exploration of our true nature. They also arise naturally as a product of healing and insight, as the wholesome expressions of our wounded patterns as they heal. Joy has the darkest outline in the group, as it is often the strongest outward expression of inner safety and connection.

The job of liberating emotions is to celebrate, explore, and embrace the miracle of life in this moment, as well as nourish and strengthen us amid our challenges. They are generally recognized by a feeling of lightness and expansiveness in the emotional body. Note the state of bliss is bracketed as a reminder that such states can be misused in spirituality to insulate us from our own pain, and thus can actually become subtle protective emotions.

SPIRALING INTO FREEDOM

In summary, these four quadrants show us how the process of healing and insight can unfold in our emotional lives. When the protective expressions of ourselves (lower left) receive the healing expressions of ourselves (upper right), they soften and reveal the wounded expressions of ourselves. When the wounded expressions of ourselves (lower right) receive the same healing energy (upper right), they transform into the liberating expressions of ourselves (upper left).

Amazingly, given the right attention, the wounded expressions can transform into their opposites. Pictured in opposite locations in Diagram 4.3's circle, sadness can bubble up into joy, doubt can alchemize into wonder, and shame can release into playfulness. As these liberating emotions subside, they settle naturally into equanimity that, in turn, generates more wholesome emotions. This cycle is a natural wellspring of authentic, creative expression.

In this way, we can also see the healing process of Diagram 4.3 as a counterclockwise spiraling into the center, starting with indifference and ending with equanimity. In the beginning, many of us tend to experience more indifference, anger, longing, and anxiety. As they soften, they reveal more shame, doubt, and sadness underneath. As we continue to practice with healing emotions, however, curiosity, gratitude, and compassion become more and more engrained in us. Before long, they are strong enough to liberate our wounds, allowing us to feel greater wonder, playfulness, joy, and, eventually, equanimity in our lives.

The process is never linear of course, nor ever final, but instead circular and ever-deepening within us. Nonetheless, the result of committed practice for a sincere practitioner is generally less and less unwholesome protection (lower left) and unmet wounding (lower right) and more and more true protection from healing emotions (upper right) and liberating qualities of heart (upper left). Using the most powerful emotions in each category, this would be expressed as moving from anger to sadness to compassion to joy, and finally, to resting in equanimity. Through the doorway of equanimity, we most readily access the essential awareness that underlies and permeates all emotions.

THE THREE HEALING EMOTIONS

When we consciously evoke a wholesome emotion and apply it to an unwholesome emotion for the purposes of healing and insight, I like to say it gets promoted to the status of an *unconditional emotion*. Instead of being joyful because of an advantageous turn of events, we invoke joy from a conscious choice, abiding within it and radiating its energy for the liberation of ourselves and all beings. In doing so, the emotion is no longer a conditioned product of favorable circumstance but exists just because we chose it. It's timeless and boundless in this way. In insight meditation, these are called "unworldly" mental states.

Any of the wholesome emotions can become unconditional emotions—wonder, playfulness, joy, compassion, gratitude, curiosity, equanimity. The stronger the force of the wholesome emotion and the deeper the place from which it emerges within us, the more liberating it can be for whatever it touches. However, there are three of the six—and one in particular—that are best suited for self-healing and self-discovery: *compassion, gratitude,* and *curiosity*.

Curiosity is an essential companion for healing and insight, for in its gentle spirit of exploration, it keeps us engaged and reveals what is hidden. In this way, it is the antidote to distraction, dismissiveness, or habitual preconceptions—especially in response to experiences that are neutral or unstimulating. It courageously draws forth hidden wisdom and sometimes hidden pain from the ordinary and mundane. In its maturest form, it is insight itself: a sustained state of discovery. In a practical sense, whenever we register the presence of an emotion, we can learn to spontaneously inquire, *What is this?* or *Who are you?*

While curiosity opens us to our experience, gratitude serves to establish a transformative intimacy. Embodying a warm appreciation, we consecrate a connection to an aspect of ourselves or our lives. In healing, this creates a fellowship with our pain that encourages inner trust and relaxation as well as an appreciation for ourselves just as we are. In its maturest form, gratitude is a wholehearted devotion to intimacy with what is without exception. We are less concerned with assessing value and more grateful that anything exists at all and that we are alive to experience it.

In particular, gratitude is the medicine of choice for protective emotional patterns that often block or constrict the tender parts of us that need healing. These patterns have been working around the clock for decades to try to shield our tender and precious hearts. By sincerely honoring them, these parts feel seen, begin to trust us, and learn to soften and transform, revealing what really needs to be healed underneath. In practice, whenever we feel tension or any protective emotion, our default response can always be *Thank you for trying to help* or *Thank you for caring so much.*

As for compassion, we've described it quite thoroughly already. Hopefully, however, in the context of this chapter, it has become clearer why it's the focus of the book. Compassion is the one emotion in the diagram that is, by its nature, designed to hold pain. In fact, the feeling of compassion itself is a cocreation with pain; it doesn't exist outside of it.

While curiosity and gratitude are critical to revealing and establishing intimacy with our pain, compassion is the force that alchemizes it by establishing inner safety. This is what finally allows our protective patterns to fully release and transform, as they don't need to protect anymore. Our wounds then begin to relax and heal, and our hearts open to deeper spiritual truths. In its maturest form, it is unconditional love, a love that doesn't hesitate to embrace even the darkest places within us.

It's common for folks to feel afraid that if they actually devoted themselves to these healing emotions, they would lose all motivation to keep progressing on the spiritual path. They would become lazy or soft, taking the "easy way out." I know I've felt this in the past. But, when we're sincere, the result is actually quite the opposite. We trade the motivating forces of anxiety and longing for life-giving, liberating ones. In this way, healing prepares us for the joy of a lifetime of deepening insight.

In other words, the healing emotions unlock the liberating emotions. Then, wonder opens us to even deeper discovery. Playfulness helps us explore lightheartedly what we used to fear. Joy supports meditative concentration to stay engaged and gives us heart-strength. All the wholesome emotions support each other in the never-ending expansion of our heart.

EMOTIONAL PATTERN LANGUAGE

As we practice mindfulness of emotions, we can learn to adjust the aperture of our attention from small and specific (momentary, discrete emotions) to large and broad (patterns of emotion across time). This often happens naturally as we observe ourselves over time, noticing the same emotions returning repeatedly or constellations of various emotions arising in succession in certain circumstances. We may even sense how our emotions have solidified into our personality traits, worldviews, and identities over the years and phases of life.

When we gain an astute sense of our emotional palette, we have the foundation built that allows us to effectively broaden our view. For example, we might notice fear in a moment. However, that may just be one emotion in a larger pattern of social anxiety, which includes not only fear but also longing for connection, shame, jealousy, sadness, and more. We can then add the dimension of time, including all the times we felt those ways, expanding pattern recognition further.

By recognizing the pattern as a whole, the practice can become increasingly transformative as we effectively expose more and more of ourselves to our healing energy, initiating more significant shifts. Taking a larger view helps prevent us from temporarily resolving individual emotions while larger patterns stay in place. Moreover, a pattern approach creates a sort of shorthand for our healing processes (e.g., the socially anxious part of me). We recognize our patterns faster and more easily apprehend their intention and origin. In one compassion practice, we can soothe an entire complex pattern that stretches back into the past. For example, by saying, *I'll support you no matter what, always,* to our entire self, we can address all the times in the past we have felt isolated and abandoned—and the ones to come.

The skill to adjust the aperture of our attention comes with time, as does the ever-deepening understanding of our own patterns. All scales of focus are valuable. However, as we add wisdom to this process (as we'll practice in part 2), we learn to zoom out even further. We notice that our smaller patterns are nested inside of larger ones. The broadest personal psychological pattern is that of the "self" itself. Healing on this level, and beyond, can open us to the transformative spiritual insights that we'll discuss in chapter 8.

COGNITIVE UNDERSTANDING TO EMBODIED WISDOM

Again, for some of us, the former diagrams and discussion will feel like an overly intellectual exercise. Admittedly, it takes some thinking and reflecting to understand any new emotional theory or methodology of healing. However, doing so with curiosity and sincerity can initiate a process of forming deeper embodied wisdom that not only prepares us for the core practices in part 2, but also, eventually, shows up in our daily lives. Bit by bit, cognitive knowledge trickles down from the head and into the heart and the gut. It goes from a concept to a way of being, from the imaginary to the cellular level.

In the meditation groups and online courses I lead, it usually takes several presentations of this information before it really starts to become accessible in practice. So don't expect yourself to have a full understanding after your first reading. For visual people like myself, printing the diagrams, interacting with them (as with the journal prompts below), and keeping them in a place where you'll see them can remind us to ask: *What am I feeling now? How am I relating to that feeling?* and *How will I now choose to respond?*

Maturation of the Heart

As we bring mindfulness and compassion to our emotional lives, a unique journey unfolds. While our experiences are never identical nor linear, if we commit to the practices, they can follow a general pattern over time.

In the beginning, we learn to stabilize our attention inwardly and become more sensitive to our inner lives. In doing so, we may actually feel stronger emotions than we're used to. However, as aversion lessens and care grows, we find the energies flow more easefully within us and we can hold more and more.

As our mindfulness strengthens, we learn to notice emotions more quickly before we add layers of resistance or get lost in narratives. With growing compassion, they are digested more completely and don't leave behind as much residue when they go. When we're triggered, we can return to calm more readily—what we might call "emotional fitness." We find we have more freedom of choice in how we relate and, eventually, how we feel.

Our increasing capacity to care invites deeper wounds to come forth to be healed while our growing devotion to our process provides the container for yet deeper transformation. Eventually, our compassionate and devoted response to our suffering becomes a refuge in and of itself.

In our daily lives, we live with less fear and, because we know how to recover when we're hurt, are better able to pursue our goals even when risk is involved. Our dependence on others to approve or affirm us lessens. We slowly begin to establish a secure attachment to ourselves, creating a spark of inner safety that isn't dependent on outer circumstances. We rediscover our authentic sense of self that emerges from knowing beyond a doubt we're enough, complete, and whole.

In this knowing, we relax, surrender, and become vulnerable to transformative insight. We see our emotions and ourselves in our essential nature and as part of a larger process of life unfolding. We are held by a larger wisdom and compassion that can help guide us. Resting in the center of our hearts ("equanimity" in Diagram 4.1), wholesome emotions flow forth through the field of awareness.

In this way, over time, our emotional and spiritual needs are fulfilled simultaneously. We care for our feelings more deeply and yet feel released from their unconscious, habitual control. They can flow through us without subsuming our attention or hardening into reaction and separation but, instead, freely offer us their wisdom. Then, just when we feel like we've got it, the most amazing thing happens: we get triggered—*again!*

Not to worry, though; as we feel our heart tied once again in knots, instead of getting frustrated, we remember we're human, not a machine, and that reminds us of our connection to all of life. With a welcome bow of humility, we gratefully apply mindfulness and compassion once again, and the process starts over. So don't worry how often you get triggered but, instead, how consistently and sincerely you relate with care anyway. This is simply our imperfectly perfect nature. Eventually, we will return to equanimity and, in our own time, allow our original hearts to sing again.

..

I want you to imagine for a moment that our healing and spiritual journeys are like taking a road trip—a family road trip. We begin the trip fused together; all our psychological parts are crammed into the driver's seat. We can't really tell whose hands are on the wheel and whose feet are on the brakes. Everyone's making a racket, telling us different directions to different destinations. All we can do is try not to crash the car.

We've tried arguing; we've tried drowning out the noise; we've thrown our hands up and let them have their way. None of it seemed to help for long. So we finally try compassion.

Lo and behold, each hand loosens on the wheel, each foot pulls back from the brake, and each of our parts crawls into the passenger seat and then the back seat—quietly now. We graciously explain to them where we're trying to go and how they can help us get there, which includes getting along with each other. In this new state, the car becomes *much* easier to operate and navigate. We even sometimes feel like a cohesive family unit, and that brings us strength and resilience. Parts of us still find their way back into the driver's seat from time to time, but we know how to work with them now.

Over time, however, on this long trip we find ourselves tired of always being the one driving and managing. We long to sit in the passenger seat, too, to trust and enjoy the journey more. We also notice our parts would benefit from even deeper and more unconditional attention, and that's hard to do while we drive. So, with a deep breath, we slowly take our hands off the wheel and our feet off the pedals and see what happens. Miraculously, the car drives itself most of the time. We slide out of the way; we aren't quite as necessary as we thought.

In the driver's seat remains an open compassionate presence (i.e., awareness). To our surprise, it's always been part of the family, and it navigates better than we ever did. We can still copilot, still express our visions and make suggestions on where to turn or stop. We can field great ideas and important concerns from the back seat and settle conflicts that bubble up. But we also look out the window more and marvel at the journey.

On the more dangerous roads, we sometimes wake up in the driver's seat again, white knuckles clenched, but we realize what's happening. We compassionately put our parts in the back, slide over into the passenger seat, and relax back into the ride once again. We know awareness can handle the stress better than we can.

Life goes on the same as it always did. Any number of things can still go wrong—and they do. And yet, it all feels different—in a reassuring way. The loving and spacious nature of awareness begins to pervade the whole car, and our sense of self lightens and expands. We're the passengers; we're the driver; we're the love that flows within the family; we're the totality of the journey itself, including all the other cars on the road too. Yet, our little trip is still important. So we stay devoted to this lifelong journey and allow the loving bonds of this little family to mature and spill out into the world.

Summary, Prompts, and Practices

CHAPTER SUMMARY

- Our emotions are particularly potent doorways to healing and insight, especially when we honor the goodness and wisdom they contain.
- Some emotions arise from and are sustained by connection. I call them the wholesome emotions, and they include the healing emotions (compassion, gratitude, and curiosity) and liberating emotions (playfulness, wonder, joy, and equanimity).
- Some emotions arise from and are sustained by separation. I call them the unwholesome emotions, and they include the protective emotions (anger, longing, anxiety, and indifference) and wounded emotions (sadness, doubt, shame, and fear).
- When we apply healing emotions to protective and wounded emotions per the practices in this book, we experience more and more liberating emotions. This supports deeper insights on the spiritual journey.

JOURNAL PROMPTS

- Draw out Diagram 4.3 on your own separate piece of paper with whatever amount of detail you desire. You'll use it in the following prompts.
- Label the emotions that are most and least common for you using a scale between one and ten for each with "1" being not at all common and "10" being very common. Take note of which you might get to know better.
- Star the emotions that are most challenging for you to be with. Write down each separately as headings. Beneath, brainstorm how each is trying to help you.
- Draw arrows on the diagram between emotions that commonly form a progression or cycle in you. For the unwholesome patterns, brainstorm places and ways you could skillfully intervene.
- Identify a singular emotion within each of the four quadrants that you're most inclined toward. Draw arrows from the healing one to the protective one to the wounded one to the liberating one. Consider how this pathway could support you.

GUIDED PRACTICES

There are two guided practices for chapter 4. The first is a meditation acquainting us with the garden of emotions. The second is a meditation on cultivating and exploring the value of wholesome emotions in our lives. Listen to the guided practices at www.justinmichelsondharma.com /thedharmaofhealing/practices or www.shambhala.com/dharmaofhealing practices.

·· Part Two

THE CORE
PRACTICES

5

THE LIVING EXPRESSION
OF COMPASSION

In part 2 of the book, we begin to shift from the principles of healing and insight into the experiential practices that catalyze them. However, before beginning with the core Dharma of Healing meditations, it's valuable to know the constituent parts of the practice and understand how they each function. This can help us relax and trust the process and guide our practice in the most beneficial direction for us. In this chapter, we will explore the four key aspects of true compassion; the methods of compassionate self-talk, reflection, and inquiry we'll use; and the precise phrases that bring them to life.

• •

True compassion remains a vacant idea until we personally experience the living feeling in our hearts. To describe it, at least for me, calls for a poetic sensibility.

True compassion is like a convergence of rivers in the center of the chest. The warm waters of care and the cool waters of sorrow coalesce into a stirring sweetness. As we dive in, the rivers widen out into a deep and spacious pool. The slightest wind of suffering sends ripples of resonance across the clear glass surface. Care bubbles up through the warm waters without resistance or constriction. Like in this nature scene, the heart in true compassion is alive, receptive, spacious, and responsive.

In compassion for the self, we peer into that deep pool and see our own reflection waving in the ripples. We behold ourselves and also feel held amid the turbulence of life. Self-compassion, however, can be a challenging place to start for many of us. We may instead need to remember a time when we received care or imagine ourselves in a scene where we can feel it. It may have been a parent, child, pet, religious figure, teacher, or perhaps a grandparent who once exemplified that heartfelt repose. For me, I love the image of a loving and wise grandmother. For a moment, let's explore it together.

Sitting right where you are, imagine yourself as a child, curled up in the lap of an attentive grandmother. It doesn't need to be your grandmother but simply an archetypal essence of the loving elder that, even if we never had, we can reach into our collective past and feel. Curled there, you stretch your little body and look up at her. When you meet her soft eyes, her face forms a knowing smile. She strokes your forehead, and you let her gaze enter you. In that single simple moment, you are completely seen, completely understood, completely cared for, and completely supported. You naturally pause in wonder at the feeling of ease flowing through you. You take a deep breath. Then, without thinking, a grin and a giggle bubble up from your body. The conditions around you haven't changed, and yet, in this embrace, all your worries have been cured. It's as if a force field of care surrounds you that nothing in the world could penetrate. You close your eyes. The moment stretches out across space and time, as if it were all there ever was.

This is the power of true compassion. When we are the recipients of its radiance, the experience transcends understanding yet delivers us home. We relax into the timeless, present moment and find wholesome emotions emerging from within. We feel safe and connected even amid the unpredictability of our lives.

The beauty of *self*-compassion, however, is that we get to be both the compassionate presence *and* the receiver of it—the grandmother and the child—all in the same moment. We radiate, receive, and ultimately relax into the deep pool of sweetness that's always been there. However, to cultivate this capacity within us, it's important to know the core components that cocreate true compassion in our hearts. Then, we can skillfully cultivate its transformative richness piece by piece.

The Four Aspects of True Compassion

Not all compassion is equal, nor do all its variations have the same healing and liberating effects. In my experience, the most beneficial form is a synergy of and balance between four specific energies within us: *seeing*, *understanding*, *caring*, and *supporting*. We could think of each of these energies or aspects as prismatic hues that combine to form the pure light of true compassion. If all are present and active, they give rise to a holistic feeling that transforms pain and supports liberation. If we are missing any one of them, the feeling falls out of balance and is reduced in its effectiveness.

If we only practice mindfulness, we might partially experience the first one. If we also seek wisdom, we might scratch the surface of the second. However, we can't experience any of them fully unless we thoroughly engage the heart. True compassion always extends its roots below the conceptual mind. It touches our hearts, our bodies, and even our essential awareness.

I will explain each of the four aspects here, their foundational role in the core Dharma of Healing practices, and how they map onto the teaching of the four noble truths we explored in chapter 2.

1. SEEING

Seeing the pain that's present is the first aspect of true compassion. It's also the necessary action for embodying the first noble truth: "There is suffering," or as I modified it, "Everyone is wounded." Until we see the pain we carry, the path to liberation can't begin. Attention to it is the first act of care.

The seeing that begins to generate true compassion, however, is not an aloof or distant observation. It's not objective and scientific. It's much more intimate, gently piercing our inner experience. It carries a warm sense of companionship, but also a meaningful vulnerability.

To get a sense of this, we might remember a time when we allowed ourselves to be seen by someone we trusted—a friend or mentor, perhaps. Or we might be able to imagine it. For that moment in time, that person recognized what we were going through clearly and without judgment. Perhaps they even read our body language or tone and knew we were uncomfortable or upset before we did. Perhaps they noticed vulnerabilities we rarely expose or witnessed our humbling mistakes, yet we still felt safe in their presence. In these ways, we discovered and explored ourselves through their supportive gaze.

In this first aspect of compassion, we turn this same intimate perception back on ourselves. We're not generating any feeling, per se. We're just learning to open up and make a simple heartfelt connection. *I see you in your sadness or your fear,* you might say to yourself. Over time, we can learn to refine this capacity to see ourselves, noticing our inner state more clearly and quickly than anyone else could.

As we continue to see and resee patterns in ourselves, the picture only becomes richer. We witness not only our immediate suffering but the patterns of past wounding associated with it. Eventually, we come to behold a full picture of our shared and vulnerable human condition within each moment. The more courageously we peer into ourselves, the more readily it leads to the next aspect of true compassion.

2. UNDERSTANDING

Understanding is the second aspect of true compassion. It is also the necessary action for embodying the second noble truth: "There is a cause of suffering." From the intimate seeing in the first aspect, we naturally begin to deepen our understanding of the causes of our pain.

The understanding that generates true compassion, however, is much less cognitive than it is heartfelt. It is heavier in empathy than analysis. It's more a "feeling into" or "resonating with" the pain itself. We're not stuck on the details of how or why. We're not trying to package our pain in concepts to create distance or move beyond it. We're moving toward deeper connection and intimacy.

To sense this, we might remember a time in our lives when we really felt understood by someone else. Or we can imagine it now. For that moment in time, this person didn't just witness us but really "got us." They understood not just what we *said* we were feeling but were willing to experience it along with us. They didn't just see us two-dimensionally but also intuited how our experience fit into the larger story of how we've become who we are. Perhaps they've been through similar things or understand our struggles from their maturity of age or experience. Either way, they don't fault us, and in this we feel a sense of mutual belonging and a confidence that we haven't been, nor will ever be, fully alone.

Relating to ourselves in this manner, we might say, *It makes perfect sense you'd feel that way.* Over time, this sense grows richer. We intuit the struggles of the past, as well. *Given what you've been through, now it* really *makes sense you'd feel/act/be this way,* we might say to ourselves. We even intuit its collective nature. *Given the unpredictable and uncontrollable nature of life as a human, it's no wonder you'd feel anxious and fearful.*

Eventually, we can even learn to appreciate how our pain is trying to help us, whether by protecting, revealing, or even teaching us. We no longer find fault in its presence. We may detect its emergence from earlier life events or simply understand it as a well-intentioned response to a scarcity of safety and connection. All of this helps to forge an intimate and empathetic relationship with our pain, creating the rich foundation that leads naturally to the next aspect of true compassion.

3. CARING

Caring is the third aspect of true compassion. When we sincerely see and understand ourselves, we can't help but activate a felt sense of care. At first, this may be a small and fleeting feeling. Eventually, though, it grows larger and more unconditional, able to transform our pain at its root. This is why I also consider it to be an essential action that makes possible the third noble truth: "There is an end to suffering," or as I modified it, "Freedom comes through caring."

However, it's a particular type of care that cocreates true compassion and leads to freedom. This care certainly doesn't tighten into controlling or fixating. We're not focused on the outcome or our preferences at all. It's much more like thatching a nest for our pain, an internal embrace where we feel safe enough to fall apart—without an expectation to come back together again.

For reference, we might think back to a time when someone who loved us deeply held us in their arms. Or we can imagine it. Perhaps it was the honeymoon phase of a new relationship. Our hearts were alive, and for that moment in time, we could feel their every look and touch as a special kindness. Perhaps we felt held completely enough to forget about the outside world, to let down our protection, and to allow everything to be fully felt. Perhaps we cried with a depth and fluidity we rarely access, for there was no fear to restrict it. We knew in our bones we were safe. In those moments, we often credit the other person and miss how our innate healing wisdom came alive. In the arms of sincere care, our systems do just what they need to heal.

Believe it or not, we can cultivate this same quality of affection for ourselves. We might start simply with a hand on our hearts, saying, *I care deeply about your sadness or your fear.* We offer a safe place for our struggles and leave expectations and pressure behind.

Over time, our capacity naturally deepens. We inch toward an unconditional embrace of even our deepest challenges. *I care about you unconditionally, without exception, always,* we might say. In doing so, the inner conditions arise for even the most stubborn wounds to begin healing. This leads naturally to the next aspect of compassion.

4. SUPPORTING

Supporting is the fourth and final aspect of true compassion. When we see, understand, and care for ourselves, we naturally want to support in whatever way we can. It is also the guiding action that underlies the fourth noble truth: "There is a path to the end of suffering," or, as I modified it, "We have the support we need within." Indeed, both the traditional eightfold path (described in chapter 2) and true compassion are fundamentally paths of self-support.

The support that's part of true compassion, however, is much simpler than eight steps. It is not a striving or intense effort. It's not strategizing or planning. It's not really a method or technique, even. At its core, it's just a sustained readiness and responsiveness of heart—an open but assured commitment to and availability for oneself. In this availability, we trust our patterns will transform *if and when* they're ready and not any sooner.

We might remember a time when someone supported us in our past. Or we might be able to imagine it. This would have been a person we could always call upon. No matter where we were, what we were doing, how we felt, or how we had acted in the past, they were still just one phone call away and would do anything they could to help. Just knowing they were there when we needed them was often enough. We felt more courageous, even fearless. We could take wise risks and get hurt because we knew they would always be there. Even when we called, just having them present to listen was often all we wanted—not some elaborate strategy or solution.

This support is not an anxious-hovering energy. It's not even offering advice or solutions necessarily. Its essential agenda is availability. *I'm available to support you, now and always, through it all*, we might say to ourselves. Amazingly, we can do this for ourselves in a way that no one else can. In doing so, it stretches the reach and depth of our care and grounds us in true allyship with our pain.

With practice, this availability and responsiveness of the heart mature. Eventually, they grow into a wholehearted devotion to ourselves *no matter what*. While this type of support is fierce in its commitment, its expression remains open and flexible. From this, practical ways of supporting ourselves may evolve (e.g., self-care practices, drawing boundaries, etc.). Yet the unshakable support that we've craved from outside of us is now satiated from within, and thus, paradoxically, we often don't need people or circumstances to change like we used to.

The wholehearted devotion of this final aspect is not only the deepest nourishment for our wounds but is where the strength and resilience of true compassion come from. Seeing, understanding, and care flow into an ocean of unconditionally supportive presence. Over time, as each of these qualities mature, we find our heart-minds mirroring the ever-present radiance of awareness itself.

• •

Many people are able to *see* some of their pain, but less are able to offer *understanding* to it. Still fewer dare to be intimate enough to *care* for it, and yet even less are willing to offer unconditional *support*—especially if that support doesn't guarantee our pain will go away. This is because, with each step, the intimacy with our own discomfort must deepen, reawakening our age-old aversion. Consequently, the deeper the suffering we experience, the sincerer our seeing, understanding, caring, and supporting must become. Again and again, we must be honest with ourselves: Do we just want this pain to heal and go away? Or do we truly want to honor it as it is, regardless of what happens?

When we express all four aspects of compassion, they synergize into a soothing and fortifying balm for the psyche. This is because they directly reflect the core emotional needs that each of us is born with, yet few of us experience fully or consistently from our caretakers, culture, or the world at large. Our needs being left unmet—not feeling seen, understood, cared for, or supported—is precisely what leaves us dissatisfied and, thus, drives our endless seeking and struggling through life. This restlessness of heart can follow us many, many years into the spiritual or healing path.

The miracle of true compassion is that we can now learn to directly meet those needs for ourselves and, therefore, discover an inner resolution that is not just profoundly fulfilling but acts as a foundation for even deeper spiritual insight. True compassion ensures that our healing and spiritual practices evolve beyond just becoming more refined protective strategies and into an honest intimacy with the totality of what is. As such, true compassion becomes the doorway to a deeper reality.

In this way, the four aspects of compassion are a personal practice, but in practicing them, they reveal their ultimate reflection. First, by mirroring the four noble truths, they convey a wise orientation to the path. Then, by meeting our essential emotional needs, they unlock and heal our hearts. Lastly, as we distill them into their purest forms, they mirror the eternal, wordless sentiments of awareness itself: the timeless presence that holds each of us in every moment, whether we notice it or not. In this way, as we practice true compassion , we are invoking the entirety of the path.

As we string together the four aspects in a progressive and cyclical flow, we generate a unified field of compassionate energy around our hearts—what I sometimes call a *field of care*. In time, we lie down in this field and soak in the warmth. In essence, we become our own archetypal grandmother.

This process is even simpler than it sounds. It happens organically through the application of resonant words and phrases that cultivate each of the four aspects. In the next section, I'll describe the key methods of mindful self-reflection, compassionate inquiry, and compassionate self-talk.

The Thoughts That Untangle Us

On the healing or spiritual path, it's all too easy to blame our thinking minds for our distress. This makes sense, as many of our thought patterns can be very challenging and confusing. Thoughts, however, are completely natural. Like our emotions, they have evolved to try to help us. Not only can they not be avoided but, in the right context, can be powerfully supportive.

For example, while thought can distract us in a meditation practice, when used wisely it can keep us focused and inspired. While thought can aggravate unwholesome emotions, it can also cultivate the wholesome ones. While thought can harden into unhelpful beliefs, it can also soften us into surrender.

As described in chapters 2 and 3, the internal language we use to consciously or unconsciously understand the journey shapes the way we practice and, thus, what comes from it. In fact, it helps shape our entire perception of self, others, and the world—and thus, how we act and react to all of it. Therefore, if we provide a compassionate structure and purpose, our thinking minds can actually heal and rewire us. As long as we don't negate our emotions in this process, the unhelpful narratives we tell ourselves can begin to transform and new liberating insights can emerge.

Using internal language and images (i.e., thoughts) in our healing, however, comes with a caveat. The thinking mind can be very cunning, quick, and profuse, easily fusing with our attention and confusing us. Because of this, there is a particular structure that I suggest here to utilize the thinking mind during portions of the guided meditations while consciously letting it go during others. In other words, we judiciously and precisely use language to enhance the processes of healing and insight and alternate that with practicing embodied, nonconceptual presence.

Before diving into the core practices in the next two chapters, I want to first explain the three modes of thinking that we'll employ together. The first mode, which I'm calling *mindful reflection*, is a mode used regularly in the end-of-chapter meditations and journal prompts and continues into the core practices. The second two, *compassionate inquiry* and *compassionate self-talk*, are used primarily in the core practices in the next two chapters. Through understanding the methodology we'll be using and distinguishing it from similar methods, I believe you'll find the guided practices will be more approachable, clear, and effective.

MINDFUL REFLECTION

In the practice of mindful reflection, instead of trying to let go of thinking as some meditative approaches suggest, we are learning to use thought to gain greater insight into ourselves consciously. There are various beneficial ways this can be done. Simply reading and reflecting on the contents of a book like this as well as using the provided guided mediations, journal exercises, and daily-life activities are some immediate examples. You've probably already been enacting it. Now I invite you to make it fully conscious.

The primary defining features of mindful reflection—and what differentiates it from mindless wandering—are (a) being aware that you're doing it and (b) leading with curiosity. Instead of focusing attention on bodily sensations as we might do in a typical meditation, we're alternating our attention between a prompt and our curious consideration of it. We oscillate back and forth until more clarity emerges. We know we've lost our presence when our mind drifts to some other topic, but we just gently return to the prompt and start again.

The primary guideline I'd recommend is to create a structure with a beginning and end. For example, we might mindfully plan: *I'm going to consider the origins of this emotional pattern for five minutes, then reflect on how it often feels in my body and mind for another five, and then plan how I might want to relate to it when it arises again.* Perhaps we even set a bell for every two and a half minutes to take a deep breath in the middle and make sure we're still on track. When the final bell rings, we consciously set down our reflection process and move into the rest of our meditation practice or the rest of our day. In this way, we engage fully and then let it go, instead of ruminating randomly throughout the day or night.

Mindful reflection is a middle way between getting lost in thought and totally excluding it from our practice. It allows us to engage in beneficial thinking processes when they seem supportive. In this book, this mode of thinking is not a primary practice but a support practice. I encourage using it at the beginning of each of the guided meditations in chapters 6 and 7, as well as at the end of each chapter in this book to enhance the other practices.

COMPASSIONATE INQUIRY

The practices of compassionate inquiry bear some similarity to mindful reflection but use thought in an even more deliberate manner. There are many teachings and modalities that could fall under this general heading. On one side of the spectrum, there are analytical investigations into one's family or cultural history, for example. On the other side of the spectrum, there are repeated question exercises (e.g., *What am I noticing right now?*) that don't have an intended result except to connect us nonconceptually to the moment. Various types of inquiry have their value and place.

In this version of compassionate inquiry, we hold an intention for healing and insight while exploring a middle way between the analytical and the nonconceptual. For example, we first identify and become intimate with an emotion as felt in our body. We then ask a particular question. We don't expect or manufacture an answer. We just listen with sincere curiosity and see what opens inside us. That might be a story, an image, or even just silence.

Our questions seek to see more clearly, understand better, care more deeply, and therefore become more available to support us. In other words, the primary object is to evoke and deepen the four aspects of compassion.

For patterns where we've established a compassionate response but they still remain restless, there are additional questions we can ask to help transform them. This is what I call *transformative self-inquiry*, an extension of compassionate self-inquiry that I will outline in greater detail shortly.

Like mindful reflection, these inquiry strategies are intended to be support practices for patterns that don't respond to the compassionate self-talk phrases. This is largely because inquiry processes are often more difficult to utilize effectively, especially when we're just starting. Once we become proficient, though, inquiry can be a potent companion for healing and insight.

COMPASSIONATE SELF-TALK

The practices of compassionate self-talk are the mindful offering of kind words, phrases, or images directed toward oneself or an aspect of one's experience. There are related practices that employ this in the form of affirmations (*I am healthy, happy, beautiful, free, etc.*); there are practices that employ this in the form of wishes or prayer (*May you be well, may you be happy, etc.*); there are even practices that employ this through holding images of positive things one wants or needs so they might be more accessible (i.e., manifestation). Each of these can have a beneficial impact at certain times in certain ways.

Our compassionate self-talk practices here, however, are different in an important way. Instead of affirming, wishing, or manifesting, we are doing something akin to "holding space" or "creating a compassionate container" for ourselves. We offer phrases that aren't intended to improve or change the recipient. The intention is simply to become warmly intimate with what is, as described through the four aspects of compassion.

Understanding this distinction is very important. It's very easy to practice compassionate self-talk from a place of unconscious aversion. We can use the phrases to make something unpleasant go away, actually cultivating more inner conflict. We might notice this in affirmations when we declare ourselves happy or healthy while actually feeling quite the opposite underneath. Wishing is similar, where we often long for ourselves or others to feel or be different from what they are in the moment. Likewise, visualizing what we want so we can attain it is often predicated on the lack or unsatisfactoriness of the present. In these examples, we and the pain within us are not being fully honored—but that is exactly what is needed to heal and transform.

Compassionate self-talk is the mainstay of the practices that follow. Unlike mindful reflection or compassionate inquiry, in this practice we are not contemplating, dialoguing, or otherwise encouraging thinking. We're simply offering the phrases like gentle gifts in hopes that they might evoke true compassion in our hearts.

• •

As we get the hang of them, these three modalities can be used in succession for the purposes of healing and insight. For example, it's natural to first contemplate the nature of a challenge we have, including the different ways we think or feel about it. In the process we might identify areas of uncertainty, then utilize inquiry to better understand our experience. After all this, we're primed to embrace our emotional and mental process with sincere compassion via kind phrases. Of course, each modality can also be used individually and as needed.

Mindfulness begins the process by extricating the witness from the unconscious flow of thinking and feeling. Then, the conscious use of words actually helps to sustain that mindful distance—be they words of curiosity or compassion or gratitude—while infusing our internal space with healing emotion. When a wise and heartfelt relationship is reestablished inside, the mindful witness gradually reunites with what's been witnessed in a wholehearted embrace, effectively inviting the pattern to reintegrate into our systems. Then we repeat.

Just like with a deep cut, we must open it up to clean it first. In this case, our disinfectant is compassion. When it's clean, we can stitch ourselves back together to complete that phase of the healing process. We'll often carry a scar as a sweet reminder of our unique human journey. Healing the small scrapes prepares us for the more serious ones and, eventually, the deepest wound of separation from life itself.

When combined with traditional meditative practices, these versions of mindful reflection, compassionate inquiry, and compassionate self-talk are potent tools for healing and insight. In this book, the balancing and grounding force for these three modes of thinking is the practice of creating an inner refuge in the present moment—often in the body itself. Through the thought-based practices of reflection, inquiry, and self-talk alongside the body-based practice of creating a refuge, the power of the mind and the innate wisdom of the body come together and merge in the heart center.

Creating an Inner Refuge

For most of us, most of the time, we don't feel fully safe in ourselves. Thus, any solution we enact—even compassion practice—often intertwines with a subtle or overt sense of preexisting insecurity or anxiety. This, in turn, interferes with the generation of true compassion. That's the catch-22: if healing requires safety, how do we hold space for our healing when we don't feel safe ourselves in the first place?

In the context of our lives, we prioritize safe places and people whenever possible, as this helps create a foundation for our inner healing work. Then, in our meditations together, we'll consciously cultivate safety simply with our attention and intention, gradually creating a refuge within ourselves. However, when creating a refuge, where we place our attention matters.

When we bring our mindful attention to something unpleasant in our experience, it's easy to feel restless or agitated, even if it's subtle. Conversely, with something pleasant, we tend to cling to it so as not to lose it. With something neutral, however, we gradually tend to feel calm and easeful—albeit often sleepy as well. This is why, in most meditation practices, we're often instructed to be with something neutral like the breath. It settles the scattered and anxious heart-mind.

But there's another option. We can embrace a pleasant experience *as an act of generosity or kindness toward ourselves*. With this warm intention, we can avoid the pitfalls of clinging to the pleasant while amplifying the benefits of feeling calm and engaged. Our body, heart, and mind more readily relax into pleasant experiences and that can translate easefully into an embodied sense of safety.

For most of us, this generally means placing our attention somewhere in our body where the sensations feel *pleasant, relaxing, or safe.* You might stop reading for a moment and explore this. Starting with the top of your head, let your attention travel downward, part by part, to your feet. As you feel each sensation, see if there's a place that feels particularly pleasant, relaxing, or safe. If so, stay there for a moment and just rest. If this is confusing, know that I'll explain it further and offer a guided practice in the next chapter.

Alternatively, we can start with something neutral like the breath, and then infuse it with wholesome emotions to make it pleasurable (e.g., a grateful breath). Again, you might give this a quick try. First, bring your attention to your breathing for a moment as you feel it in the center of your chest. Then, placing a slight smile in the corners of your mouth, you can say to yourself, "Breathing in and out, I'm thankful to be alive." Say it a few more times slowly and notice if the experience of your breath becomes more intimate and enjoyable.

This orientation to practice can be particularly supportive if you struggle with sustaining focus or discipline in meditation or daily life. Instead of striving to stay present and becoming tight and tense in our spiritual discipline—which naturally has counterproductive results—this approach harnesses the nourishing nature of pleasure to grow our concentration. The more we "pour" our attention into a nourishing refuge within ourselves, the more supportive it can become. As we learn to *enjoy* being present, we naturally want to make space to meditate and heal. When we practice, we're often able to stay focused for longer.

Most importantly, perhaps, accessing a refuge within us makes us more available for healing. When we are feeling relaxed and safe in ourselves, the sentiment of self-compassion is sincerer and impacts us more profoundly. We are more likely to approach our pain fully without secretly wishing it would go away—hard to do from a place of anxiety. Moreover, having a refuge to return to when we're confused helps us avoid overwhelm, fatigue, and unnecessary struggle in our practice. We can even skillfully move our attention back and forth, alternating between our refuge and the sensitive edges of our healing work. This also generates an empowering sense of agency.

If finding a refuge within seems like a tall order, don't worry. We all just start sincerely where we are. The phrases will begin to work on us, and our sense of safety will naturally expand. We can then offer self-compassion a little more unconditionally, and in turn, our sense of safety deepens yet a little further. In this way, our refuge practice and our compassionate self-talk practice evolve together until, eventually, they merge in the deepest embrace.

Self-Compassion Phrases

Each phrase below mirrors the four aspects of compassion and the four noble truths. But due to the natural variation in the ways each of us perceives language, the wording of these phrases will sit differently with each of us. Moreover, these words are not intended to be ends in themselves. They are simply there to assist us in attuning to our innate capacity for compassion.

These phrases came from my own journey of healing and insight refined over the years through teaching and sharing. After meditating with them for a while and sensing the energy they intend to create, consider how to make them your own. I freely encourage you to explore how they land with you and what adjustments would create a better connection.

One of the common questions people have is about the words *you* and *your*. Why wouldn't we only use *I* to reference our own experience? Well, you certainly can. However, speaking to ourselves in the second person functions to further support the establishment of healthy space from our emotions/thoughts. In doing so, it also helps to grow a healthy meditative self that becomes an increasingly mindful and caring force within us.

In practicing this way, we end up personifying our patterns to some degree, as you've heard me do in this book at times. This is a technique that draws on our deep relational nature, inviting even more care and sweetness into our inner lives. So I invite you to play with speaking *to* emotions or patterns and see how it feels. In later stages of practice, we'll drop the pronouns altogether, as well as the words themselves, and rest in a unified state.

TABLE 1. SELF-COMPASSION PHRASES

		PHRASE STEM	CONTINUED PHRASE	OPTIONAL MOD./ EXT.
1.		I see you	in your _____ [sadness, fear, doubt, pain, etc.]	and I feel what you're going through.
		Alternative for protective emotions (e.g., anger, anxiety, longing, indifference)	and honor your _____ [emotion, pain, work, etc.]	with humility and respect.
2.		I understand	and it makes sense you'd feel that way	given what you've been through... [Recount the circumstances.]
		Alternative for protective emotions	Thank you for trying to help. Thank you for caring so much.	I see what you've been trying to do for me. [Explain.] We're on the same team.
3.		I care	about you and your _____ [challenge, hardship, etc.]	but also your joy and liberation.
		Alternative for protective emotions	I care about you too	your struggle and also your well-being.
4.		I support you	no matter what happens	even if... [Speak to the fear of what might happen.]
		Alternative for protective emotions	I'm here to support you	and help you rest.

TABLE 2. SELF-COMPASSION PHRASES SIMPLIFIED

I'M HERE	CARING FOR YOU	THROUGH IT ALL.

EXPLANATION OF TABLES 1 AND 2

In Table 1, the leftmost column gives us the "phrase stems" that hold the core energy of the statement. They can be complete on their own but are often much more effective when refined with more specifics. The center column offers a suggestion for an elaborated phrase to clarify the energy. The rightmost column provides an optional modification or extension that may better suit the needs of a moment or circumstance.

Lastly, in the rows below each main phrase is an alternative that may work better for *protective* parts, patterns, or emotions. Here, each of the four aspects of compassion transforms ever so slightly. Seeing shifts to *honoring*, understanding to *thanking*, caring to *becoming a teammate* or *friend*, and supporting to *relieving*. Poetically, we might say that, instead of thatching a nest for our pain, we're making an altar to it. These shifts recognize the tireless work of our protective parts and support their softening and letting go.

And for those who may want an even greater simplicity, I offer a single summary phrase in Table 2 that encapsulates the overall spirit of the practice—*I'm here caring for you through it all.* We could also say, *You're always welcome here* or just simply *Welcome,* as I say at the beginning of every phrase series in every guided meditation.

MECHANICS OF PRACTICE

These six steps are the basic nuts and bolts of using these phrases in a meditation practice. We'll explore this process experientially in the next chapter.

1. We stabilize our attention on a pleasant, relaxed, or safe aspect of our present-moment experience, often somewhere in the body. I call this our *refuge* within us.
2. We bring our attention to a troubled aspect of our experience—generally, an emotion as felt in the body. Or sometimes we'll bring our attention to an image of ourselves.

3. We welcome the emotion or image, and in doing so, notice any aversive or contrasting attitude that might arise.
4. We speak the phrases directly to this emotion or image slowly and sincerely.
5. We repeat the phrases sequentially until a compassionate connection is firmly established, or as long as desired.
6. We return to the refuge anytime we're confused, distracted, or overwhelmed and/or for the final portion of the meditation.

One common question is how to offer these phrases to ourselves when we are acting unwisely, for example, when dealing with an addiction. We worry that if we welcome our feelings, we will encourage our own unhealthy patterns. In practice, when we feel the pain of the pattern and sincerely offer the phrases to that pain, it's much more likely the opposite will happen. Instead of acting *from* the pain, we disarm the pain so we no longer have to act from it. We are freed up to choose the most appropriate action.

In doing so, we naturally cultivate wisdom and ethics in our lives from the inside out. We also refine a variety of helpful skills and capacities, including directing and focusing our attention, creating a sense of safety within ourselves, recognizing and welcoming our thoughts and emotions, cultivating balanced effort, deepening our concentration, and more.

There is no way to fail. If we get lost, we just go back to the beginning. The most important part of the practice is always our own attitude. Learning to be deeply genuine in our care for ourselves will always outweigh any attainment of a particular technique, state, or imagined outcome.

RECIPIENTS OF THE PHRASES

These phrases can be directed toward an image or felt sense of ourselves, an emotional energy in the body, a thought process, a physical sensation, or even toward awareness itself if we want to get creative. We can also imagine receiving these words from someone or something else within or outside of ourselves. Each approach has its own value. However, our emotions as felt in the body will be the primary object of attention in the core practices.

Compassionate Self-Inquiry Questions

Sometimes, when we practice with the self-compassion phrases, we may find it difficult to access one or more of the aspects of compassion. We may not quite be able to see or understand what we are looking at, or we may struggle to muster care and support. We may also begin to feel impatient or tense around the practice. When this happens, we can take the self-compassion phrases a step further into self-*inquiry*.

Because of our conditioning, however, it's easy for an inquiry practice like this to become overly analytical, busy, and effortful. So I recommend that you focus initially on the self-compassion phrases and, only once there is a clear sense of what true compassion feels like for you, then explore inquiry as needed.

TABLE 3. COMPASSIONATE SELF-INQUIRY QUESTIONS

	CORE QUESTION	OPTIONAL ALTERNATIVE	OPTIONAL RESPONSE (based on self-compassion phrases)
1.	What are you feeling **right now**?	What's the emotion, and where do you feel it right now?	I see you in your _____ [sadness, fear, doubt, etc.].
2.	What's creating this feeling for you **right now**?	What's the story of the pain right now?	It makes sense you'd feel that way.
	Alternatives for protective emotions (anger, anxiety, longing, indifference, etc.)	How are you trying to help me right now?	Thank you for caring so much. I see we're on the same team now.
		What are you afraid would happen if you didn't protect me right now?	Thank you for working so hard to prevent that. I see your care and concern.*
		Consider returning to the self-compassion phrases to work with the fear or other emotions underneath.	

	CORE QUESTION	OPTIONAL ALTERNATIVE	OPTIONAL RESPONSE (based on self-compassion phrases)
3.	Can I hold you in your pain **right now**?	Can I be here with you as you go through this right now?	I care about your pain and also your joy and liberation.
4.	How can I best support you **right now**?	How can I *show* you my care right now?	I'm here to support you no matter what, even if [what you're afraid of] happens.

TABLE 4. COMPASSIONATE SELF-INQUIRY SIMPLIFICATION

1.	Is there anything you'd like to share?
2.	How can I best support you **right now**?

EXPLANATION OF TABLES 3 AND 4

In Table 3, the leftmost column shares the primary inquiry questions. In the middle column are the alternative questions that may suit you or the moment better. In the rightmost column are potential phrases to use to reply to any response we receive.

After experimenting with the suggested questions and getting a feel for the practice, we may naturally customize them to our needs. If you want greater simplicity to the inquiry practice, I offer two potential summary questions that encapsulate the spirit of the practice in Table 4.

In addition, under the second and third questions, there are suggested modifications for protective emotions or patterns. For example, the questions *How have you been trying to help me?* and *What are you afraid would happen if you didn't feel this way?* are intended to reveal the wounds underneath our protective strategies. If we ask what would happen if we let go of our anger, the answer might be that we're afraid we'd be taken advantage of again. This reconnects us with the past wounds of betrayal, sadness, or even shame. Then, we can either start the inquiry over, asking questions to the newly revealed wounded emotion, or return to the self-compassion phrases with that wound.

MECHANICS OF PRACTICE

The basic mechanics of this inquiry practice are very similar to offering phrases above. However, there is a slightly different cadence.

1. We stabilize our attention on the refuge within us, which, again, is a pleasant, relaxed, or safe aspect of our present-moment experience, often somewhere in the body.
2. We bring our attention to a troubled aspect of our experience—generally, an emotion as felt in the body. Or we can use our sense of self as a whole.
3. Again, we first welcome the emotion or sense of self, and in doing so, notice any aversive or contrasting attitude that might arise.
4. We ask a question *to* that aspect or sense slowly and sincerely. We wait and listen. If a response emerges, we can then respond briefly and kindly.
5. We then ask the next question and listen again. The questions repeat sequentially until sufficient understanding is gained to better care for a part of ourselves.
6. If we've gained deeper intimacy with our emotion, we may choose to shift out of inquiry and return exclusively to self-compassion phrases or a simple compassionate embrace.
7. We return to our refuge whenever we're confused, distracted, or overwhelmed and/or for the final portion of the meditation.

This type of inquiry practice comes very naturally to some people and can be counterintuitive to others. I personally remember being quite surprised to discover that an emotion in my body could deliver a response in words. But sure enough, given the chance, our psyches can operate this way.

Does this mean we actually have other beings inside of us? No. We just retain the imprints of countless past perceptions, which become narratives in our minds. If we become aware of this, we can then dialogue with our own old ways of seeing and relating to the world to catalyze healing and insight.

As we know, humans tend to care most readily through the empathic resonance of stories. Hence, once we hear directly from the wounds within ourselves, it can be more compelling to respond with compassion. In doing so, we also democratize our healing process, giving marginalized parts of ourselves a voice instead of our dominant habits always taking the reins.

Remember, the overall goal here is not to always be talking to ourselves or to get to the bottom of every issue but to learn how to listen and how to cultivate present-moment care. That's why the words *right now* are emphasized. We might be tempted to list a thousand ways we felt or might feel, that used to support us or might in the future, but healing and insight only happen now. They come from what we can offer to our embodied experience *in this moment*. When the context is narrowed to that, things get simpler. In terms of support, we usually just want a nurturing presence and that's always something we can learn to give.

Like the phrase practice, inquiry can be used with any pattern or part, including sickness or pain in the physical body. However, for our purposes here, it is most effective when applied to our emotional body.

TRANSFORMATIVE SELF-INQUIRY

Once we have sincerely met ourselves with true compassion, a new opportunity opens to us. We can consider asking ourselves questions that catalyze even deeper wisdom and transformation. This can be particularly important for patterns that, despite our devoted care, continue to be rewounded and reactivated in the same ways time and time again.

Remembering the five natural forces of healing, everything within us wants to heal *and* knows how to heal. Our wounded and protective emotions, through being embraced in our own care, are getting ready to transform into liberating forms. Sometimes they just need to be prompted and given permission. Below is a three-step inquiry process for protective and wounded emotions, respectively.

For protective emotions (anger, longing, anxiety, indifference), we first notice the effect they have on our system (e.g., tension and exhaustion). Feeling it intimately helps to slowly teach ourselves that although we're *trying* to help, it's actually hurting us inside (and likely outside, too). With this deepened awareness, we are more willing to consider other options.

Second, knowing that this emotion is just trying to protect us, we see if we can find a more beneficial form of protection within our present-moment experience. We inquire about an embodied place that is "strong but relaxed" within us. We may discover that our initial, habitual protective strategy is not the only protective force we have access to and, if we do, we embrace the alternative to whatever degree we can. Even if nothing arises, we stay curious and without an agenda, just planting the seed of possibility for the future.

Lastly, we return to the protective emotion to inquire if there's another approach to the situation that would be easier on everyone but protect just as well—if not better. If we find there is, we affirm and feel what it would be like to enact that approach in our lives or practice. Often, but not always, the new way forward involves bringing to life the embodied protection we found in the previous step. Again, whatever comes to us is perfect.

To illustrate this, I'll use a simple example from one of my students. She applied this process to an anxious pattern. With the first inquiry, she noticed the tightening in her belly. She realized it was trying to protect her from the vulnerability of aging, change, and uncertainty, but was also preventing her from seeing the beauty in her life now. To her surprise, with the second inquiry, she discovered a feeling of deeper ease and strength spreading through her body. Then, with the third inquiry, she could feel that ease come forward, filling her belly and helping her realize she could walk safely *with* life instead of needing to shield herself *from* it. You could say that she, and her anxiety, discovered a new form of protection that didn't hurt and, in fact, protected much better. And for that moment, at least, she broke open an old neural pathway and embodied another way.

With transformative inquiry, we can repeat this process as many times as we'd like, as it deepens every time. In each step, we take our time to feel into the answers in our bodies. We don't have to complete or master any of these steps, just begin to inch into the experiences so we might eventually repattern our responses.

We don't try to force any answers either but just let ourselves learn at our own pace through the open-ended prompts outlined in Table 5. Also, notice the optional responses in the rightmost column, which can help us stay in a compassionate relationship with ourselves and reinforce the impact of the experience.

TABLE 5. TRANSFORMATIVE SELF-INQUIRY
FOR PROTECTIVE EMOTIONS

	TRANSFORMATIVE INQUIRY QUESTIONS FOR PROTECTIVE EMOTIONS		ALTERNATIVE QUESTION	OPTIONAL RESPONSE
1.	Notice the Impact	Do you notice the impact this [protective emotion] is having on us **right now**? Describe.	Where do you feel the pain of this response in the body **right now**? Describe.	I know you're trying to help [enumerate the ways], but it's also causing pain for us and others.
2.	Explore a Deeper Protection	Where is a place in the body that feels strong but relaxed **right now**? Describe.	What would it feel like to be completely protected from all harm **right now**? Describe.	Breathe here. This powerful place is always available.
3.	Consider a New Approach	Is there another response that might be easier for you and protect us even better **right now**? Describe.	If you could choose, what new emotion or strategy might you rather use to protect us **right now**? Describe.	I support you in choosing this new approach. [Feel what that could be like.]

For wounded emotions (sadness, doubt, shame, fear), the process is slightly different. We are often already well aware of the impact of the wound on us from our previous self-compassion work. Instead, what we tend to lack is a strong sense of safety to impart to the emotion. For that reason, we begin by establishing a deeper refuge *beside* the pain. We inquire into the safest place imaginable in our present-moment experience, often in our bodies. This may be the refuge we've already been working with, or another secure place might spontaneously reveal itself. It could even be an image or a memory. Regardless of the result, we stay curious and move to the next inquiry.

From this new foundation, we may be able to see other possibilities. We inquire with the emotion how else it might *choose* to feel, if it could. Lo and behold, by giving ourselves permission we often find it possible to begin to choose something more wholesome than the wounded emotional pattern. This can also initiate an emotional release from the part of us that's felt trapped in the pain. But even if nothing happens, we've started a process of inquiry that can come to fruition later.

If we do find ourselves bolstered by a safe place inside and empowered with a choice in how we feel, we are primed for the third step: letting ourselves consider what it would feel like to release the burden of the original wounded emotion. We do so in the spirit of exploration, as a theoretical exercise and not with any expectation. We might find we're actually willing to go there now. If we are, even for a moment, we let that process unfold in our body and allow it to shift or release as it needs to. The object of the practice is not to achieve a letting go but more to lean into the possibility and let that potential start to work on us.

In my practice, my safest place is often awareness or its expression as radiant spaciousness. Resting there for a time after the first inquiry, I take a deeper breath and then turn back to the wounded emotion in my body. As I ask the emotion what it might choose, it often brightens and I delightfully support its joy or ease. Then, when I further inquire what it might feel like to let go, we playfully explore the possibilities, often leading to an emotional release or calming. Sooner or later, as the emotion recedes, awareness tends to come forward again—but now even more radiantly, unrestrained by the initial wound.

Whatever letting go is possible in the last step tends to lead naturally back to whatever semblance of safety we found in the first step, but now in a more embodied way. This in turn can liberate a greater sense of choice, which in turn can reveal a greater potential for letting go, which in turn can establish a yet greater sense of safety, and so on. We can cycle back through this process as many times as we'd like.

TABLE 6. TRANSFORMATIVE SELF-INQUIRY
FOR WOUNDED EMOTIONS

TRANSFORMATIVE INQUIRY QUESTIONS FOR WOUNDED EMOTIONS		ALTERNATIVE QUESTION	OPTIONAL RESPONSE
1.	Explore a Deeper Refuge	What is the deepest and safest refuge you can feel within you **right now**? Describe.	Can you imagine a place within you that is completely and absolutely safe **right now?** Describe.	Breathe here. This safe place can always be available to you.
2.	Consider a New Feeling	If the emotion could choose, how would it wish to feel **right now**? Describe.	Can you imagine this emotion's most liberated internal expression **right now**? Describe.	You're always welcome to choose to feel this way.
3.	Imagine the Release	What might it feel like **right now** for this wound to heal and be liberated? Describe.	What might it feel like in your body **right now** to set down the weight of this pain? Describe.	Healing is possible for you. Feel the wisdom in the wound.

While the questions are designed sequentially, they are also mutually interdependent. Each question works to facilitate the others. So if you feel drawn to a particular question or to a different order of questioning, I invite you to experiment and explore. For example, you might find that imagining the release first makes it easier to explore a deeper refuge and then consider a new feeling. Or, for protective emotions, you might find resting in a deeper protection within makes it easier to then notice the pain of the pattern. Be creative.

The overall intention of both sets of questions is to facilitate the transformation of ingrained painful patterns by catalyzing the realization of choice or agency, finding a new protection or refuge inside of us, and feeling into the potential release or transformation. In summary, they empower us to discover more harmonious ways of relating to ourselves and life. The mechanics of practice are very similar to those described in the compassionate self-inquiry section above.

Again, due to our deep habit of wanting to change ourselves from a place of judgment, lack, or aversion, I recommend you practice with the self-compassion phrases first. Transformative inquiry works best when it's offered within a preestablished field of care.

THE NATURAL MOVEMENT TOWARD SIMPLICITY

Employing phrases and questions is only necessary because our heart-minds and our healing are complex and multilayered. There are countless mental and emotional patterns that can remain unseen even decades into a spiritual practice. The phrases and questions we've discussed use the power of the mind to reveal, transform, and liberate every layer of suffering they touch. They "untangle the tangle," as one of the ancient Buddhist texts phrases it.[1]

It's not uncommon to feel resistance or doubt around adopting an active self-compassion practice like this. I remember it took one of my students with a long-term Dharma practice quite a while to give it a try. But as she recounted to me, "As I finally let go of trying to rationalize it and just followed the instructions to soften, listen, and care for myself, it all started to unfold. I first began to feel and soften my spiritual striving, which then revealed an inner world of hidden emotional pain. Applying compassion to each part, the pain eased, the mind quieted, and a sense of spaciousness revealed itself. Indeed, my pain was *empty*, as I had heard so many times, but actually feeling it in my body was a new experience that has never left me."

Regardless of our background, the phrases and questions above can feel like a lot to consider or practice with. However, the guided meditations make it easy to give it a try. Then, with practice, we can gradually learn to embody true compassion with greater ease, quietude, and contentment. We eventually distill compassion to its essence, radiating the energy of the phrases and questions without even saying them—perhaps just with a smile. This growing simplicity of practice helps us merge compassion with mindfulness, bringing the head down into the heart and then opening to awareness. Think back to the image of the archetypal grandmother at the beginning of the chapter. She didn't have to say a thing.

Summary, Prompts, and Practices

CHAPTER SUMMARY

- The four aspects of true compassion are seeing, understanding, caring, and supporting. When they combine, they generate a field of care that is powerfully healing.
- Thoughts are not our enemy. Instead, they can support healing and insight, especially when used consciously through mindful reflection, compassionate inquiry, and compassionate self-talk.
- These practices are much more effective when used in conjunction with cultivating and establishing an inner refuge or place of rest inside of us. This will be included as part of every guided meditation.
- A series of phrases and questions based on the four aspects shared in the tables of this chapter can help us generate and sustain true compassion.

JOURNAL PROMPTS

- Return to a moment in your life when you felt seen, understood, cared for, and supported. This could be from another person, a pet, nature, or something else. Reexperience what you saw, smelled, tasted, heard, and/or felt in that moment, and take it in as if you were back there again.
- Write in your journal the versions of the phrases and/or questions that most resonate with you currently—one for each of the four aspects.
- Brainstorm five troubled patterns or challenging circumstances that you'd like to tend to in the guided meditations in the next chapter. Make sure some of them are easier, more surface-level challenges and some are harder and deeper patterns.
- Find an image of yourself, or draw one, at an age that is easy for you to care for. It could be your present-moment self or when you were a child.
- Scan through your body slowly with your attention. Where in your body might feel like a place of refuge to rest your attention? List a few ideas.

GUIDED PRACTICE

Our guided practice for the fifth chapter is the practice of receiving compassion from a benefactor in our lives. Through this, we can begin to sense what the four aspects of compassion feel like in our bodies, hearts, and minds. Please follow along and enjoy the guided meditation at www.justin michelsondharma.com/thedharmaofhealing/practices or www.shambhala .com/dharmaofhealingpractices.

6

TURNING THE
WHEEL OF HEALING
Surface and Depth

All the ideas and practices we've explored in this book so far have been in preparation for the core guided meditations in this and the next chapter. These core meditations comprise four sequential progressions I call *turnings of the wheel of healing*. We'll start with the recommended preparation and foundational practices, then move into the meditations of the first and second turnings, which, like the end-of-chapter meditations, can be found online as guided audio tracks. For each section, the intended skill development is outlined and daily-life support practices are offered— including exercises for deeper trauma we may hold.

$$\cdot \cdot$$

When the Buddha first taught the four noble truths after his enlightenment, he is said to have set in motion the "Wheel of the Dharma."[1] For the past 2,600 years, each Buddhist practitioner has helped to keep this wheel turning. In the Dharma of Healing, we explore a modern variation of this same wheel: the *wheel of healing*, which we turn to heal and liberate ourselves through the power of true compassion.

Just like with any wheel and axle, it's the first movements of true compassion that require the greatest effort. Then, as we continue to roll ahead in our practice, it develops its own momentum and the turning becomes easier. As the wheel spins faster, the four aspects of true compassion blend into a unified feeling. We then allow this feeling to work its way into ever deeper layers of our self until it touches every last part of us.

Even though the nature of a wheel is to cycle circularly—and in turning it, we find ourselves back at the beginning over and over—we don't actually stay in the same place. For example, we may revisit the same meditation cushion day after day, but each time we return, we have traveled slightly farther down our path, just as a wheel rolls down a road with each rotation. This progression or evolution may be subtle, but it is inevitable if we stay on course.

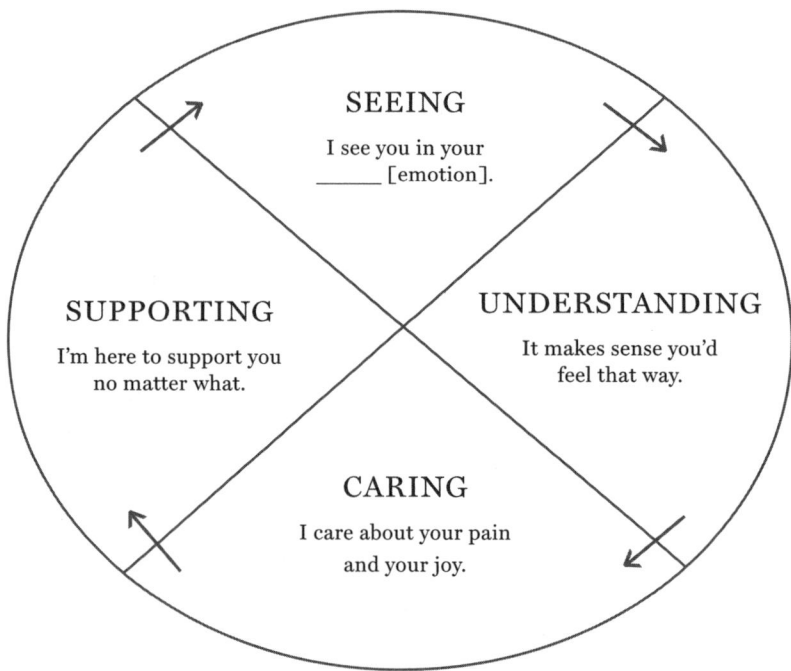

FIGURE 6.1. THE WHEEL OF HEALING

The Four Turnings

The core practices are divided into four sections or turnings of the wheel—two in this chapter and two in chapter 7. In each turning, the spirit of compassion doesn't waver, but how we use it evolves. As we modulate where, how, and with what understanding we apply our compassion, the simple act of caring matures into an act of liberation.

The first turning takes us through the surface layers of our consciousness, developing our initial capacity for self-compassion. The second turning brings compassion into our deeply rooted patterns, stretching us to cultivate ever more unconditional care. This is where we eventually meet our "original heart": the radiant and precious tenderness at our core. The third turning honors our suffering as part of the larger unfolding of ancestry, culture, and nature, further widening our experience of compassion. This is where we deepen into the fundamental interconnection of all things, a place of greater belonging and fullness. Lastly, the fourth turning invites us to relax our effort and surrender into awareness. This is the release into the deepest refuge, a place of pervading spaciousness or emptiness that permeates us and our wounds. Through the synergy of the four turnings arises the jewel of the "awakened heart," a concept we'll explore further in chapter 8.

In this way, we first spiral inward to the center of ourselves, honing and strengthening our compassion. Then, we spiral back out in widening circles, reconnecting with everything around us before releasing into spaciousness. We move from effortful, personal healing into effortless universal knowing—and back again—until it becomes one seamless experience.

OVERVIEW OF THE GUIDED MEDITATIONS

Below is a list of the complete practices in the Dharma of Healing. While the list might initially appear overwhelming, remember it's not necessary to do all of the meditations in one go. There are different meditations for different purposes, as I will explain. To work with a particular emotional challenge, you may only need a single meditation you resonate with, or perhaps one meditation from each turning.

The first five guided meditations are the foundational practices, which introduce the prerequisite skills. Then, there are nineteen core practices that employ the four aspects of compassion through phrases and inquiry. Many of the meditations bear resemblance to one another but contain important changes to the wording, as well as to the placement of our attention. The repetition of instructions is an intentional feature of the practice that helps us deepen our experience and understanding with each pass.

There are primary self-compassion practices (2/3, 6/7, 12/13/14, 17/18). There are inquiry practices for when an internal process requires additional understanding (4/5, 10/11, 15). And there are supportive practices (1, 8, 9, 16, 19) that further enhance or provide additional depth to our healing and insight. Each meditation will be outlined individually and accessible online via the links provided.

Foundational Practices

1. Finding Your Refuge
2. Recognizing Emotions in the Body
3. Noticing Attitudes and Judgments
4. Generating Inner Warmth
5. Caring for the Body

Core Practices

FIRST TURNING

1. Compassion for the Whole Self
2. Protective Emotion Practice
3. Wounded Emotion Practice
4. Protective Emotion Practice—Compassionate Inquiry Variation
5. Wounded Emotion Practice—Compassionate Inquiry Variation

SECOND TURNING

6. Honoring Our Protectors
7. Embracing Our Core Wounds
8. Coming to Terms with Life
9. Somatic Movement Compassion Practice (for Additional Support)
10. Honoring Our Protectors—Transformative Inquiry Variation
11. Welcoming Our Core Wounds—Transformative Inquiry Variation

THIRD TURNING

12. Family and Ancestral Wounding
13. Cultural and Societal Wounding
14. Evolutionary Wounding
15. Third Turning Inquiry and Mindful Reflection

FOURTH TURNING

16. Healing the Meditator
17. Opening to Receive
18. The Deepest Refuge
19. The Awakened Heart

The simplest approach to this progressive practice is to start from the beginning, listening to each foundational meditation and then to each core meditation one by one. You can make a note of which resonate the most with you. Then, on your second time through, you might only do one or two of the most resonant meditations per turning, focusing on a specific pattern you're healing through.

A key aspect of the practices is their cyclical nature. So it's very valuable to work through the turnings multiple times, even with a single emotional challenge. The repetition develops an understanding of the connections between each turning and helps you learn to traverse them with intuitive ease. At some point, I recommend experimenting by guiding yourself through the meditations without a recording. This is important for establishing confidence, increasing capacity, and opening up to creativity in your practice and process.

Alternatively, you may prefer to choose a meditation that's suits you in that moment. For example, if I am triggered in my daily life and feel mildly angry or frustrated, I might use meditation 2 in the first turning to soothe my protective energy. That might be sufficient, or it might reveal sadness underneath. So I may choose then to do meditation 3 for wounded emotions. However, if that anger is very strong and habitual, I might go straight to meditation 6 in the second turning to more deeply honor it. That might reveal a core wound underneath, in which case I might then use meditation 7 on "Embracing Our Core Wounds." Or if I've worked with this pattern many times and understand its origins in family dynamics, for example, I might go direct to meditation 12 and start there. You get the idea. Once we feel confident with the process, we can choose the work that's right for us.

PREPARING TO ENTER A SYSTEM OF FORMAL PRACTICE

As we enter the practice phase, please take this moment to assess and prepare as an initial act of self-care. This is particularly relevant if you're newer to meditation, but it is also certainly worth doing even if you've had many years of experience. Of course, you're welcome to read through the entire book before doing the meditations. However, when you do begin, please consider the following four recommendations:

One: Your formal practice will be more beneficial if you create a dedicated practice space. It is hard enough for any of us to justify healing practices amid our busy lives; we need to make it as easy and accessible as possible. This can be as simple as a special cushion, bench, chair, or blanket that you keep in a corner of your bedroom. It can become more elaborate with an altar containing meaningful objects or pictures, or it can be the dedication of an entire room without any screens or distractions. Be creative with what you have. Every bit of intention helps.

Two: Your formal practice will benefit you more if you create a schedule up front. Choose a reasonable time of day, length of time, and frequency (the meditations are between fifteen and thirty minutes long), and add at least ten minutes of integration time afterward, if possible. Then, take a moment to program it into your calendar with a gentle reminder alarm. The practices are most effective if done every day but do what you can and be easy on yourself.

Three: Your formal practice will be more beneficial if you stay committed to the full process. If we can commit to a practice for at least a month, we are much more likely to deeply understand it, continue it, and reap the benefits for our lives. If we are diligent with the foundational practices, repeating them until we feel confident, then the core practices will be much easier. Likewise, if we don't just complete the core practices but cycle through them at least three or four times, we will realize their deeper spiritual significance and transformative potential. I do hope you'll journey with me as far as you can.

Four: Your formal practice will be more beneficial if you get enough rest. Due to the nature of our society, most of us are much busier and more stressed than we want to be. Many of us have been running on fumes for years, if not decades, overcaffeinated and underslept. Because of this, when we sit or lie down to meditate, we often go straight from wired to tired, falling asleep and missing the experience. Being rested supports us in learning how to relax while staying fully awake—an important aspect of deep healing and insight, as well as integrating the lessons we learn.

If you have questions as you read through the practice descriptions in the next two chapters or if you're feeling challenged as you practice, please see the troubleshooting guide at the end of chapter 7. This guide answers many of the common questions that arise for people. You may also find it helpful to read it over *before* starting any of the practices.

Foundational Practices

Each of us is entering this practice at a different experience level with meditation. To get the most out of the core practices, it's *critically important* to establish a handful of key meditative skills: the ability to (1) stabilize your attention in a pleasant, relaxed, or safe place in the present moment; (2) recognize emotions as felt in the body; (3) notice hidden attitudes and judgments; (4) generate a basic felt sense of heart-warmth; and (5) care for your physical body.

To be honest, it took me well over a decade into my path to establish these foundations, and even longer to refine them, because I had to feel around in the dark to arrive at this template. When I watch students of mine consciously lay these foundations from the beginning, their healing and spiritual growth is exponentially faster than mine was. So even if you are an experienced meditator, I encourage you to review each foundational practice thoroughly. As a teacher, I can confirm that countless longtime meditators have *not* gained these skills. Again, repeat each meditation until you feel confident with it—or at least twice. Then move on to the next.

FOUNDATION 1: FINDING A REFUGE

Creating an inner refuge is very supportive to healing and insight. Our first foundational practice involves exploring our present-moment experience to find places that feel particularly pleasant, relaxed, or safe. Then we can return to this refuge(s) throughout the core practices, anchoring our attention in the present and gradually deepening a sense of safety and connection in ourselves.

While we can discover multiple refuges within or be spontaneous with what feels good in a particular moment, it is generally most helpful to be consistent. This supports the stabilization of our attention in the present moment, an experience that has become rarer and rarer in the digital age. Part of the training of this foundational practice—and an essential support for healing and insight—is the ability to sustain focus for a period of time. This, in turn, allows us to provide steady care for our pain.

And while our refuge can be anywhere in the present moment, it's preferable to find a place in the body to support stability of attention, as our bodies tend to be one of the stablest aspects of our experience. More importantly, a nonconceptual, body-based attention helps us sit with our emotions without getting lost in narratives, as well as learn to access a greater awareness. When in doubt, I often recommend defaulting to the sensations of the breath as felt in the center of the chest. This location merges with our energetic emotional center, making it a natural spot to hold our emotions in a refuge of warmth.

For those with body-specific trauma or chronic pain and illness, there may be nowhere in the body that feels pleasant, relaxed, or safe. As someone who has struggled intimately with chronic illness, I'm very familiar with this experience. It's not a problem. You can first explore whether you can just find somewhere that feels neutral in the body. If so, you can plant the seed of safety there to potentially grow over time. Alternatively, you can explore placing your attention on comforting sounds or sights around you, a soothing and repeated phrase, or even a safe image or memory. The core intention of this practice is to learn to relax our nervous systems regularly, which then supports the natural unfolding of healing and insight. So get creative. For example, if you use an image or memory, try to immerse yourself in it, engaging each imagined sense until you fully feel yourself there. What are the sights, sounds, smells, etc., in that memory?

For one of my students with a transgender identity and body-based trauma, it was using the Dharma of Healing compassion phrases, instead of finding a refuge, that helped him discover a safe place inside. Instead of repeating phrases like *You can do it* or *I believe in you* as he'd done in the past and that felt like trying to trick himself, the four aspects of true compassion helped him see that all his struggles were actually based in care. This, in turn, helped him to finally soften to himself, and as protective walls came down, he could explore the possibility of safety in his body. So even if the refuge practice doesn't work for you, you can still continue with the core practices and trust you'll return to this in time.

FOUNDATION 2: RECOGNIZING EMOTIONS IN THE BODY

After finding a refuge, the next foundational step is to recognize our emotions in our body. As described in chapter 4, feeling emotions as sensation has a variety of benefits, such as helping stay grounded and keeping us from becoming lost in the associated narrative. Moreover, if we can't isolate an emotion, it will be challenging to offer phrases to it or practice inquiry with it to help it heal.

Emotions can be felt anywhere in the body from head to toe. For most of us, there are a few particular areas where we notice tension or tenderness. For me, it's often my belly or chest; for many others it's shoulders or hips. Sometimes the feeling is more diffused.

In this foundation, we curiously investigate the perceived size, shape, texture, movement, or even color of our emotions as they appear in our bodies. As we practice, we become increasingly familiar and comfortable with their various expressions. If we find difficulty with this guided exercise, we can still continue to the core practices, as the phrases themselves often help to reveal hidden emotions and the places they reside in the body.

FOUNDATION 3: NOTICING ATTITUDES AND JUDGMENTS

Simply recognizing emotions in our bodies doesn't necessarily prepare us to offer sincere compassion. Our attitudes or judgments *toward* the emotions very often prevent it.

As I described from my own experience in chapter 2, we can meditate for many years without noticing the unhelpful and sometimes subtle attitudes, judgments, or reactions we bring to our practice and path. They can remain intricately hidden within the spiritual sense of self that manages our practice, embedded within our assumptions and agendas around healing and liberation.

I've never known or worked with anyone who hasn't harbored unconscious tendencies of aversion toward their emotions—whether fear, impatience, distraction, or even repulsion. So we can expect our fledgling intentions toward self-compassion to be constrained initially by our hidden attitudes. The key learning in this foundational practice is to discover how to *notice* them. After recognizing an emotion, we then practice "turning our attention around" to witness how we feel toward it. Many of us will notice an aversive thought first, but if we follow it, we can uncover the corresponding emotion underneath. In this way, we're learning to find an emotion *about* an emotion.

In my healing process, impatience was always the most challenging attitude. *This is* still *here?* I would think. *Oh my gosh. I just practiced with this.* It would show up as a voice in my head, but also an exasperation I felt as tension in my chest. When I saw this—or my mentor helped me see it—I could then work to thank it for trying to protect me, soften it, and surrender to intimacy with the original emotion. Without that step, healing wouldn't have been possible for many of my wounds.

In fact, people often find that the majority of the discomfort and dysfunction associated with a wounded or protective pattern comes from our less-than-compassionate attitude toward it. For example, we may be terrified to experience the looming monster of our shame or depression for years, but once we heal the fear *of it* and turn back to it, it reveals its tender innocence.

Hence, this subtle redirection of mindfulness is an essential skill, first learned here, and then incorporated into all the core practices. Again, if you find this practice confusing, just continue to the core practices, as these attitudes are often revealed by the repetition of the phrases themselves.

FOUNDATION 4: GENERATING INNER WARMTH

The previous foundations are important, but they don't necessarily lead to a felt sense of compassion. We might notice an aversive attitude, for example, but then are annoyed instead of grateful. Now we're annoyed about an attitude about a wound, and we're even more tangled. Here, we practice cultivating a memory of heart-warmth, even before we add the phrases. Learning to do this also makes it much more pleasant to be present, and our concentration tends to increase significantly.

In the guided meditation for this foundation, we'll practice simple techniques that are incorporated into the core practices but can also be practiced in daily life. It's easier than we might think. For example, we'll place a supportive hand on our bodies or a slight smile on our face or imagine a place or time when we felt joyful or cared for. If we have trouble with those, we can also imagine someone or something else caring for us. Feeling that warmth even once, we'll then have something to draw upon.

Again, if you have challenges with this, simply continue to the core practices and the repetitive phrases may well eventually inspire it to emerge.

FOUNDATION 5: CARING FOR THE BODY

Even with all the other foundations in place, it can be all too easy to overlook our bodies on the healing and spiritual paths. We can think they are just a vessel to carry out our spiritual journey. We can forget they bear much of the burden of our stuck emotions and thoughts, including the deepest existential ones—and that comes with a cost. Moreover, we forget that the body has its own deep and innate wisdom that can support our journey. Overlooking our bodies, therefore, inevitably limits our healing, insight, and our daily-life integration of both.

It's also important to remember the way we think and feel affects our physical systems.[2] Unwholesome emotions tend to have harmful effects, while the opposite is also true. As we heal, it's helpful to extend our compassion to the body as it recovers from the wounds and less-than-helpful habits we've burdened it with.

Leading with compassion, we can learn to listen to our body during the healing process and actually let it help. In particular, our bodies can remember how to release stuck emotions and welcome new energies. Like our hearts and minds, they too know the five forces of healing from chapter 3, but we may have to support them in recalling them. As we sensitize to our bodies, they can also intuit deep insights into the nature of life. This is because they are not just flesh and bones but a sacred expression of our true nature itself.

In this simple meditation, we will use a series of physical movements to nurture and relax our bodies. We listen and include our bodies in a compassionate way, eventually becoming trusted friends on the path. I welcome you to employ these techniques whenever you need to. In meditation 9 in the core practices, I also include a more in-depth somatic practice.

..

You can access the five foundational practices online at www.justin michelsondharma.com/thedharmaofhealing/practices or www.shambhala .com/dharmaofhealingpractices.

The First Turning: Surface Consciousness

The first turning of the wheel is the application of self-compassion to our everyday thoughts and emotions. This is the surface layer of our heart-minds that reacts and responds to the circumstantial ups and downs of the conditions of our lives. It's natural for us to feel frustrated, sad, anxious, doubtful, confused, or angry when things don't go as planned—in our practice, on the job, or in a relationship. In this turning, we learn to make self-compassion our first response.

Entering the first turning begins with making contact with the ways that we avoid pain. Understandably, many of us have developed a thick skin to navigate this chaotic world. Some of the most common surface-level protective strategies are staying busy, distracting ourselves, or seeking relief in addictive substances or behaviors. In meditation practice, especially in the beginning, we often experience self-protective mechanisms such as racing or distracted thoughts, trouble sitting still, or boredom. When practicing self-compassion in meditation, they are often skepticism, impatience, defensiveness, or numbness. For me, it was the judgment of compassion as less than wisdom, weak and ineffectual.

These are what I call our *master protectors*. They are the outermost patterns of thought and emotion that prevent us from acknowledging and feeling our backlogged emotions, from relating with care instead of resentment, from allowing ourselves to be supported, and from finding the humility and courage to try new things. We may be able to notice them as tension in the body or repetitive thinking in the mind, or we may need to wait until self-compassion practice pushes them into view. For example, if you hear the phrases and are immediately annoyed and irritated, that's obviously a protector to meet. Instead, if you don't feel anything, it may take a few repetitions to discover the subtle protective strategy that's blocking your access.

Once we've broken through this surface tension, it's much easier to identify, feel, and begin to warm up to a whole host of day-to-day emotions.

We soften and connect to ourselves in a new and intimate way, growing our heart capacity one opportunity at a time. When there's tension in our marriage, we feel anxious about money, we make a mistake at work, we're late for an appointment, or on many other occasions—we pause, put a hand on our hearts, and let out a breath. Within just days or weeks of practicing sincerely, we notice a greater tranquility of mind, restfulness of heart, and regulation of our nervous systems.

MEDITATION 1
Compassion for the Whole Self

This is the general entry practice to soften and ease the heart-mind. It can be used as preparation for deeper emotional work or other spiritual practice or simply as a stand-alone practice for calming and connecting.

Preparatory Reflection: Recall an image of yourself or find a picture of yourself. It could be in the present day or all the way back to childhood. Consider what is easiest for you to feel compassion toward.

Method Summary: Find your refuge. Call to heart the image above, or instead just a felt sense of yourself. Offer self-compassion phrases to that image. If it's challenging, imagine you are receiving these phrases from a benefactor.

Suggested Phrase Variations:

- I see you . . . just as you are, your gifts and your imperfections, the challenges you've been through, the things you couldn't have known.
- I understand . . . better than anyone, why you'd feel the way you feel, why you became who you did, shaped by all the ups and downs of your life.
- I care about you . . . your needs and your dreams, your one-of-a-kind heart, your pain and also your liberation.
- I support you . . . always, now and into the future, no matter what unfolds, I'm here.

Quick Tip: If an image of yourself is hard to conjure or hold, don't worry. Just use your name in the phrases or a felt sense of yourself.

MEDITATION 2
Protective Emotion Practice

This meditation is for surface-level protective emotions such as variations of anger, longing, anxiety, or indifference. It can be used as preparation for deeper healing work or spiritual practice or as a stand-alone response to life's ongoing challenges.

Preparatory Reflections:

- What's a recent time you felt a protective emotion? (It may be helpful to choose a feeling that arises regularly in response to a stimulus in your life, so you're familiar with it. Choose something meaningful but not too intense to start.)
- Where did you feel it in your body?
- How was it trying to help in that situation?

Method Summary: Find your refuge. Bring to heart the recent protective emotion (or use one that's present). Offer self-compassion phrases to the emotion.

Suggested Phrase Variations: Use the original self-compassion phrases from chapter 5.

Quick Tip: Identify protective emotions by how they feel tense, dense, or constricted in the emotional body.

MEDITATION 3
Wounded Emotion Practice

This meditation works with surface-level wounded emotions such as variations of shame, doubt, sadness, and fear. You can use it in preparation for deeper healing work or simply to respond to daily challenges.

Preparatory Reflections:

- What's a recent time you felt a wounded emotion? (It may be helpful to choose a feeling that arises regularly in response to a stimulus in your life, so you're familiar with it. Choose something meaningful but not too intense to start.)

- Where did you feel it in your body?
- What might it be trying to show you?

Method Summary: Find your refuge. Bring to heart the recent wounded emotion (or use one that's present). Offer self-compassion phrases to the emotion.

Suggested Phrase Variations: Use the original self-compassion phrases from chapter 5.

Quick Tip: Identify wounded emotions by how they feel tender, raw, or vulnerable to the emotional body.

MEDITATION 4
Protective Emotion Practice— Compassionate Inquiry Variation

This supplemental inquiry practice is for protective emotions that remain consistently hard to notice or engage with.

Preparatory Reflections: What protective emotions or patterns within you do you feel unclear about or struggle with? Choose one.

- Where do you feel it in your body?
- How is it trying to help you?

Method Summary: Find your refuge. Bring to heart the protective emotion or emotional pattern. Ask questions to see, understand, care, and support with greater clarity and sincerity. Respond with self-compassion.

Question Variations: Use the original compassionate self-inquiry questions from chapter 5.

Quick Tips: Don't pressure answers to come. Listen without expectation, leading with curiosity and patience. Anything is welcome as a response, from words to bodily sensations to simply silence.

Wounded Emotion Practice— Compassionate Inquiry Variation

This supplemental inquiry practice is for wounded emotions that remain consistently hard to notice or engage with.

Preparatory Reflections: What wounded emotions or patterns within you do you feel unclear about or struggle with?

Method Summary: Find your refuge. Call to heart the wounded emotion or emotional pattern. Ask questions to see, understand, care, and support with greater clarity and sincerity. Respond with self-compassion.

Question Variations: Use the original compassionate self-inquiry questions from chapter 5.

Quick Tips: Same as meditation 4.

. .

For the questions or challenges that inevitably arise, please refer to the troubleshooting guide at the end of chapter 7. The above five meditations of the first turning are available online at www.justinmichelsondharma .com/thedharmaofhealing/practices or www.shambhala.com/dharmaof healingpractices.

LESSONS FROM THE FIRST TURNING

Even though it's just the first layer of self-compassion, in some ways, the first turning is the hardest of them all. Our protectors get nervous and try to pull various internal strings to convince us to turn around or distract ourselves. I know I stalled here for many years. Of course, these forces within us are just trying to protect our precious hearts from our own pain, so again, we try our best to be grateful.

We might hear ourselves say something like, *OK, I tried it. Yeah, it was fine, but I'm already pretty nice to myself. Maybe I'll pick it back up again when I need it.* Or *Yeah, I'm just not very good at it,* or *It's a little too sappy and sentimental for me.* This is, in fact, where most people stop: right before it actually starts making their lives easier. Instead, they wait until compounding crises befall their lives as they do for all of us at some point and push them far too quickly into the second turning, tumbling overwhelmed into their wounding. I can tell you from experience, at that point, the road is much steeper and rockier.

The primary intention of the first turning is just to establish ourselves in self-compassion practice so that whenever we awaken from a triggered moment, we instinctively use it. This means growing confidence and proficiency in our personalized approach that helps us compassionately resolve the regular inner challenges in meditation and everyday life. Doing this, however, requires specific skill development, as acquired through the foundational and first turning meditations above. With practice, we grow our capacity to more and more gracefully

1. stabilize our internal refuge
2. unfuse with our emotions/thoughts
3. identify or name them within us
4. notice any unhelpful attitudes toward them
5. decide how to compassionately respond through phrases or inquiry or touch
6. combine the four aspects of compassion into a unified feeling of true compassion in the heart
7. sustain our attention with them until there is a sense of completion for the moment

The longer-term goal of the first turning is to slow and then end the *accumulation* of wounding from daily experiences—essentially staying caught up with our healing. When we become self-aware of our common patterns and proficient in the process, we can learn to heal in real time or shortly after a triggering incident. When this is the case, then a portion of our meditative energy can naturally redirect into the second turning: working with the deeper wounds and patterns in our subconscious.

Ideally, our healing process is steady and predictable, the level of challenge (inner and outer) increasing as our internal capacity does. However, in reality, it can sometimes be much more volatile. Indeed, for some of us, life is already emotionally overwhelming. This might be from big life changes or stressors, reactivated past traumas, experiences of marginalization, or the like. If this is the case for you, please take a look at the tips for working with trauma and marginalization at the end of this chapter and consider moving more quickly into the second turning practices.

EVERYDAY SUPPORT PRACTICES—FIRST TURNING

In addition to the formal meditation practices, it's very supportive to discover ways of integrating aspects of the practice into the rest of your day. Here are seven suggestions, from least to greatest effort:

1. *Notice when wholesome states arise.* Feelings like joy, gratitude, compassion, and calm arise more often than we think. They come and go, and we don't usually take the time to stop and take them in. Instead, when something good happens or you see something beautiful, pause and fully take it in. Breathe into it so it circulates through your entire body. Be thankful you feel this way, even for a moment.

2. *Bring a slight smile to the corners of your mouth.* This simple act can easily accompany virtually any activity. It's a subtle but potent reminder of the warm presence within us. By employing it, we're not pretending to be happy; we're generating warmth to be applied to whatever arises. No one has to know but you.

3. *Place a hand on the body.* We can incorporate this simple offering of self-support periodically during many activities—walking, reading/ writing, speaking/listening, cleaning, driving, weeding, etc. It is a physical reminder of the care and companionship we are deepening for ourselves, and it keeps us grounded in the present-moment sensations of our body.

4. *Offer abbreviated phrases to yourself.* The summary phrase I offered in chapter 5 was *I'm here caring for you through it all.* To easily incorporate it into our day, we could shorten that to simply *I'm here, I care,* or any other variation we resonate with, such as *I got you, It's OK,* etc. People often find that repeating a simple phrase silently to themselves with regularity helps them continue their compassion through daily activities.

5. *Set a mindfulness reminder at least three times a day.* Ideally, we're looking to tie together the formal practice periods with daily-life integration practices to have a more or less continuous flow of mindfulness and com-

passion. Setting an alarm on our phone can help to remind us to pause, take a breath, and enact any of these practices for at least one minute.

6. *Try the Two-Minute Mirror Meditation.* Most of us look in the mirror before starting our day. When you do, try standing still, taking a deep breath, and then taking an extra two minutes to gaze into your own reflection. Essentially, as an eyes-open version of meditation 1, you can offer compassionate inquiry or phrases directly into your own eyes.

7. *Maintain a daily journal practice.* Journaling supports ongoing mindful reflection in our healing journey. It can be a process of discovery or of reification of an important insight. It is often most rich directly after a formal meditation practice. Your first journaling session can be about creatively incorporating these practices, or some of your own, into your daily schedule!

The Second Turning: Depth Consciousness

The second turning is the journey beneath the surface of the heart-mind and into the murky depths of our psyches. This is the realm of formative life experiences, lifelong patterns, and strong and sometimes dark emotions—ones that have often mushroomed in the shadows of our inattention. It's the realm of the somatic where the cells of the body meet and merge with the conditioning of the heart-mind, where stagnant emotion hardens into physical aches, pains, and illness. It is where our deepest loves and fears intermingle, emerging into our most intimate life relationships. It's where the true roots of our actions reside.[3]

In this subconscious realm, the smattering of impressions we take from past events swirl within us for decades, creating a self-referential web of associations that is anything but linear and logical—let alone accurate in the objective sense. Navigating it can feel more like being in a dream than waking life with irrational fears, distorted projections, and illogical associations as well as harmless childhood parts and innocent traumas disguised as dark monsters of the past. The way we relate to ourselves in this realm is fractal in nature. We become a friend, a partner, a parent to ourselves, each act of self-compassion reconditioning each relationship archetype within. This symbolic subconscious ecology, formed from innumerable interactions and experiences, challenges our conventional sense of self.

Given the nature of this realm, it is ideally approached only when one has gained confidence with practices such as those in the first turning. Too often in typical spiritual practice, a practitioner will stumble across or recklessly dive into this dimension of themselves without the awareness, support people, or the tools to navigate it. They are caught unaware and unprepared by overwhelming emotions and/or realizations and instinctually have a strong fight, flight, or freeze response. Then, instead of having a hidden and dormant wound, they have an active wound *and* a new psychological complex in contention with it (e.g., they actively fear their past fear). Without ongoing support, the result is often the inadvertent reinforcement of or entanglement within the very wounds they sought to overcome.

To approach these deeper patterns in meditation, we'll need to develop a new level of presence and skill. We must be able to secure a sense of safety in our refuge, separate out our fears and projections from the wounded emotions themselves, and wholeheartedly open to larger waves of pain. Our hearts and their healing emotions must evolve into their most courageous and devoted versions, for we can't fully inhabit ourselves until we have looked kindly into the eyes of our deepest fears. In the process, we might encounter the treasure resting on the bottom: our original hearts in their perfect tenderness and innocence.

..

To access the second turning consciously, we can use doorways similar to those we accessed in the first. Often, to seal off the subconscious, we also use some of the same protective strategies we've employed to prevent us from feeling the small things—just stronger. We can consider the ways we protect our most tender emotions in intense situations or intimate relationships. We might get angry or lash out to avoid being vulnerable or admit fault. We might hide to avoid being seen by others. We might just shut down or dissociate. It's often the case that the more robust our protective reaction, the deeper the wound.

Despite our protective efforts, however, core wounds still emerge periodically at the surface of lives. We might recognize them as racing, repetitive thoughts or highly volatile emotions, especially those that we know are out of proportion with the objective circumstances of the moment as when something small feels like a huge deal. We can pay particular attention to narratives that use the words *always* or *never* (e.g., *I'm never going to be good enough*; *I'm always going to be alone*; *I can never do this right*, etc.). Many of these deeper wounds stem from a core lack of safety or belonging but, with compassion, can be powerful doorways to transformation.

In addition to protective strategies and wounded emotions, we can also access the second turning through the raw sensations of the physical body. With mindfulness, we can discover persistent pockets of tension or tenderness in our body that are often connected to our deeper emotional lives. Indeed, the body can be seen as an unconscious extension of the mind, storing anything significant we've experienced or are experiencing. For me, this is the doorway that welcomed me into the deepest chambers of my subconscious that I never knew existed.

· ·

Note: The following meditations are intended to bring us into contact with deep wounding within us. If you have a history of trauma, please read "Additional Considerations for Trauma and Marginalization" at the end of this section before beginning practice. In general, moving slowly and cautiously in this work is advisable. Rushing or pushing may bring painful setbacks in your growth.

MEDITATION 6
Honoring Our Protectors

This intensive practice is designed to soften deeply held protective patterns that keep us reactive and triggered in work, relationships, and life. It builds upon meditation 2 in the first turning.

Preparatory Reflection: List three of your deepest-held or strongest-felt protective patterns, perhaps drawing from the examples above. Consider times when you shut down, lash out, obsess, please others, or escape. What emotions are energizing those actions? Where do you feel them in the body?

Method Summary: Find your refuge. Bring to heart one of the deeply held protective emotional patterns. First, offer sincere gratitude. Then, offer sincere self-compassion phrases. Open to the wound underneath.

Suggested Phrase Variations:

- I see you . . . but this time I bow deeply in respect and humility.
- Thank you . . . thank you for your devotion to my protection, for caring so fiercely and ceaselessly for me.
- I care too . . . for my well-being, but also about yours and for the deep stress you carry.
- I'm here now to support us . . . so you might finally rest after all this time.

Quick Tip: Consider what this protective pattern might be afraid of happening if it didn't protect you in this way. This can cultivate gratitude and compassion and lead to the wound underneath.

MEDITATION 7
Embracing Our Core Wounds

This is an intensive practice designed to approach the deepest wounding within us. It inclines our hearts toward an unconditional care that can heal and reconnect us to our original hearts. It builds upon meditation 3 in the first turning.

Preparatory Reflection: List five core wounds that could use your healing attention. Consider times of great fear, doubt, shame, or grief. Many people feel they're not good enough, worthy of care, safe to be as they are, or even that something's deeply wrong with them.

Method Summary: Find your refuge. Call to heart the core wound, experienced as an emotion in the body. Offer unconditional self-compassion via the self-compassion phrases. Open to your original heart.

Suggested Phrase Variations:

- I see you . . . and I feel your profound tenderness and vulnerability.
- I understand . . . it makes perfect sense you'd feel this way; I trust your wisdom.
- I care . . . about you unconditionally, letting go of *any* need for you to change or even heal.
- I'm devoted to supporting us always so we might grow together in deeper intimacy.

Quick Tip: Take the long view. Don't expect or pressure any particular transformation. Just devote yourself wholeheartedly to the process.

MEDITATION 8

Coming to Terms with Life

This is a support practice that works directly with the universal challenges of being human: in particular, old age, sickness, death, and ultimately, the eventual loss of everything we care about. Said differently, we reflect on our inherent vulnerability to life's ever-changing and uncontrollable nature. These underlying themes of life are aspects of almost all our wounds and protective strategies, especially those deepest ones in the second turning. So, by healing our relationship to these realities, we unlock healing in every other aspect of life. These topics are also the subject of standard reflection in insight meditation, called the five remembrances.

Preparatory Reflections:

- Consider how you relate to old age, sickness, death, or the general changing and uncontrollable nature of life. What is one specific life challenge you face right now related to these themes? What emotions arise for you in response?
- Consider how the core wound or protective pattern you worked with in the last two meditations relates to these themes. Are you trying to protect from something such as loss or change that is actually the nature of life? Are you wounded not just by a particular circumstance but by this impersonal nature of life?

Method Summary: Find your refuge. Offer phrases that reflect on these universal human realities. Bring to heart a specific emotion related to these realities. Offer self-compassion phrases.

Suggested Phrase Variations:

- I see you . . . in your pain, your natural response to the deep instability of life.
- I understand . . . it makes sense you'd feel the way you do—why you'd wish it to be otherwise, why you'd try to protect from these realities.

- I care . . . about your loss, but also about your liberation, even within this challenging human condition.
- I'm here to support you . . . through all of it, no matter how it all unfolds.

Quick Tip: Go slow and remember you're not alone. Let yourself grieve and follow the grief back home.

MEDITATION 9

Somatic Movement Compassion Practice (for Additional Support)

This is an additional support practice that ensures we include the wisdom of our bodies in our healing process. It's particularly relevant in the second turning when we are working with deeply held emotional patterns often trapped within our bodies. Mindful movement can help to bring emotions to the surface, loosen and open them, and expose them to compassion to process and integrate.

Preparatory Reflection: Is there a place in your body that regularly holds emotional tension? Or a wound that feels hard to access or stuck?

Method Summary: Find your refuge. Scan your body to find any places of tension or tenderness. Soothe these with self-compassion. Allow the physical body to express its wisdom through free-form movement. Return to your refuge.

Quick Tip: Let the physical body lead. The physical body knows how to support healing in the emotional body. Don't try to release or get rid of the emotion. Let the body compassionately dance with it.

MEDITATION 10

Honoring Our Protectors— Transformative Inquiry Variation

This is a transformative inquiry practice for deeply rooted and persistent protective strategies with which we've already established a compassionate relationship.

Preparatory Reflection: What protective emotions or patterns keep coming up even after being held in unconditional compassion? Consider persistent triggers in life and, especially, relationships.

Method Summary: Find your refuge. Call to heart the protective strategy in question. Ask abbreviated compassionate inquiry questions, then transformative inquiry questions.

Question Variations: Use the transformative inquiry questions from chapter 5.

Quick Tip: Be patient and curious, letting your pain answer the questions honestly. Don't pressure or rush your healing.

MEDITATION 11

Welcoming the Core Wounds—
Transformative Inquiry Variation

This is a transformative inquiry practice for deeply rooted and persistent core wounds with which we've already established a compassionate relationship.

Preparatory Reflection: What core wounds (i.e., wounded emotions) keep coming up even after being held in unconditional compassion? Consider persistent triggers in life and, especially, in relationships.

Method Summary: Find your refuge. Call to heart the core wound in question. Ask abbreviated compassionate inquiry questions, then transformative inquiry questions.

Question Variations: Use the transformative inquiry questions from chapter 5.

Quick Tip: Same as meditation 10.

• •

The six meditations in the second turning can be found at www.justin michelsondharma.com/thedharmaofhealing/practices or www.shambhala .com/dharmaofhealingpractices.

LESSONS FROM THE SECOND TURNING

The overall intention of the second turning is to strengthen and refine our self-compassion practice to meet progressively deeper pain within us.

For folks who have arrived here gradually from the first turning, this progression is natural and intuitive. However, it's valuable to summarize the specific skill development to keep your eye on. Specifically, for the second turning, additional skills include developing

1. a stronger sense of internal refuge, both as a refuge *from* our pain and a refuge *for* our pain;
2. an intuitive body-based recognition of subconscious protective layers and wounds;
3. a refined capacity to notice subtle agendas and projections within the meditative mind (e.g., attitudes of impatience, projection of fear, or manipulation of one's experience);
4. an instinct for what healing approach is needed and learning to be creative and adaptive in your application (which healing emotions, phrases, or questions, etc.);
5. a growing resilience with painful internal experiences;
6. a growing unconditionality and devotion with our compassion; and
7. the ability to sense and touch our essential tenderness and goodness of heart, underneath all the wounds (i.e., the original heart).

From a psychological perspective, we could describe this as the process of healing trauma, regulating and restoring our nervous systems, and rewiring our neuropathways for healthier patterns. From an insight meditation perspective, we could describe this as not just soothing but *uprooting* the causes of our suffering—aversion, desire, and delusion—allowing us to finally connect to the present moment with relaxed, embodied clarity. Both perspectives move us toward the reestablishment of inner safety and connection and, with it, the fundamental sense of well-being that is our birthright.

It is natural to hope that such deep work would heal or transform everything from our past. We often equate healing with the extinguishing of specific unwanted emotional patterns. While of course this *can* happen, this orientation can actually be counterproductive. Instead, developing an unwavering confidence in our ability to care for anything that arises within us—regardless of perceived progress or outcome—is a more liberating goal. We know we're truly embodying this when the falling away of a pattern doesn't trigger exasperated relief but instead a twinge of sorrow for the ending of that loving relationship.

In this way, the second turning also begins a critical shift that is continued in the next two turnings. This is the paradigm shift from a linear, outcome-based mode of practice to a nonlinear, timeless, and unconditioned mode marking the transition from healing into insight. We are accustomed to thinking, *If I do this practice, I'll get this outcome. If I'm kind to my pain, it will heal and go away. If I'm dedicated to being present, I'll have an awakening sometime in the future, and all will be well.*

This makes sense in a conventional way, but in spirituality, it means we're embarking on a never-ending path. By focusing on getting or avoiding an outcome, we keep our success and salvation always one step away from us, just out of reach. So, instead, we now move toward the realm of the "no matter what," the "always welcome," and the "already whole." It's a courageous way of living that is beyond goals and rewards, devoted to what already is and who we already are—even if we never heal or awaken—*no matter what*. And this is precisely what opens the door to liberating insight.

EVERYDAY SUPPORT PRACTICES—SECOND TURNING

Here are a few suggestions for continuing the deeper work off the cushion. These can be used along with those listed for the first turning.

1. *Find creative ways to feel held while also holding yourself in care.* Laying on the earth, taking a bath, being held by a partner, weighted blankets, float tanks, burying yourself in the sand on the beach, etc.— anything that helps us viscerally feel held can also support us in holding ourselves in care. Even while your partner is holding you, practice holding yourself too. We amplify our healing capacity when we practice self-compassion with extra support.

2. *Reconnect with your body.* Regular body-based activities can support the regulation of our nervous systems and the movement of stuck emotion, especially when combined with mindfulness and self-compassion. Exercise, dance, yoga, or even sports can help bring our awareness down into our bodies. Or simply engage regularly in tactile experiences, noticing what you see, hear, touch, smell, and taste in your environment. Consider somatic healing exercises or therapy to support the wisdom of the body.

3. *Talk it out.* Find a friend or a therapist to talk with about your process—someone you feel safe with. This can reveal new insights and clarify your self-understanding. In turn, this can help you care for yourself even more deeply.

4. *Find community.* You'll likely be more inspired, have more fun, and feel more supported if you connect with others who are also devoted to the path. This might be through local or online groups, self-compassion retreats, or with close family or friends.

5. *Make the time.* Treat healing like an intimate relationship or marriage. Think long term and devote ongoing time and commitment. When you create your schedule, block out time to focus exclusively on this work. When you do a deep dive, always schedule time to integrate and rest.

6. *Map your path.* To engage your mind in addition to your heart, consider mapping out your experiences. For example, draw or name your protective patterns and the wounds they protect. Track your evolving relationship with them over time.

7. *Consider enjoying the process.* It's radical, but it's more than possible to enjoy and celebrate the healing process, especially when you do it with other people. Consider making this a central intention, rather than the relief of suffering itself. When you do, you'll have arrived no matter where you are.

ADDITIONAL CONSIDERATIONS FOR TRAUMA AND MARGINALIZATION

If you have experienced intense emotional trauma and/or marginalization, it's essential to consider additional support to your practice. This also applies if you are in a particular period of intense emotional upheaval from life changes. Below is a list of suggestions.

These are not meant to be exhaustive. Since each of our histories and social locations are unique, we may each benefit from instruction that addresses our particular circumstances. If we're regularly overwhelmed, we may even need to step away from intensive healing practices altogether for a time to focus solely on improving our practical realities. For more resources, please see books and articles on trauma-informed mindfulness and local groups led by or therapists who specialize in folks who share your experience.

1. *Remove yourself from the source of pain, if possible.* Remember, compassion never means resigning yourself to hurtful circumstances. If you can distance yourself from ongoing re-wounding, please consider that a priority before attempting to practice.

2. *Increase safety, stability, and simplicity in your life, if possible.* Healing blooms in a safe and stable environment. Before trying to practice, consider creating safer spaces for yourself in your daily life. This might include removing yourself from unhelpful influences or environments, even for a short period every day.

3. *Find dedicated support people, if possible.* Before diving into yourself, it's ideal to secure the support of a trusted therapist, mentor, friend, or family member. This could be someone in the room with you while you practice or someone you can speak to when needed. Alternatively, consider how meaningful objects from your life or images of inspiring figures might support you in your practice. For example, you could set up an altar at home.

4. *Give yourself the space to fall apart, if possible.* The container we create shapes our healing process. In particular, to address deep wounds, consider planning a longer, sustained period of personal retreat—at least a full day, if not several. This allows you to alternate practice, rest, and reflection before returning to daily responsibilities.

5. *Reassure yourself that you're worth it.* Abuse or marginalization transmits the message that we're not worth our own care, let alone care from others. Or we can feel it's selfish to invest in ourselves when so many around us are suffering. Both of these beliefs can prevent us from practicing self-compassion. However, caring for ourselves actually helps us take our power back from oppressive circumstances while also allowing us to help others more effectively. Perhaps start with a simple morning affirmation: *I'm worth my own care.* Then tend to the emotions that arise in response with kindness.

6. *Welcome pleasure when you can.* Embracing the pleasant aspects of life as an act generosity to yourself is often the quickest way to regulation. Before, during, and after your practice, bring your attention to something pleasant in the moment. Consider explicit self-care practices like bathing, soothing music, or being in nature. Pleasure can be deeply medicinal when used not as a distraction but as a conscious support to healing.

7. *Take breaks regularly.* Healing doesn't mean martyrdom. We enact our compassion by going slow and knowing our limits. Our capacity to stop and take a break from our healing process is just as important as our willingness to engage.

Summary and Practices

CHAPTER SUMMARY

- The four turnings utilize true compassion to take the practitioner through the surface, depth, collective, and universal aspects of their experience in a cyclical and ever-deepening process.
- Through a series of preparatory actions and foundational practices, the practitioner learns the essential skills needed to turn the wheel of healing.
- Through eleven guided meditations in the first two turnings, the practitioner progressively dives deeper into their protective and wounded emotions, learning to first approach and then unconditionally embrace their pain.
- Additional support practices for integration into daily life, as well as considerations for trauma and marginalization, are included throughout.

GUIDED PRACTICES

Access the foundational practices, as well as the first and second turning practices at www.justinmichelsondharma.com/thedharmaofhealing /practices or www.shambhala.com/dharmaofhealingpractices.

TURNING THE
WHEEL OF HEALING

Collective and Universal

This chapter follows a very similar format to the last. It includes guided meditations, intended skill development, and daily-life support practices, while adding a troubleshooting guide at the end for additional assistance. Now that we've explored the first two turnings and strengthened our capacity for unconditional compassion, we are ready to infuse the practice with wisdom. Establishing a psychological wholeness within, we're now equipped to expand the self beyond conventional boundaries. In the process, we'll be reminded our healing doesn't ever end; it just stretches out into liberation.

The Third Turning: Collective Consciousness

As our capacity to stay present amid intense, unwholesome emotion grows, we grow too. We widen ourselves beyond the edges of emotion itself and realize we aren't fully defined by their urges, nor their comings and goings. We let a long breath out, freed to see our emotions more impersonally—almost as visitors from somewhere beyond ourselves. In fact, they are not just ours but are a phenomenon of our shared human consciousness across space and time.

While this may sound esoteric, it's quite well studied. The term *collective consciousness* has been used for many years to describe the shared set of perceptions, beliefs, and feelings that occur within groups—some of which are conscious, but many of which are not.[1] We are cocreated by our social and natural environment much more than we often realize.

For our purposes, I will divide our collective consciousness into three related layers, which we can imagine as concentric circles around the individual. The first concentric circle outward is that of our families and ancestry. The second is that of culture and society. The third is that of our evolutionary biology or nature. Surrounding those circles is the universal aspect, which I'll speak to in the fourth turning.

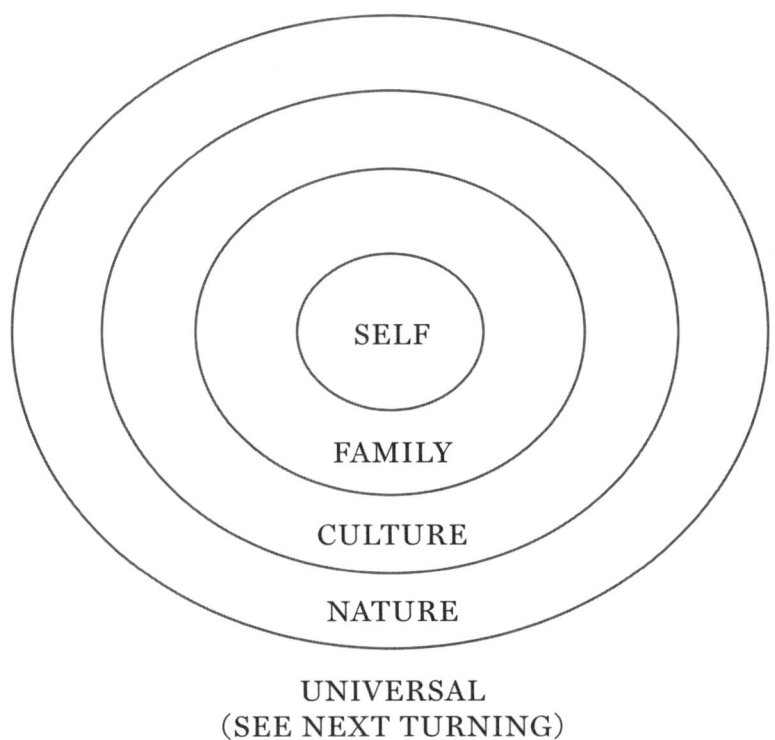

UNIVERSAL
(SEE NEXT TURNING)

FIGURE 7.1. COLLECTIVE CONSCIOUSNESS

The transformative power of collective consciousness is how it can expand our individual sense of self in a direct and experiential way. We can discover that the emotions and thoughts we experience every day are not siloed. They are the descendants of our shared past and connected strands of our present paradigm. Echoes of a vast and ancient human struggle resound in each wounded pattern that inhabits our body in the present.

In effect, nothing arises independently. As the Buddha taught thousands of years ago, everything coarises in concert with everything else based on an intricate web of causes and effects. In Buddhism, this concept is known as *dependent arising* or *dependent origination*. As we affect the world, it simultaneously affects us. Perception happens through relationships. We all mutually condition one another in unexpected ways across space and time. In other words, the collective thinks and feels us into being just as much as we contribute to it.

We are always part of a larger process that started before us and exists beyond us. Ultimately, the contents of any moment are the result of a process as old as time and as wide as the farthest edges of space. Not a single thought or emotion happens purely from us. Our heart-minds are well beyond our control or complete comprehension.

In the evolution of healing and insight, this truth of the third turning invites us to see our pain in a new and expansive light, meet it with an even greater compassion, and set down what is no longer ours to carry.

• •

To enter this third turning, we can use the same wounds and protective strategies we've been working with, but now we illuminate the collective aspects of family, culture, and nature within them.

In the context of our family of origin, we can likely see certain mannerisms, belief systems, and emotional patterns that we've taken from our parents, caretakers, or relatives. Indeed, our formative perceptions of self and world emerge from our family systems[2] and reveal themselves through our healing journey. This familial conditioning transfers through various means, including learned mimicry, direct wounding from familial interactions, and even epigenetics. In fact, the ways your family tried to help you, such as through worrying about you or looking out for your safety, may have actually become the protective strategies that now constrict you. When we look with this understanding, we begin to see the familial aspect of collective consciousness in so much of what we think, say, and do.

In the context of culture, the same is true. For example, we can likely see many ways public schooling, advertising trends, media narratives, and peer pressure have shaped our perception of ourselves and the world. This has become increasingly powerful and true in the digital age. In terms of wounding, this is the realm of group belonging and social approval—or the lack thereof—and the aloneness that so many feel. There's something about us that isn't acceptable, doesn't fit the norms, or garners stereotypes and prejudice, and we grapple with those less-than-compassionate perceptions of us. This includes all the isms that pervade our society. We may have been judged or treated differently because of our race, sex, class, etc., and feel inadequate (i.e., internalized oppression) or indignant. Or we may have judged and exiled others and, in doing so, found ourselves isolated and alone.

Ironically, this aspect of collective consciousness is also the realm of wounding from being *successfully* acculturated and accepted. When we're raised in a wounded culture, we can be praised and rewarded for traits that are actually harmful to us, like rugged individualism, status-seeking, excessive materialism, or even narcissistic behavior. Or for others like myself, we receive praise for self-sacrifice and martyrdom to solve the world's problems. To heal and liberate ourselves, we need to address the ways the status quo conditioning around us has confined and confused us. The culture cocreates our wounds through cocreating the ways we see and relate to ourselves.

In the context of nature, we are part of a larger collective consciousness of living organisms on this planet with a long evolutionary history. Of course, this expresses itself in many ways, as it underlies all our activity—and our wounds. Each of our emotional patterns has evolved to try to help us over millions of years, their unifying intention aimed toward securing our safety and well-being for ourselves as well as those we love. In healing, we might notice our longings for stability, security, or predictability, our fears and anxieties around change and death, or the rage and jealousy we carry to safeguard what we care about. Deeper still, we might notice the felt sense of the fragility and vulnerability of our design—a speck amid the waves, winds, and quakes of nature. In addition, we feel the pain of our modern separation from the natural world and the pain of the Earth's destruction we witness. In these ways and many more, our biological nature cocreates our wounding.

Reflections on collective consciousness reveal how we inherit our protective and wounded patterns from family, culture, and nature. To see this most easily, we can look to our protective emotional patterns and inquire if they might be direct emulations of our caretakers' or cultural icons' behavior—as they often are. For example, if our caretaker regularly used anger to protect themselves or yelled at us when we were young, we may now habitually use anger to both repel others but also to attack ourselves. Looking inside, we might discover not just a wound of shame from being yelled at in the past but also anger we've used to suppress that same shame—perhaps just like our caretaker did with their own wounds. In this way, we inherit protective strategies—often even the ones that hurt us—and use them to continue wounding ourselves and others. Until we heal, the cycle just gets passed on again.

For our purposes, we don't need to analyze the genesis of every aspect of our personal wounding to have success here. In fact, that can sometimes be counterproductive. We just need enough understanding to trust that the collective aspect of a given wound is real. Then we can use this perspective to liberate our pain from the confines of a strictly personal worldview and so increase our capacity for healing and insight.

This is not without its challenges and risks, however. Expanding our perspective can bring new triggers as we acknowledge the others implicit in creating our wounds. If this is the case for you, you may wish to regularly use the forgiveness meditation that appears at the end of this chapter alongside these practices. Moreover, acknowledging the connected nature of our pain can elicit empathetic pain for those who suffer with us or for the Earth itself. Welcoming new triggers and collective pain is all part of the process of heart maturation as we learn to encompass the heartbreaking complexities of the world with our growing compassion.

MEDITATION 12
Family and Ancestral Wounding

This meditation speaks compassionately to our wounds' familial and/or ancestral origins. Common inherited protective strategies include self-critical voices, as well as ways we protect ourselves in intimate relationships, such as closing down or lashing out. Common inherited wounds include feeling unworthy or unaccepted, as well as feeling unsafe or unseen.

Preparatory Reflection: What is a wounded or protective emotion that you hold that you sense might originate from a family member or ancestor? It could be the same pattern you've been working with or something new. If it's a protective emotion, how has it been trying to help you? If it's a wounded emotion, what might it be revealing to you? Where do you feel it in your body?

Method Summary: Find your refuge. Bring to heart the emotion or pattern arising from family/ancestral patterns. Offer self-compassion phrases. Invite in benevolent members of family or ancestry to assist in holding the pain.

Suggested Phrase Variations:

- I see you . . . in your pain, not just as mine but as a blameless part of an older process, passed down through family and ancestry.
- I understand . . . it makes sense you'd feel that way, as your struggle is a product of others' confusion they couldn't yet fully see or heal.
- (For Protective Emotions: Thank you . . . for trying to protect my family and ancestry from their own pain they couldn't hold, for caring so deeply about us.)
- I care . . . about you too, the heavy ancestral load you carry, and your liberation from this burden.
- Know that I'm here to support you, no matter how far back the hurt goes, no matter how many generations. I'm here for as long as you need to heal.

Quick Tip: Focus less on what others may have done to you and more on your capacity to set down what's not yours and move forward with the wholesome protection of compassion. It wasn't your fault, but it is your responsibility now.

MEDITATION 13
Cultural and Societal Wounding

This meditation brings compassion to the cultural or societal aspects of our wounds. Common protective strategies also include self-critical voices internalized from the culture, anxiety about social performance or approval, or anger and longing for justice and equity. Common wounds include a lack of belonging, inadequacy and shame, self-doubt, or other forms of internalized oppression.

Preparatory Reflection: What is a wounded or protective emotion that you hold that you sense might originate from—or in direct cocreation with—a pattern of the culture, a cultural group, or a societal system? It could be the same pattern you've been working with or a new one. If it's a protective emotion, how has it been trying to help you? If it's a wounded emotion, what might it be revealing to you? Where do you feel it in your body?

Method Summary: Find your refuge. Bring to heart the wounded or protective emotion arising from the culture. Offer self-compassion phrases. Invite in a benevolent cultural figure or social group you trust to assist in holding the pain.

Suggested Phrase Variations:

- I see you . . . in your pain, not just as mine but as part of a larger process created by the culture around you, its wounds becoming yours.
- I understand . . . it makes sense you'd feel that way, as your struggle is a result of collective suffering that we haven't yet been able to heal. (For Protective Emotions: Thank you . . . for trying to protect the collective heart-mind from its own pain that it can't hold, for caring so much about all of us.)
- I care . . . about you too, the heavy cultural load you carry, and your expansion beyond these limitations.
- Know that I'm here to support you, no matter what others think, say, or do, no matter how far and wide the hurt echoes; I'm here for as long as you need to heal.

Quick Tip: Rather than focusing on the harm others may have inflicted on you, cultivate your ability to release what does not belong to you, restore your connection to yourself, and move forward held by and in service to compassion.

A NOTE ON DIVERSITY, EQUITY, AND INCLUSION (DEI) WORK

This meditation can bring us into the territory of all the societal isms such as racism, classism, sexism, and so on. No matter our social location, these systemic patterns affect us somehow. They create powerful wounds for oppressed groups but also for the privileged—albeit not equally and not in the same ways. We all have healing to do in this realm.

By taking our wounds related to one of these isms as the object of this meditation, we can begin to heal the internalized aspect of these oppressive patterns. We can use our own personal experience of inequity or our empathetic pain for others' experience. (Note: if this is an overwhelming place of pain for you, please see the advice for trauma and marginalization at the end of chapter 6.)

Especially for those in more privileged social locations—in the United States; white or wealthy or heterosexual or male—it's essential to humbly feel these collective wounds and bring awareness to our implicit participation in systems that perpetuate them. However, this requires uncovering the cunning protective strategies that shield us from feeling the pain of inequality and our part in it. While this work can be heartbreaking, if we are sincere and skillful—careful not to create new complexes of guilt and shame—it can enhance our self-awareness, deepen our heart's resiliency and capacity for compassion, and orient us toward a life of greater humility and service to others.

For me, my unearned privilege has been a very powerful motivator for inner and outer growth, as well as service work in the world, but my relationship to it hasn't always been wholesome. I've carried guilt, depression, and desperation; I've created more social division through my passion or judgment. But with the help of mindfulness and compassion, I've learned to prioritize wholesome connection—within and without—and alchemize the pain to fuel my life in a healthy way. On a larger scale, this type of healing work will hopefully lead to an increased understanding and repaired trust between diverse people so we might better address our collective challenges together.

Note this type of internal equity work is an in-depth and ongoing journey that benefits from a tailored container with supportive resources and peers. Thus, the practices in the third turning alone can't come close to fully addressing it. Please see writings by many wise, BIPOC spiritual authors, such as Ruth King, Rev. angel Kyodo williams, Zenju Earthlyn Manuel, and more—as well as workshops in your local area. In addition, two extra guided meditations focused on this topic (numbered 13.1 and 13.2), as well as links to additional resources, are provided at www.justin michelsondharma.com/thedharmaofhealing/practices or at www.shambhala .com/dharmaofhealingpractices.

MEDITATION 14
Evolutionary Wounding

This meditation speaks compassionately to the evolutionary nature of our pain. While this dimension of our experience underlies all emotional experiences as they all have natural origins,[3] those related to safety and survival are often most relevant here. For example, we might consider fears of loss, longings for security, or even loneliness. Or we might feel the pain of our ecological crises and our separation from the natural world.

Note that if the familial or cultural dimension of a given wound is strong, we may not be ready to see it in this greater context yet.

Preparatory Reflection: What is a wounded or protective emotion that has deep roots in your natural, evolutionary past? It could be the same pattern you've been working with or a new one. If it's a protective emotion, how has it been trying to help you? If it's a wounded emotion, what might it be revealing to you? Where do you feel it in your body?

Method Summary: Find your refuge. Bring to heart the wounded or protective emotion arising from evolutionary origins. Offer self-compassion phrases. Invite in supportive elements of the natural world to help you hold this pain.

Suggested Phrase Variations:

- I see you . . . in your pain, not just as mine but as part of a greater process of nature, from deep in our evolutionary past, well before and beyond me.
- I understand you . . . It makes sense you'd feel that way, as your struggle is a result of the confluence of countless natural processes that conditioned your biology—as old as the Earth itself.

- (For Protective Emotions: Thank you . . . for trying to protect human life in this unstable world, for caring so much for our unique human expression.)
- I care . . . about you too, the heavy evolutionary load you carry, and your liberation from this burden.
- Know that I'm here to support you, no matter how deeply embedded the conditioning is. I'm here for as long as you need to heal.

Quick Tip: Focus less on the limiting aspects of whatever conditioning you carry and more on letting everything within you feel the nourishment of being part of this mysterious miracle of life. Allow this to be a place beyond good or bad, right or wrong.

MEDITATION 15
Investigative Inquiry—
Third Turning Compassion Practices

This is the supplemental inquiry practice for wounded or protective emotions that have not responded to the meditations of the third turning. It combines compassionate inquiry and mindful reflection to deepen our understanding of the collective origins of our wounds. When completed, use the answers you receive to then reengage in the previous three meditations.

Preparatory Reflection: Is there a significant emotional pattern that you feel unclear around its origins with family, culture, or nature? If it's a protective emotion, how has it been trying to help you? If it's a wounded emotion, what might it be revealing to you? Where do you feel it in your body?

Method Summary: Find your refuge. Bring to heart the wounded or protective emotion. Ask inquiry questions to the emotion, or just contemplate and reflect using a journal. Offer compassionate responses.

Inquiry/Journaling Questions:

- Is there anything you'd like to share?
- When did you first feel this way?
- What influences from your family/culture/nature cocreated this feeling?

- What part of this pattern are you willing to set down or transform?
- How can I best support you in that process right now?

Quick Tip: When you ask a question, just wait and listen for an intuitive response before analyzing. Then, if no answer arises, shift to journaling and mindful reflection.

• •

The meditations above for the third turning can be found at www.justin michelsondharma.com/thedharmaofhealing/practices or www.shambhala .com/dharmaofhealingpractices.

LESSONS FROM THE THIRD TURNING

The overall intention of the third turning is to reconceptualize our pain as a natural expression of collective consciousness and, in doing so, expand and mature our compassion while enhancing our capacity to let go. In other words, the addition of wisdom reflections makes our healing more effective. Doing so requires some additional skill development, so if the practices feel complex or challenging at first, that's normal. Additional skills include growing

1. enough familiarity with the fundamentals of the practices thus far that we can layer on wisdom perspectives without distraction or overanalysis;
2. the ability to refrain from arresting oneself in guilt or blame while also taking responsibility for relating with compassion going forward;
3. increased steadiness to follow changing emotions in the body elicited by the compassion phrases without losing the overall thread;
4. the ability to propose the possibility of letting go without any expectation or pressure (i.e., *You can set down what's not yours when you're ready.*);
5. expanding our internal refuge, thus facilitating greater trust in the goodness of life that is before, after, and beyond us; and
6. the ability to experience more extensive collective pain without personalizing it, trying to fix it, or letting it crush us. Instead, we relax into it and trust its wisdom.

Practicing in this way, we can develop significant insight over time. In particular, seeing that our pain is not just ours, we can set down some or all of the heavy, personalized weight of carrying it, as well as the guilt and blame we burden ourselves with. Likewise, seeing that everything we experience is shared can help us to shed the feeling we're alone. Moreover, we realize we have a choice in whether we perpetuate family, cultural, or biological conditioning or enact something different.

The longer-term goal of the third turning is to reconnect with and relax back into our shared, collective heart. In doing so, we realize that the resolution of our pain is less in its absence and more its being held within the embrace of deep interconnection. Fortified by a deep sense of belonging, we learn to be soft and strong, to be fully open and vulnerable *and* supported and resilient.

EVERYDAY SUPPORT PRACTICES—THIRD TURNING

1. *Look for connections* to family, culture, or nature within your thoughts and emotions—or even just when relating to friends, movies, or social media memes. When you notice a connection, write it down to include it in these practices.

2. *Consider studying* your ancestry, cultural origins, and even evolutionary origins. This can support your sense of being part of a larger process unfolding.

3. *Practice forgiveness* for harm that has been done to you and the harm you have done to others. Make an effort to understand the pain and confusion that lead to causing harm. See the forgiveness practice at the end of this chapter.

4. *Find simple phrases* that keep this perspective alive throughout the day. For example, you might say, "This, too, is nature unfolding." Or you might just playfully say "Hi, Mom," when your anxious, protective patterns arise—assuming they came from your mom, of course. If she's not the source of the pattern, say hi to whoever it may be instead.

5. *Spend time in nature with big views.* From time to time, surround yourself with an environment or landscape that evokes a sense of spaciousness and interconnection within you. See if you can feel into the paradoxical, but liberating, experience of being fully open and vulnerable but also fully connected and supported by nature.

The Fourth Turning: Universal Consciousness

The fourth turning of the wheel of healing finally expands our compassion practice beyond our own reach. Now we learn to relinquish our effort and control, receive unconditional care, and surrender into the vastness. In doing so, we find freedom from the constrictions of our own agenda and a home amid the universal dimension of life. We release our hands from the wheel, slide over into the passenger seat, and give the keys to awareness itself.

The spirit of devotion we've been cultivating—the embrace of the "no matter what" or "always and forever"—is deeply powerful. However, without this next letting go, it's also self-limiting. As we approach an absolute embrace of our pain—the event horizon of freedom itself—we often find ourselves unable to surrender completely into unification. This is because even though we yearn to experience the unconditional and absolute, the part of ourselves managing our healing journey can't merge with the universal from its small self-referential worldview. In fact, it's hopelessly conditional—no matter how hard it tries, it's subject to distraction, forgetting, and the constant oscillations of mind.

Paradoxically, for our practice to evolve and our care to become perfected, we have to release everything we've brought to this point, including ourselves. In other words, the growing expanse of our care from the second and third turnings has to be balanced with an equal and opposite letting go. In doing so, we naturally evolve from loving our wounds to realizing their—and our—nature as loving awareness itself.

· ·

We could say universal consciousness, which we've also called awareness, is simply a more inclusive form of collective consciousness. It's a field of potential that holds the totality of all things across space and time, the formless counterpart to the dynamic world of form. Therefore, while we can't sense it with our five senses, we can access it anywhere and through any aspect of our experience. When we allow this consciousness to be felt, we experience the deepest healing refuge yet.

The first step is to once again turn our attention around. However, instead of looking for an attitude, we're looking for the meditator, the healer, or the spiritual seeker themselves. When we find them in the form of thoughts, emotions, or body tension, we offer our gratitude and compassion for their tireless and courageous efforts to help liberate us and give them permission to relax. We then do the same with our deepest spiritual longing. This process resolves any remaining goal orientation and returns us more fully to wholeness in the now.

The second step builds on the first, inviting us to not just relinquish our excess exertion or attachment to outcome but to learn to effortlessly receive. We allow ourselves to rest back into interconnection and be completely cared for by something greater than us. Our faith in the goodness and wisdom of life inevitably grows.

The third step establishes a refuge in the universal. We take our practice of creating a refuge inside of ourselves we've used at the beginning and end of every meditation and evolve it. Now, we pour ourselves into that refuge entirely until there is no inside or outside—just a translucent home in the center of everything. We expand into the silence, stillness, and spaciousness surrounding us in all directions. Our personal refuge becomes a doorway to a universal refuge.

The process reveals through direct experience what is already known to science: 99.9 percent of everything is actually space. That includes us: our thoughts and emotions and even our journey of healing. We could say our wounds heal by realizing themselves as space. However, this space not a cold and empty vacuum. It radiates with a wordless warmth from the fires of our alchemical human heart.

Lastly, in the final meditation, we marry the emptiness of universal consciousness with the fullness of interconnected form. The personal and universal aspects of ourselves, form and formless, merge into the unified whole of the awakened heart—a concept discussed further in chapter 8.

MEDITATION 16

Healing the Meditator

This guided meditation offers compassion to the hardworking self who helped get us here. We treat this meditative self as we would any other protective pattern that covers over our wounds—that is, we offer it gratitude and care. In doing so, we allow ourselves to surrender to the relief of already having arrived.

Preparatory Reflection: Just by turning your attention around, you may be able to notice the voice or energy that has kept you "on track" in your practice. You may be able to feel the striving in your body. This is the first protective part we'll be honoring.

In addition, we all have a deeper emotional longing for freedom. This part can be invited out through inquiry. We might ask ourselves, *How would you feel if you could never meditate or do healing practices again? If you could never complete the path of healing or liberation?* Feel not just the grief but the longing and resistance in your body. This is the second protective part we'll be honoring.

Method Summary: Observe the part of you that manages your healing and spiritual journey. Offer self-compassion phrases. Observe your deeper spiritual longing for freedom. Offer self-compassion phrases.

Suggested Phrase Variations:

- I see you . . . and I honor you, for your noble and tireless effort to heal and liberate us.
- I thank you . . . with sincere gratitude for your devotion to helping us, for caring so fiercely for our well-being.
- I care . . . too about this cause, but also about the stress you carry.
- I'm here now to support us . . . unconditionally, even if we never find healing or liberation, never feel safe, relaxed, or whole.

Quick Tip: Don't be afraid to compassionately feel the fear, the loss, the guilt, the shame, etc., associated with releasing an effortful devotion to practice. Paradoxically, it will only bring your practice closer to the place you've longed for.

MEDITATION 17
Opening to Receive

Once we have soothed the meditative self and relaxed our effort even more, we can open our heart-minds to receive the compassion that's already here. To practice this, we will imagine that compassion is emanating toward us from another entity or from life itself.

Preparatory Reflection: Consider from what or whom you will practice receiving compassion. Perhaps choose the most vast and loving thing you can conceptualize. Nature? The Earth? Awareness? The Universe? A god or goddess of compassion? Write a few options down or visualize them as clearly as you can.

Method Summary: Find your refuge. Imagine a benevolent entity with you. Effortlessly receive self-compassion phrases. Relax and let it in deeply.

Suggested Phrase Variations (to receive):

- I see you . . . fully in your essential humanness: all your fears and joys, your confusion and clarity, your longing for safety and protection—all of it.
- I understand . . . you completely just as you are, in all your perfect mistakes and imperfections.
- I care . . . about you unconditionally without exception, holding your rare and precious human heart in its wisdom and goodness.
- I'm here to support you through the ups and downs of life and always, no matter what has or will happen, no matter what you do or what you become. I'm here.

Note: You can experiment with replacing the word I with the name of the vast and loving presence (e.g., "awareness sees me fully in my essential humanness . . .").

Quick Tip: Notice if there is a skeptical, protective part of yourself that is concerned that this is all imaginary. *Am I actually receiving compassion from something else? Is compassion already here just waiting to be received?* Thank this part for its concern and see if it's willing to just give it a try for a moment and find out what happens.

• •

MEDITATION 18

The Deepest Refuge

This is the guided meditation for bringing oneself home to the deepest refuge within. Here, there is no doing, nondoing, giving, receiving, or separation. There is just the still expanse of the universe breathing through us and our wounds, radiating with boundless compassion. In this, there is a sense of total completion.

I recommend doing this meditation several times to really get a feel for it before moving onto the next.

Preparatory Reflection: Reflect on the refuge you've been cultivating through the meditations so far. Does it feel deeply safe? If not, what is the safest place or time you've ever known? Imagine yourself there now and re-feel it. You're welcome to use this as your refuge for the meditation.

Method Summary: Find your refuge. Expand it throughout your body and outward until it encompasses you. Dissolve into silence, stillness, and spaciousness. Feel the radiating warmth and let it permeate every wound and every part of your life.

Quick Tip: Find a particularly quiet and safe environment. Stay at least partially upright to promote wakefulness. Relax and repeat until you can stay with it through the entire process.

MEDITATION 19
The Awakened Heart

This is the final meditation in the series of core practices. It brings together the essence of each of the four turnings into a unified whole, encouraging us to include everything and cling to nothing. Just as the four aspects of compassion unified into true compassion, the four turnings unify into a liberated wholeness.

However, this meditation will be more accessible and powerful if we've (a) already cycled through the four turnings several times and (b) read through to the end of chapter 8. At the least, repeat meditation 18 until you feel very comfortable with it before doing this meditation.

Preparatory Reflection: Consider the journal prompts at the end of chapter 8.

Method Summary: Find your refuge. Call to heart an image of yourself. Offer self-compassion phrases to the surface, depth, collective, and universal aspects. Reflect on the duality of personal and universal, form and emptiness. Let go of each and rest on the threshold between, feeling a sovereign and unified sense of being.

Suggested Phrase Variations: We cycle through the four aspects of true compassion for each of the four turnings as well as consider additional reflections. See the guided meditation for exact phrases.

Quick Tip: Continue practicing until you can switch between turnings effortlessly. Using the same emotional pattern or self-image, you can learn to see it on the surface, in its depth, collectively, or universally.

• •

These meditations can be found at www.justinmichelsondharma.com /thedharmaofhealing/practices or www.shambhala.com/dharmaofhealing practices.

LESSONS FROM THE FOURTH TURNING

The overall intention of the fourth turning is to learn to let go, receive and surrender into the deepest refuge of awareness within us. In this all-encompassing and eternal embrace, we don't need the tense protection we've carried with us. With the backing of awareness—the part of us that is never triggered—we can say we'll be here for ourselves *no matter what* and mean it. In doing so, our remaining wounds heal more readily, and we process future pain more gracefully as it comes. Healing and insight unfold with a spacious ease.

In addition to the skills of the previous turnings, the fourth requires the skills of

1. learning to recognize when we are holding any tension, weight, or striving in our practice and learning to turn to that habit with sincere compassion;
2. learning to be in an effortless, receptive orientation to our present-moment experience without losing mindfulness;
3. learning to pour ourselves into our internal refuge with abandon, thus allowing ourselves to let go, receive, and be held by something greater than us;
4. learning to recognize awareness in our own embodied experience, including in our pain, through the qualities of silence, stillness, and spaciousness; and
5. learning to access and reaccess awareness to utilize its radiance of safety and connection.

6. shifting from *loving* our wounds and ourselves to *realizing* our essence as loving awareness itself.

One of the key aspects of the fourth turning is refining our understanding of wise effort—a factor on the eightfold noble path from chapter 2. For much of our practice, wise effort is a balancing act. If we try too hard (striving), clinging to an outcome, we fall into the experience of tension or contraction. Naturally, we correct by releasing effort, but as we let ourselves relax, we fall off the other side into spacing out, dullness, not caring, or sleepiness.

In the first three turnings, we evolve this process by choosing compassion as the guiding force behind our effort—a force that, when pure, doesn't cling to outcome or create tension. This helps the pendulum between tension and distraction near the still point at our center. Now, in the fourth turning, we're courageously letting go of *any* self-oriented agenda to explore a new paradigm of effort altogether. Relaxing back into awareness, we find an awake energy coming forth through the heart that steadies us without trying at all. This further stabilizes us in the present moment and liberates wholesome emotions to join in the deepening exploration of practice.

On the somatic level, the fourth turning encourages us to finally release the need for the body to protect us from emotional harm, bear the weight and pain of our lives, or be the ultimate refuge of safety for us. We're giving those responsibilities back to life itself. In other words, in this turning, somatic healing is not about releasing a singular trauma but learning to set down an entire tension-based mode of inhabiting the body. As we relieve the body of our heart-mind's existential grip and return to connection with awareness, the body can express its innate wisdom without constriction.

The longer-term goal of the fourth turning is, again, not the extinguishment of pain or suffering but the gradual emergence of an equanimity and contentment within us that the ups and downs of life can never take away. In the embrace of the universal, we realize no matter what our lives or healing journey looks or feels like, we always have a home inside where all is well. Eventually, we realize that we and our wounds are, in essence, also awareness. In doing so, we find the deepest reassurance that we will always be safe and connected.

This resolves much of the heaviness of our suffering, but that doesn't mean we stop healing or stop engaging in life—quite the opposite. We turn the wheel of healing with renewed, wholesome vigor. We take this energy back to the first turning and turn the wheel again and again, learning to synergize these different modes of being into one seamless whole.

EVERYDAY SUPPORT PRACTICES—FOURTH TURNING

1. *Stop doing everything* for a moment. Periodically break from the task at hand. Close your eyes and find the silence, stillness, or spaciousness of the moment. When you reengage, see if the movement can come *from* awareness instead of your personal effort.

2. *Craft experiments.* Some mornings, commit to not getting up from bed from a place of protection or wounding (the sense of "I have to" or "I should"). Lie there with curiosity and kindness, waiting for a wholesome part to take the lead. We might even ask, *How can I start this day from the safest place within me?*

3. *Find simple phrases or questions* that keep these perspectives alive throughout the day. I like the question, *Who or what is caring for this?*—with *this* being whatever is in front of me. For me, the answer is awareness, and in asking, its care comes forward into my life. Or ask yourself, *What would I do right now if I were* completely *safe and connected?* before making important decisions.

4. *Radiate compassion.* Bring a slight smile to the corners of your mouth during the day. Let that simple gesture merge with mindfulness, silently radiating compassion inwardly and outwardly.

5. *Create longer, quiet solo time or retreat time in your day, week, month, or year.* Sometimes, we need ample rest and space to relax enough to allow a deeper letting go and the insight that follows.

6. *Search out the most relaxing experiences*—float tanks, dark rooms, hot baths, deep embraces of a loved one, hold a grandchild in your lap, etc. Stay present and practice self-compassion (especially the final meditations) when you are in them. See what happens.

Continuing the Work

We can practice the four turnings as a progressive and linear process or learn to intuit the most appropriate meditation for a given challenge. We might sense whether an arising emotion is on the surface, from deeper down, or part of the collective. We might sense whether it needs personal care or a vast, surrendered embrace. We might sense whether it needs a question to reveal itself, a phrase, or maybe just silence.

When in doubt, however, I always recommend starting with a personal approach and widening from there. Likewise, I always recommend starting with being more active and effortful and then letting go from there. This also correlates with using more words (phrases/inquiry) early on and then softening into prioritizing warm spaciousness and silence as we become comfortable with the process. Remember the five healing forces in chapter 3. Everything wants to be free, and knows how to be. We mainly just show up to hold compassionate space for that process.

Once we get the hang of it, we may traverse the four turnings, from surface to universal, in a single sitting. Or we might focus on just one. Over the longer arc of our practice, we may naturally gravitate toward the most liberating and healing insights of the fourth turning—just don't skip right there without doing the preparation work.

Eventually, I encourage you to make it your own, shifting from a prescriptive approach to a creative one. Let yourself be guided at first and then become your own teacher, trusting your inner wisdom. As your trust grows, you may find yourself relaxing into a sense of faith in the larger unfolding of your life and life itself.

· ·

However you choose to practice the Dharma of Healing, there's one main rule: *don't try to get to the end.*

I remember sitting in front of my Zen teacher Joan Sutherland in my early twenties and asking her innocently, "So are you at the end of the path?" She looked at me with compassionate concern and said, "Oh dear, no, thankfully not." I remember being confused and rather disappointed at the moment. Not only did this path I got on not end, but my teacher didn't even want it to!

I remembered her remark as it seemed to stand in contrast to traditional Theravada Buddhist conceptions of nirvana and enlightenment, of "reaching the other shore" and not returning to human incarnation. Over the years, her words worked on me and melted my limiting concepts.

Indeed, if interconnection were the guiding principle, as it felt in my heart, there could be no lasting distinction between enlightenment and ignorance, endings and beginnings, or even connection and separateness. Why would I want it to be otherwise?

This, too, is the spirit of the Dharma of Healing. Whether we want it to or not, at some point we realize that ending isn't really an option. We may have a grand spiritual experience after years of hard work, but the next day, we are delivered back to the first turning, tending to the next triggers or mundane arisings. It is the nature of the universe to always keep unfolding, and we either align our healing and insight with that and keep deepening or we don't and stop.

True compassion, however, invites us one step further. It shows us that it's possible to actually *enjoy* the sweetness of caring for suffering, and not just for our own sake but for all beings. We consciously choose to keep coming back to the path because we want to. So perhaps that is the best guidepost for an "ending point" of our spiritual and healing path, if we insist on having one. We face our suffering heart-on until we actually don't need or want it to end. Suffering can disappear from us or the world if it would like, but it will always be welcome while it's here. The door of the awakened heart is always open.

In this way, not only is the ancient drive of aversion completely quenched, but there is a wholesome force of enjoyment greasing the axle upon which the wheel of healing spins. Then, we don't need to worry about ensuring we've completed all the healings or collected all the insights. Whatever Dharma-gates are to be opened, they will open in just the right way and at just the right time for each of us.

Troubleshooting Guide

Below I list questions or concerns people often share when doing the Dharma of Healing practices. I offer a brief response to each, hoping you will find it helps clarify your path and keeps you going. I encourage you to bookmark this page so you can return to review these tips when you feel stuck.

1. I just feel like I can't get the practice right.

Fortunately, it's not about getting it right or getting anywhere. It's just about meeting your pain with care. In this question, it's the feeling of "not-rightness" that's calling out for your attention. Where in your body do you feel the struggle? Is it a grief in your chest, a pocket of doubt in your gut, the tension of self-judgment in your jaw or eyes?

Meet that part of you that feels like it's doing it wrong, and care for it. Reassure yourself that it doesn't matter if you ever figure it out: you will be there holding yourself no matter what. Or meet the part of you that is desperately trying to fix yourself, leaving you anxious and exhausted. Reassure yourself there's nothing wrong, give yourself a break from practicing, and just let yourself rest in a pleasant experience in the moment. All of a sudden, you're doing the practice.

Trying to do it right is a common stumbling block. It certainly was for me. I remembered what happened when I would do it wrong as a kid: there could be big consequences. The same was true in school, in relationships, at work. So with my practice, I needed to do it right so I wouldn't get reprimanded by someone else—or myself. I had to learn over many years that in healing and spirituality, there is no right way; there's just *your* authentic way.

2. I'm constantly lost in thought, and I can't locate an emotion in my body.

This is common at the beginning. Don't worry. The first step is to continue to practice the foundational meditations.

If you still find yourself struggling, don't try to meditate yet. Instead, just speak to yourself kindly. Start by thanking your thoughts and emotions for trying to help the best way they know how. Then let them know that you care about them, and you want them to be well. Repeat this sincerely until you start to calm.

Then do something active with your body, like a form of exercise you like. Go until you're tired. After that, come back, shower, eat, and try the foundational meditation again. This time just let yourself relax and receive—don't try to do it right.

If none of this helps, try doing something nice for others first. Volunteer at a soup kitchen. Give a gift to your spouse. Smile at the clerk at the checkout counter. In the Buddha's time, he actually instructed people to practice two years of generosity before even meditating. In our practice here, this helps ripen the heart so we can then be truly generous to ourselves.

3. I'm not a visual person or I'm not a verbal person. Some of the practices don't work for me.

Each of us naturally has different processing styles. Some of us are more visual; some more verbal, more energetic, or more kinesthetic. Some will have a more challenging time holding an image in their mind, while others will have difficulty finding phrases, and still others will have trouble feeling emotions in the body.

I know that I always had trouble holding images in my mind, but certain phrases really worked for me. Maybe for you, it's just placing a hand on your heart that ignites the process. Any doorway that engenders warmheartedness is the right place to start for you. Be exploratory and find your own path of resonance with these practices.

4. When I offer myself the phrases, my mind talks back to me.

It's been my experience that at least 10 percent of people initially face inner arguments in response to the phrases. For example, an aggravated or skeptical inner voice might reply, *No you* don't *see/understand/care/support me!* In other words, some part of ourselves doesn't believe us.

This often happens because of an entrenched inner conflict and/or history of neglect. We may have unintentionally abandoned, betrayed, or oppressed parts of us, and/or others may have done so. At first, our inner voices might not trust us or anyone. This is painful, but it isn't an impediment to practice. It's actually an excellent opportunity to meet what's likely to be a deep wound.

The general recommendation is to direct your attention to the aggravated voices and practice the compassion phrases *with them*. For example, *I see you in your mistrust; it makes sense you wouldn't believe me since I haven't been kind in the past*, etc. If it helps, you can even soften the phrases by saying, *I want to learn to care for or support you.*

Alternatively, some folks find it's best to take responsibility, say sorry, and feel the grief of that inner schism. Then they might offer compassion phrases to the grief. If the contention remains, however, it's often best to shift to inquiry and ask what we could do to help repair it. If we get a clear response, it's important to abide by the request, even if that means no longer practicing in that moment. We can check back in at a later time.

Ultimately, such situations require a personalized and intuitive approach only you can discover. Don't give up. Just be humble, sincere, and devoted, like you're working to repair a relationship with someone you have hurt or are taking care of a child who has been mistreated. You're rebuilding trust through patience and care.

For one of my students with a significant trauma history, my phrases would sometimes really aggravate him. His parts didn't believe him nor did they want anyone else to tell them what to do. So, instead, on many occasions we shifted to inquiry, like asking, *What would help you feel safest right now?* When more trust and safety could be established, then he could be creative about how to relate and his healing became much more accessible.

5. I experience overwhelming emotions when practicing.

For some of us, our deeper wounding isn't buried in the subconscious but easily bubbles to the surface with the slightest invitation. While this may seem like a problem at first, once we get the hang of working with it, we'll be able to access a lot of healing that many people can't. So stick with it. I'll offer a few thoughts here, but please also refer to "Additional Considerations for Trauma and Marginalization" at the end of chapter 6 for various tips.

In general, we first want to calm the overwhelm. Often, the easiest way to do this is to stop the practice and do something else that relaxes us, engages us, or wears us out. Then, when we return to practice, we find the safest, most comfortable, and relaxing place to do a short meditation. We make it our exclusive goal to establish a refuge within our present-moment experience (see foundation 1 meditation practice).

Once we develop a refuge inside, we can practice titrating our exposure to the overwhelming emotion by doing very short practice periods with our pain in times/places we feel very safe, returning to the refuge whenever needed. We slowly build confidence and the capacity to feel and relate to increasing emotional energy without being overwhelmed; eventually, healing does happen and things become easier. A key piece of this process is learning to see the attitudes we bring to the overwhelm itself (foundational meditation 3). Often, it's our fear of or resistance to the emotion that makes it much bigger than it otherwise would be.

6. I don't feel anything when I practice self-compassion.

For some of us, our protective strategy has been to numb, suppress, or dull our emotional experience. When we sit down to practice self-compassion, we either can't feel our emotions and/or can't feel the emotional resonance of the self-compassion phrases. This is common, and there are a variety of ways to address it.

The first doorway I often suggest is to locate the experience of numbness or suppression in or around the body. We are sensing into the subtle sensations of the emotional shield we carry—it might just feel like static or a wall. If we can't locate it, we can simply ask ourselves directly where it is (*Where is the numbness in my body?*) and listen for an answer. If we still can't, we can instead turn our attention to the frustration or grief that we may feel about the numbness. Once we sense the numbness or our reaction to it, I recommend meditation 2 for protective emotions. Repeat regularly. The numbness may *slowly* melt as trust is reestablished.

The second doorway I often suggest is practicing meditation 1 using an image of yourself from a younger age when you remember having a vibrant emotional life. Alternatively, we can use an image from a time when we were very hurt and offer self-compassion phrases to that image. Remembering an earlier emotional time can reawaken our capacity to feel.

The third doorway is to practice inquiry, as suggested in meditations 4 and 10. In particular, we might get curious about what wound this numbness protects us from remembering and feeling. When we get in touch with the pain, we can then continue with the standard self-compassion phrases. Lastly, any of the trauma-informed practices at the end of the second turning can also be good for softening a hardened or numb heart.

I remember one of my students struggled immensely with this. For decades, he had kept trying to push past the numbness into the feeling he wanted, but instead, he'd end up going from feeling nothing to feeling manic with energy and then crashing later. In this practice, he worked to honor the numbness, thanked it, and didn't try to make it go anywhere. In doing so, he realized he didn't have to wait for the numbness to leave to feel something. He could feel *for* the numbness. Surely enough, when he could do this, his heart started to thaw and he could explore and heal the emotional terrain that had been frozen over for so many years.

7. I can't get an emotional pattern to heal. It keeps coming back.

Yes, some of our deepest patterns are very ingrained. However, they never heal from impatience, no matter how subtle or justified. The best medicine is to turn to the impatience, exhaustion, or exasperation without trying to get it to heal. If you can offer that protective emotion gratitude and care, it will often soften. Then we can turn back to the pattern we're working with and summon truly unconditional care: *No matter if you ever heal or ever go away, I will always welcome you with open arms. Always. No matter what.* When this sentiment is *sincere* and continuous, it doesn't matter if it heals—which ironically is the exact time when it starts to.

I've had to learn this over and again on my path. The mythical idea of "being done" is ever ready to hijack our path. That's why in the core practices every recording starts the phrases or inquiry with the word *welcome*. For me, I like the phrase *you're always welcome*. If I say that *before* responding in any way, it short-circuits the tendency to manipulate the experience subtly. If it's always welcome, then my prerogative is inherently transformed. I readily open my heart in care to what might be a painful, but ultimately beautiful, expression of life moving through me.

If and when such an unconditional care has been established, then you can *curiously* explore transformative inquiry or the meditations of the fourth turning to alchemize additional healing and insight.

8. I don't resonate with the phrases or questions.

Great. I'm glad you know what *doesn't* resonate because that means you'll be able to discover what *does*. We're not looking for the right words; we're looking for words that elicit a compassionate or caring response within our own hearts. Sometimes, that's just silence with a smile and a hand on the body. Sometimes, it's a simple phrase like *I'm here.*

Consider using just the beginning and end of the core practices. In the middle, instead of using my phrases, begin to speak authentically and compassionately to yourself. Intuit what you might need to hear right now, based on what you're going through. Or you might imagine someone you trust is offering you reassurance. What might they say or have said? This is a great opportunity actually to listen and learn what we need. Then write down the phrases so you can use them in future practice.

Also, know you're not alone: I've had various students who feel the same way. We all receive language differently. I encourage you to use the principles in the book to craft the custom messages that your wounds are waiting for.

9. *The practice feels too complicated, cumbersome, and tiring.*

For those familiar with simpler meditation practices or those new to meditation, this practice may initially feel complex and cumbersome. This is understandable. First, don't try to do *everything* in the guided meditations. Just listen and allow, and see what feels inspiring. Second, I always recommend that practitioners do the simplest form of this practice possible that still creates the intended effect. That might just be creating a refuge or just placing a hand on your body. Third, feel free to use these practices as a tool to supplement an existing practice as opposed to an everyday primary practice if that feels more appropriate for you at this time. Lastly, like any practice, it will get easier over time, and if you continue, there will be a moment when it feels simple and easy.

As long as you're relaxing and staying present, you're doing the practice—even if you're in the bathtub. If you add a little warmth of heart in there, you're doing great. Sometimes less is more.

10. *I can do the practice, and it helps, but part of me keeps feeling unsafe and fearful.*

First, see the advice under the heading: "I can't get an emotional pattern to heal . . ." In addition, I'll offer two other perspectives.

If you're feeling this way, I would recommend focusing 80 percent of your practice energy just on establishing a refuge inside yourself. This is introduced in foundation 1, is at the beginning and end of every other meditation, and in its most expansive form in meditation 18. If there is still a lack of safety, consider your outside circumstances. When we have consistent and strong stressors in our life or regularly feel unsafe, it can be hard to establish a safe refuge on the inside. Sometimes we need to make substantial practical changes to decrease stress during this healing period, if possible. Or plan a period away for intensive practice.

The second perspective is that sometimes we can use practices like self-compassion to justify not taking risks that would ultimately support us. We can inadvertently use the phrases to indulge or coddle our fear. A helpful metaphor might be when a child regularly cries until their parent gives them what they want. Perhaps it's time for them to grow in some way, but instead of helping them be brave, we give into the wounding.

In healing, we want to be an inner parent who honors our emotional pain while also guiding ourselves toward developing more resilience. If we build a trusting and caring bond with our wounded parts (i.e., secure attachment), they will likely naturally expand their edges. If not, we may need to secure our fear to our chest like a baby and continue taking the risks that our lives require. Doing things we're afraid of doesn't mean we don't care for our fear. If we embrace ourselves lovingly while doing it, it can be very healing. In the end, *we* are driving the vehicle of our lives— along with awareness—not our scared parts.

I know for me it took a while to walk this line. There were times when deep wounds were exposed and parts of me were literally afraid to leave my house. I wanted to be compassionate and not push myself into triggering situations, as that had been an unhealthy pattern in the past, but I also couldn't stay home all day. So I had to learn to carry my wounds lovingly and confidently with me through my daily life—to work, to relationships, to the grocery store. In doing so, the wounds eventually came to realize that the world wasn't as unsafe as they had remembered because they were now held in my unconditionally loving embrace.

11. Nowhere in my body feels safe.

For some folks, there will be nowhere in the body that feels like a refuge— at least at the beginning. First, I always recommend a body scan to see if there might be part of your body that you've simply overlooked. There may not be a safe place, but there may at least be a neutral space that can be a good place to start. You can even include the space around your body.

If still nothing feels OK, I encourage you to get creative. You can bring your attention to pleasant sounds, perhaps through ambient/nonlyrical music or being immersed in nature. You can also open your eyes and bring your attention to sight. In this case, it's often easiest to settle the eyes downward so the gaze can be simple, soft, and undistracted. Alternatively, some folks will hold an image in their minds that soothes them and/or repeat a settling phrase (e.g., *I'm here with you*). You can find what works just for you through courageous and committed trial and error. Over time and from that refuge, you can begin to slowly grow and spread that sense of safety and use it as a foundation for healing.

Also see the "Additional Considerations for Trauma and Marginalization" at the end of chapter 6 for more tips.

12. *Why do you use gratitude (saying thank you) instead of compassion for certain practices but not for others?*

Curiosity, gratitude, and compassion are the three healing emotions I recommend using. One might be out front, but the other two are in the wings. In the reflection and inquiry processes, curiosity leads the exploration. In working with protective emotions, gratitude is out front to honor our hardworking parts. For everything else, compassion takes center stage. However, in every practice, any of those three emotions will enhance the healing experience. So I encourage you to experiment with what works best for you.

13. *I can't see the meditator/healer/seeker.*

In mediation 16, when we turn our attention around to see the meditator, we're just looking for another mental-emotional pattern. It's the thoughts and feelings involved in managing our healing or spiritual journey, especially the ones that are trying to encourage or motivate us. This part evaluates our progress toward specific goals, often judging ourselves if we don't reach them. It also protects against others' judgments about our path. You may feel its emotional energy in your body somewhere as pressure, tension, or striving.

Alternatively, we might be able to notice the *idea* of us as a meditator or spiritual person—the identity we carry. What would it be like if you couldn't meditate ever again? What if someone tells you you're doing it wrong or won't get "there"? What part of you reacts?

However, if you turn your attention around and don't see anything, don't worry about it. In fact, in the insight tradition, it's a powerful insight to *not* find the self. With anything we notice, we can ask, Who *is noticing this?* "Me, of course," we might say. But then we can ask, Who *is noticing me?* All we might find is an open compassionate space, and that might be quite liberating. (See chapter 8 for a continued discussion.)

14. I don't know where my wounding is coming from— family/culture/biology?

Not to worry. You don't need to find the origin of any wound to heal it. What matters is, again, the quality of care and presence you bring to it. Moreover, you don't need to know the exact source to trust that it must be connected to conditioning from family, culture, and nature. That's where everyone's conditioning comes from. Remembering that is much more important than remembering the details.

I certainly came across this in my own healing process. My memories were incomplete and jumbled and I wondered if I was just making things up. Eventually, I realized it didn't matter so much. Sure, it was sometimes interesting to research to understand aspects of my personal history. But the primary value of whatever information I gained was not its accuracy but instead the self-compassion it then could help me generate and the permission it gave me to loosen my grip on the pain.

15. I can't see/feel/understand awareness or universal consciousness.

These concepts can be elusive and confusing, admittedly. This isn't intentional. Unfortunately, no word or phrase can encapsulate awareness, because it isn't contained within thought. We can't grasp it through our mind. It's not even something we can see, smell, taste, hear, or touch, at least not in the traditional sense. We have to have a direct, unmediated experience.

Fortunately, there are many intermediaries. For example, the qualities of silence, stillness, and spaciousness are dimensions of every moment that we can bring our attention to. In time, they draw us into the experience of awareness. Alternatively, if we create enough safety in ourselves, letting ourselves relax completely, we naturally dissolve into the moment. Awareness is the field of potential we become.

Most importantly, remember that striving after this experience will only block your access to it. Letting go of it, it comes closer. You might relax the need to understand it for now, and instead continue wholeheartedly with the core practices, trusting that it will make sense at the perfect moment for you.

16. I'm confused about all the terms. What is awareness, the awakened heart, life itself, the original heart, etc.?

That would make sense. I've used various terms throughout the book to try to describe ineffable aspects of the human experience. Each word or phrase has an intended purpose and meaning in the context of the book and the path described. Here's a brief summary:

1. *Wounded heart* refers to our personal wounds and protective strategies on the surface and subconscious layers of the heart-mind.
2. *Original heart* refers to our unique, individual heart underneath or before our wounding. It is tender, open, and innocent.
3. *Heart of life* refers to our interconnected or shared heart with all other beings across space and time. Our original hearts are but a node in a vast heart of life.
4. *Awareness* refers to our deepest refuge or the universal dimension of ourselves that is most readily known through spaciousness, silence, and stillness. I also call it *universal consciousness* in the fourth turning.
5. *Awakened heart* is the complete home for the heart on the spiritual path, an experience of unification of all aspects of ourselves (surface, depth, collective, universal) that is free from clinging to any aspect. (See chapter 8 for further discussion.)
6. *Brahmaviharas* are the natural, radiant expressions of the awakened heart. They can also be practiced and cultivated. They are loving-kindness, compassion, sympathetic joy, and equanimity.
7. *Life itself* refers to the totality of the known and unknown universe across space and time—both what we perceive and what we don't—radiating with its mysterious and unexplainable intelligence. The four turnings are what we can perceive, but that is just one iota of the totality that is.

Summary and Practices

CHAPTER SUMMARY

- Through four guided meditations comprising the third turning, the practitioner learns to expand their sense of self and their compassionate heart to include the familial, cultural, and evolutionary aspects of their pain.

- Through the final four guided meditations comprising the fourth turning, the practitioner learns to relax their striving and let go into the wholesome embrace of the deepest refuge within.

- Just as the four aspects of compassion unify into true compassion, the four turnings are intended to be repeated until they, too, unify into a holistic perception of life. This can culminate in the liberating realization of the awakened heart.

- The troubleshooting guide answers common questions and concerns that arise in the practice.

GUIDED PRACTICES

Several of the third turning practices, in particular, can sometimes trigger anger and blame toward others. Healing these wounds is often supported by practicing forgiveness. Hence, the additional guided meditation practice for chapter 7 is a process for learning to forgive others. Access this and other meditations and resources at www.justinmichelsondharma.com /thedharmaofhealing/practices or www.shambhala.com/dharmaofhealing practices.

Part Three

THE REALIZATION

8

THE JOY OF THE
AWAKENED HEART

In part 3 of this book, we shift from the experiential, meditative practices of the Dharma of Healing to an exploration of how those practices are made real in our lives. This chapter begins by probing the most profound, personal truths of the path. This includes what I call the deepest protection and the deepest refuge, as well as the awakened heart that integrates the personal and the universal aspects of ourselves. These and other ideas may sound esoteric or lofty, but they point to natural experiences accessible to everyone. I encourage you to have a curious approach, taking in whatever resonates with you and setting down the rest.

• •

The path described by the four turnings is not easy, but it's also not complex. We first use the warmth of compassion to melt our resistance and transform the hurt we carry. We do so day after day, down and down into ourselves, until we hold our most precious and tender original heart in our hands (first and second turnings). We then apply the wisdom of interconnection to return this heart to its home, repairing the broken threads until we are once again woven wholly into the fabric of everything (third turning). This helps us surrender completely into the deepest refuge within us: awareness (fourth turning).

In each turning, we become lighter and more transparent until, in the end, we may disappear altogether in the embrace. In the next moment, however, the bell rings or the alarm goes off. We open our eyes and reengage with our lives, and before long, we get confused and bruised again. Not to worry—the warmth of compassion transforms yet more hurt and melts yet more resistance, helping us to return home once again—now more fully. We then reengage in life with even greater capacity.

The positive feedback loop continues. Each cycle, we let go and reengage with more wholeheartedness until we realize there is no difference between the most mundane aspects of our lives and the deepest experiences of practice. In this unification, we glimpse the jewel of the awakened heart—the placeless place at the center, at the threshold between the human and more-than-human worlds. Here blooms a very rare and precious kind of joy.

• •

The need for safety pervades our lives as humans. To address this on the physical level, we work to provide for and protect our basic needs. On the emotional level, we employ self-compassion to soothe and transform. On the spiritual level, however, the creation of safety comes through suturing our most primal wound: *the wound of separation from life itself.* However, fully healing this wound at the core of us requires more than spiritual skill or healing techniques. We must touch our deepest spiritual longing and follow this wise guide all the way back to its original source.

We might ask ourselves now, *What is our deepest spiritual longing?* As we do, we might find it reaches far beyond self-improvement and personal growth, even beyond physical and emotional safety or healing itself. We long to experience something that's not *in any way* limited or transient. We long to experience something that's not *at all* breakable or losable. We long to experience something that's not even ours, nor created by us, but is much, much vaster. We can trust this longing; it remembers the goodness and wisdom at the center of things.

Following this longing, we can intuit our way into the full embrace of interconnection, the complete release into awareness, and, ultimately, into the sovereignty of the awakened heart. The following sections take inspiration from various aspects of insight meditation—most notably the teachings of emptiness and nonself. In chapter 2, I noted that these teachings can be confusing and potentially harmful—if we haven't done enough healing. At this point, we may be ready to approach them again with a greater degree of safety and connection inside.

Yet even with a mature self-compassion practice, stepping farther into the unknown naturally feels risky. It may sound appealing to return home to interconnection, but when we're at the edge of leaving our familiar way of being behind, we can hesitate. This is one more paradox on the path: it's through taking spiritual risks—with wisdom and compassion—that we allow ourselves to fall into the ultimate safety. This letting go is an intimate and personal act that we allow if and when we're ready. For now, we can just try on the following perspectives and notice what stirs in us.

Interconnection: The Deepest Protection

Our normal means of psychological self-protection include various expressions of creating distance, ranging from subtle hesitation to aggressive pushing away. As we grow on our spiritual path, we come to see that all of these strategies hurt us more than they help. Fortunately, there are ways to protect ourselves that *don't* sever our internal connection with others, ourselves, or life itself. In fact, the deepest protection actually comes *through* connection—especially through connection to the heart of life.

This realization is guarded, however, by a deep psychological habit that remains hidden well into our spiritual journeys. It is the chief protective habit that manages all others and fail-safes the foundational sense of separation in the psyche. Due to its central role in maintaining psychological stability, for much of the path we must work within its boundaries. However, after dedicating ourselves to creating internal coherence through self-compassion, we may be safe and stable enough to reconsider the basic assumptions of the self.

THE LIMITED PROTECTION OF THE SELF

The self is one of the earliest and most tenacious protective mechanisms that we each evolve. Just as the physical body evolved to have skin around our organism, the heart-mind evolved its counterpart in thought and emotion. It did so as a survival strategy in response to pain. By creating the concept of a separate self, we could organize our mental-emotional strategies in relation to the threats and needs "outside," and thereby navigate the world with less hurt. This started very humbly, but over time evolved into the multilayered, multicentric sense of self we've been exploring in healing practice.

This becomes clearer when observing an infant. In the earliest months and years, we tend to lack fear of many things. We don't know to fear a snake or the edge of our crib. We don't know we need to feed every two hours. We initially learn those things through direct and painful feedback from the inside and out. This naturally teaches our perceptual and nervous systems to differentiate,[1] and aversion, desire, and delusion begin to grow in us. The self forms to protect us not just from a single pain, however, but from all *potential* pains that could arise if we let down our guard. As a by-product of this gracious effort, it formalizes the wound of separation from life and inadvertently prepares the soil for future suffering to sprout.

As described in chapter 1, when we experience pain in the absence of a *felt sense of safety and connection*, we inevitably initiate protective processes that further separate us. The self, as our fundamental, overarching protective mechanism, worked the same way—and still does. The more threatened or endangered we felt and feel, the stronger the walls of the self—and the aversion that holds it in place—tend to become. However, since the sense of self is the foundation from which other protective strategies emerge, it can't rest like other protective strategies. It feels it has to reinforce itself again and again through identification—e.g., this or that is "me" or "mine"—hardening the sense of separation over time until it becomes so thick and heavy that we can't see or feel past it.

Even with all this well-intentioned effort, however, the self can't quite fulfill its promise of complete protection through separation. Indeed, none of our strategies could or can because there's no way to eliminate our fundamental vulnerability to life. And thank goodness for that! If we could truly close ourselves off—as we at times want to—we would only suffocate ourselves just as surely as if we had shrink-wrapped our skin in plastic. This unconscious dream of complete isolation from any danger is not only impossible but would actually mean the death of our organism. We will always be subject to the impacts of life—both the painful and the liberating.

In this way, it's not that the self isn't *real*, as we sometimes hear it put. It's that the idea that it has ever or could ever actually separate us is a falsehood. This is because the self isn't what we think it is. It's not a "thing" any more than our reaction to taking our hand off a hot stove is a "thing."

The self is a mental-emotional *process* by which we manage threats. It's a strategy or a tool—a verb, not a noun. Therefore, it's not a cause of grief unless we keep making it solid and opaque. Hence, we're not looking to annihilate the perception of selfhood (that would be suicide), but instead make it conscious and then encourage it to become relaxed, transparent, and fluid again.

To do so, we use the same medicine and logic that we do with every other protective strategy. We offer unconditional curiosity, compassion, and especially gratitude—not contempt—and we can watch it begin to soften and open. When we truly see it for the generous protective force it's been, when we no longer deny its allyship, we can honor it for working tirelessly to protect our vulnerable and precious human bodies, hearts, and minds for decades on end. It's a miracle, really. We don't need to blame it for not satisfying our deepest longing or being our forever home. It was never meant for that; we were always meant to return to a more funda-mental protection.

It makes me chuckle, and it also makes me tear up. For so many years, I would have *never* thought to be grateful to my sense of self in meditation. Like so many spiritual seekers, I tried to watch it, outwit it, or fight against it, subtly or overtly. But once the self truly realizes we're not out to destroy it but instead seek to honor it, we're on a whole different playing field. We enter into a conscious and curious coexploration of the pain that the per-ception of separation brings and the alternative ways of seeing and being that might protect us better with even less effort. Then transformation is not a fight against delusion but a cocreation with life.

In this exploration, a series of humbling questions might arise: *If I can't provide the best protection for myself, if I can't sustain a stress-free rela-tionship with life, if I can't satisfy my deepest longing, then what can? And how can I make space for that to come through?*

THE LASTING PROTECTION OF INTERCONNECTION

The irony is not lost on me that one of the final acts of self-compassion is finding the safety to let the walls of the self come down. We finally feel the exhaustion from the constant reassertion of the self and have mercy on this ancient pattern. This compassionate act returns us home, at last, to the heart of life.

We were born from interconnection, and we die back into it. The water used to create our cells was once ancient lakes, then clouds and rain. The minerals used to form our bones are the dust of ancient mountains. Our thoughts and emotions are just higher-order expressions of the same natural elements. We were literally assembled from everything around us. In fact, we still are in each moment. There is a pregnant field of care from which you were constructed and to which you will return. This is why so many practitioners, including my teacher and myself, have practiced extensively in nature, as it vulnerably exposes these essential truths.

In this book, we've been rediscovering the nourishment of this interconnection one puzzle piece at a time. We've reconnected ourselves to each thought, emotion, and sensation. Then we've extended that connection out to everyone and everything around us. Now let's put the final piece back into the jigsaw puzzle of life: ourselves.

We shift from connecting *to* everything and learn to live *as* everything. Instead of interacting *with* our life from behind glass, we step out into it, lie down, and *become* it. Like two droplets of water that surpass their surface tension and merge, connection amasses into *inter*connection, or as Thich Nhat Hanh called it, *inter-being*. We feel ourselves being rewired into the circuitry of all things—the trees, the mountains, the soil, and the heart-minds of all the ones around us—as well as before and after us.

This feeling is the deepest protection not because we erect new and improved walls to keep out danger but precisely because it dissolves all barriers and divisions. The energies of life surge toward us but have nothing solid to impact. Instead, like flowing water, they find the pathways to move under, over, and through us and back into the ocean of life. Moreover, instead of feeling alone, we can now draw upon the nearly infinite resources of this web we're a part of—including its ancient wisdom and goodness. Something greater than us has our back, and we are never without companionship. We are even protected from death itself, for not even death can break the web of interconnection. Death is, in fact, a servant to it—dutifully returning our forms to be reorganized into something new.

In feeling this, even for a moment, we become fortified in an indescribable way. Yet we also realize our immense vulnerability. The web of interconnection that makes us indestructible is also what allows us to get hurt and eventually spells the dissolution of everything we've come to know and love. In this way, this deepest protection also necessitates the deepest humility. The riddle is finally solved. This is how it's possible to feel completely protected and completely vulnerable at the same time. For me, this realization was such a relief. I could allow my heart to stay soft and open without fear of being destroyed.

To explore this in our lives, we might inquire as to what protection is necessary in any given moment. Do we need the countless forms of aversion right now? We might, or might not. Do we need the sense of separation carried in our conception of self? We might. When you are navigating the New York subway or the remote wilderness of Alaska, maybe they're helpful. But when we're in meditation or we're home in bed, we might be able to start to set them down and explore the deeper protection that's flowing underneath. I've enjoyed reminding my troubled mind, *Thank you for caring so much about me—and just so you know—we're already safe and whole one step deeper down.*

THE PROTECTIVE RADIANCE OF THE HEART

I've stated that when we feel safe and connected, the natural liberated qualities of the heart emerge; the wholesome emotions arise effortlessly. Like a puzzle of a beautiful sunset, as we carefully fit the pieces together, the scene comes alive, and with the last piece in place, the light radiates forth. This is the promise of realizing interconnection: the depth of our newfound protection initiates a whole new level of heart capacity. Imbued with unfathomable support, we can not only feel the warmth inwardly, but courageously radiate it outward in all directions. It's this outward flow of the heart that becomes our best protection for navigating the complexities of our *daily lives* while still staying open and vulnerable.

Each of the wholesome emotions can be both received from and broadcast into the field of interconnection surrounding us. It may become a field of wonder, joy, gratitude, compassion, playfulness, or even equanimity. Instead of preemptively protecting by creating a barrier, these emotions protect when needed by generating a radiance. Instead of sending out worried thoughts, they send out wordless heart-prayers. The potential of these heart-radiances is truly unlimited.

I'm reminded of a story of a Tibetan monk named Palden Gyatso, who was tortured in Chinese prisons and upon his release spoke about the compassion he had cultivated for his torturers.[2] This radiant spirit kept him alive during his thirty-three years of imprisonment. Nelson Mandela's story is another famous example. If such things are possible, then compassion can shine anywhere, and we can each aspire to deepen our capacities.

In the insight meditation tradition, these protective energies are loving-kindness, compassion, joy, and equanimity, collectively called the brahmaviharas. These are tools we can use to heal ourselves and others, and they are the natural protective expressions of an open, fearless heart rooted in interconnection. They were taught by the Buddha to be *radiated* outward in all directions, throughout all space and time.

Loving-Kindness

When an open, fearless heart sees ourselves or another living being, it naturally radiates loving-kindness, or *metta* in Pali, the ancient language in which the earliest Buddhist texts are written. This protects us in many ways.

First, it protects us from the self-inflicted pain of our own aversion, judgment, or ill will toward ourselves or others. When this radiance is strong, it can help us stay rooted in nonharming even when we're being harmed. Moreover, it can soften or sometimes even deflect the emotional or energetic impact of that harm. In the traditional teachings, the Buddha is said to have instructed monks to use this art of radiating loving-kindness as a preventative means of protecting against evil spirits in the forest.[3]

More practically, by radiating friendliness toward others, we are simply much more likely to be treated with friendliness back and, in the process, create a strong social network, thus providing further protection.

Compassion

When an open, fearless heart sees ourselves or another being in a state of suffering, it naturally radiates compassion, or *karuna* in Pali.

This protects us in similar ways as loving-kindness does. However, it's many times more powerful in this capacity, especially when combined with wisdom, as it naturally is in the brahmaviharas. When this compassion is strong and focused on the source of suffering, it disarms destructive forces within us—and with skillfulness, in others as well. The disarmament and subsequent healing protect us from the proliferation of harm. By seeing the suffering in others, this radiance helps us take things less personally and short-circuits our defensive reactions that make things worse. Moreover, it prevents pitying or judging others, keeping us connected and equal.

Sympathetic Joy

When an open, fearless heart sees ourselves or another being in a state of happiness or well-being, it naturally radiates joy, or *mudita* in Pali. In fact, this empathetic capacity of heart can reflect and amplify any wholesome quality we encounter. In doing so, it amplifies their protective nature.

Joy, in particular, is like friendliness or compassion; it often breeds goodwill and benevolent connections with others while protecting ourselves from self-inflicted patterns of internal suffering. When this radiance is strong, it celebrates others' joy even when we aren't included and even when we're hurting. This protects us and others from the harmful effects of jealousy, envy, and comparison.

Equanimity

When an open, fearless heart is not activated by kindness, compassion, or joy, it simply abides within equanimity, or *upekkha* in Pali. This capacity could also be said to underlie the other brahmaviharas, since, without it, they couldn't be sustained in the face of adversity. Equanimity's genius is its ability to hold anything that passes through it without reacting. Its spacious and inclusive nature mirrors that of awareness itself, and when it's present, wholesome emotions flourish.

Through equanimity's radiance of peaceful and calm energy, it heals our restlessness and worry. People in our presence naturally feel safe to relax and be themselves, building trust and goodwill. Mostly, however, equanimity protects us by preventing countless unwise or harmful decisions in our lives. Imagine all the grief we could have forgone if we wouldn't have thought, said, or done all those things we did from a place of insecurity and reactivity. Especially at a time when so many are losing their cool, there is nothing more self-protective than the capacity to stay centered, not escalate, and respond wisely.

Gratitude

While gratitude—*dana* in Pali—is not technically a brahmavihara in the insight tradition, sometimes it seems like it should be. When an open, fearless heart receives a gift, it naturally radiates gratitude. Gratitude protects us from all harms arising from lack and dissatisfaction, as it inclines the heart-mind toward wholeness and contentment.

The brahmavihara type of gratitude is unconditional. It's not dependent on traditional gifts or even favorable conditions. It's a natural response to the miracle of existence itself—the fact that anything is happening at all and that we get to be a part of it. This is a gift appearing in every moment. As the radiance of gratitude shines outward, those around us feel held and appreciated and, in turn, shower us with the same.

THE PROTECTION OF GOODNESS

The brahmaviharas are an inspiring and reassuring balm for the protective parts, patterns, and emotions within us. When our anxiety, anger, and longing truly see that there is a way to protect us that doesn't require constant stress *and* actually protects us infinitely better, they're ripe for a transformation. They realize they can then choose to retire from their protective duties into the arms of interconnection or to evolve into an esteemed role as one of the supreme radiances of heart.

As they mature within us, the brahmaviharas offer final confirmation of the fundamental goodness of life and of our own heart-minds. Indeed, these radiances arise from letting go and *not* from our own manufacturing; they flow from interconnection and out through our hearts. In that way, we can verify that they reside at the core of us, even beneath the unwholesome roots of desire, aversion, and delusion. Moreover, we can realize our protective strategies have not just been trying to help; *they have always been the brahmaviharas in disguise.* Realizing themselves as love, they can finally relinquish their contracted nature.

When we experience this transformation from *self*-protection to *inter*-protection—even for a moment—our whole being undergoes an evolutionary shift. We then know our primal duty to keep ourselves safe is no longer only ours. It arises from something we don't have to create or sustain. It's not dependent on outer conditions.

Accessing this innate, protective goodness may not bring us material wealth, social status, or influence. But it makes what we already have come alive with a deeply fulfilling radiance—and that's a far greater gift than all the riches of the world alone could bring. What we might sacrifice in material gain to discover these gems is paid back a hundredfold again and again.

Awareness: The Deepest Refuge

A refuge is a place safe from harm, a place we can feel at home. All beings long for a refuge. Some creatures burrow a tunnel. Others build a nest. Still others camouflage themselves in the open. For humans, we not only seek physical refuge; we seek refuge for our emotional and spiritual hearts.

Without any spiritual training, we naturally try to find refuge in anything and everything around us. From the bond with our first caretakers onward to the myriad people, places, and things in our lives, we try to find a home for our heart-minds. Even when we are discovering a spiritual path, the tendencies easily transfer, and we seek refuge in ideas, identities, practices, teachers, etc. All of this is natural and can be healthy for a time if we choose wisely. However, in the long term, many of us arrest our development, settling for refuges that may be comfortable and familiar but don't support our deepest aspirations.

A healthy spiritual journey is a little like the life of a hermit crab. Our initial cozy homes nurture us for a spell, but in time we grow out of them. The spiritual heart, intuiting a deeper and more expansive place to rest and express, leaves the safety and familiarity of one refuge after another. Over time, we naturally shift from taking refuge in the conditions of the outer world toward the more reliable refuges of the inner life. For example, we might take refuge in the sensations of our breath or the feeling of a pleasant or relaxed place in our present-moment experience or even the energy of wholesome emotions like compassion or joy. However, if we keep courageously following our heart, we'll eventually see through the world of the five senses altogether. We'll discover the deepest refuge that underlies all things.

The same logic applies to our healing journey. The transient, outer refuges of people, places, and things may provide enough safety for our smaller wounds to heal. But we need deeper refuges to generate enough safety for our more profound suffering to transform. Thus, the healing path also naturally evolves toward the deepest refuge possible so we may eventually heal even the deepest wound of separation from life. We then discover this wound isn't just a separation from our heart-minds or other people, places, and things in the world of form. It's also a separation from the vast expanse of awareness that underlies everything. Yes, through interconnection, we can feel fearless in the world of form; through the radiances, we can gracefully protect ourselves from emotional harms; yet, until we retrieve the other half of ourselves—the formless—we can't be truly whole.

This organic process of evolving our refuge is actually quite beautiful and natural. It means that our protective walls and the deepest traumas they cover can end up becoming our greatest benefactors. The walls generate the longing to restore interconnection, and the traumatic pain generates the longing for lasting relief in the formless. In other words, our very suffering is what compels us to seek our liberation and eventually return home.

For many of us, however, the process will not *feel* particularly logical or linear, except in retrospect. All of us, myself included, usually only realize the refuges we've been hiding in when they are broken by life. We lose our job, our home, our relationship, our health, our reputation, etc., and we're exposed and vulnerable again. Each of us can recall the key changes or losses that were the most revealing for us.

Without wisdom, we scramble to rebuild from the same limited and anxious strategies, not knowing that there is a deeper refuge possible within. However, after repeated disappointments, we may eventually realize that nothing in the world can provide the truly lasting safety and sense of home we crave deep down. With great relief, we realize the "failures" weren't our fault. It was the conditions of life that weren't designed to last or be tidy. In fact, the disappointments were actually our benefactors as well, as they ushered in a wiser approach and grew the courage within us to pursue it.

In this way, we realize that while healing and insight can be supported by beneficial conditions, they can also be propelled forward by the crumbling of those very conditions—if we see them with wisdom. Indeed, our natural nemesis of impermanence, which keeps taking what we love again and again, is the greatest maturing force for our spiritual hearts. It breaks us free from complacency and forces us to keep looking deeper for a refuge that finally can't be broken.

I've used the concept of awareness as the primary pointer toward the formless dimension of our experience and world. In insight meditation, the traditional term would be *emptiness*. I prefer the concept of awareness because its multiple meanings and uses help us understand how to experience it.

Awareness can refer to the activity of attention or mindfulness (a verb), as in being *aware of* something, like the breath. It can refer to a characteristic or quality of a person, as in someone who is aware (an adjective). It can also refer to the fundamental expression of consciousness itself; we can possess awareness as a living being (a noun). In other words, we are (a) effortlessly expressing awareness already by virtue of being conscious, (b) enacting awareness through directing our attention and mindfulness, and (c) in doing both, centering it as the defining characteristic of who and what we are.

In this way, awareness is a bridge concept, whereby the ineffable, spiritual dimension can be seen and interacted with in our direct experience via our mindful attention. We might imagine our attention like the beam of a flashlight, our sensory/cognitive systems like the hardware, and awareness the source of the light-energy. In this way, our deepest refuge can be both limitless and extra-personal, and yet intimate to every moment of our embodied experience. We have control of it through attention, and we also have no control over it because we can't turn off consciousness at will.

Seen in this way, accessing the deepest refuge of awareness is not distant or abstract. We reaffirm our connection to it through the simple act of mindfulness itself. We awaken it not through cultivation but through healing the constriction of its natural expression (i.e., wounds and, particularly, protective layers), letting it shine brighter through us. We witness awareness directly when we turn our attention around to see where it's been emanating from. We merge with it by releasing our existential grip on the world of form, including our separate sense of self.

But what does awareness look and feel like? How would you know if you experienced it? In meditation, when we turn our attention around, there's nothing there. But if we sustain that gaze, we might begin to feel into a spacious, silent, and still field of aliveness without borders. It won't have any shape, size, weight, texture, etc.—yet we can sense it's pregnant with potential. It doesn't have a source; it doesn't come from or go toward anything else. It just *is* without any explanation.

SPACIOUSNESS, STILLNESS, AND SILENCE

Spaciousness, stillness, and silence are qualities of every moment and also potent doorways into experiencing awareness. Instead of resting our attention in the body, we can actually attend to these three qualities in our meditation (as we do in meditation 18). We experience them subjectively, but they are also objective aspects of reality. Scientists have confirmed that 99.9 percent of everything in us and around us is just empty space.[4] Naturally it follows that because it's empty, the space is also still and silent.

If 99.9 percent of everything is actually just space, that's pretty radical. It means our body is space. Our thoughts are space. Even our irritation and anger are space. Your job is space. Your family is space. Even you—the one trying to heal and awaken—are almost entirely space. Yet, 99.9 percent of the time, we are hyperfocused on stuff and things. Amazingly, our habit of perception is a *direct inversion of reality*. No wonder we suffer! Again and again, we make something out of nothing. If compassion is the hopeless romantic, wisdom is certainly the comedian.

Realigning our lives with this basic scientific truth is a core, liberating insight. To explore what this might be like, try some creative exercises. For example, you might sit with your eyes closed and imagine the sensations of your body are floating in empty space—like you're an astronaut in zero gravity. There's no real up or down or sideways, just space extending in all directions. Learn to relax within this lack of orientation. Or next time you experience emotional tension in your body, sense the space *within* that perceived density. The same with your restless thinking. Or, in a still and quiet moment of meditation, you might curiously ask yourself, *What is sitting here meditating, anyway?* Scientifically speaking, it's just space. We're no less sacred; we're just much less solid than we thought.

Using the concept of space, we can see awareness need not be some esoteric mystical state to seek after. It's simply part of the structure of reality. Without it, nothing could move or flow. This realization can give us relief from the feeling of density and self-importance that often characterizes our lives. This can also relieve us from the heaviness that can come from periods of intense emotional processing, like the work we do in the first three turnings of the wheel of healing.

If you combine awareness with the warmth of heart we've been cultivating, then the vast empty space can radiate with a warm and loving presence. This is a beautiful expression of the balance between wisdom and compassion and can help us feel that, even with its boundless and amorphous nature, awareness is safe to relax into. When we do, this warm and loving presence can provide the deepest healing environment yet for our pain.

EFFORTLESS ABIDING

It's said that if someone approached a black hole, they would notice that time slows down. If they were to enter it, time would stop altogether.[5] I like to think of awareness as the same, just reversed. In order to approach it, *we* have to slow down, and to enter it, *we* have to fully stop. If we don't, the motion of our spiritual effort itself will block our view, keeping a veil between us and this deepest refuge.

Obviously, our wise and skillful effort is necessary at times on the path. However, in relation to the deepest healing and insight, our doing becomes what actually moves us farther away. As with experiencing the protection of interconnection, we must let go of the very thing that has gotten us this far: the meditative self with its effortful practice.

This letting go is a natural and inevitable part of the path. Our own well-meaning effort simply becomes too heavy and awkward to come with us into this conceptless space. This is because it, too, arises from protective impulses rooted in a perceived lack of absolute safety. Therefore, it reinforces the insecurity it seeks to overcome. Even our trusted spiritual longing can become entangled with a subtle goal orientation.

Now, truly letting go requires accepting the possibility of never being safe, of never arriving. We accept the possibility of being trapped forevermore within our pain or being crushed by shame and hopelessness. Yet, in doing so we reveal quite the opposite: we are safe and free in the arms of what's always and already been here—which effort has inevitably overlooked. We are OK without a justifiable reason, unexplainably complete.

When I think about it, it makes sense. For something to be the absolutely deepest refuge, it can't require *anything* of me. It can't only be there if I try hard enough or in a certain way. In fact, a deepest refuge couldn't be "mine" at all, because then it would be subject to my unpredictable nature—my moods, whims, wants, etc.—and thus, not truly a stable refuge. We each know this intuitively. To fully trust, we have to feel safety emerge from something more than just us. Then we know it's reliable.

The four turnings prepare us for this effortless abiding by soothing the preexisting, wounded restlessness that permeates our consciousness, freeing ourselves from our own control and giving that control back to life itself. Then, when we do surrender, we fall back into awareness instead of into our old, disconnected conditioning. We experience the reality that is present before we filter or manipulate it. And it turns out, when we do, there's not anything there.

THE GREAT NOTHING

No one would sign up for the path if they were told up front that there was a whole lot of nothing at the end! Again, wisdom is here as the comedian. We want a big something after all this work. We want bright lights and bliss. However, the simplicity of nothing turns out to be a most unexpected gift.

We finally get a taste of an ancient restfulness, a break from all the anxious seeking that's weathered our bodies, hearts, and minds over all these years. Don't get me wrong: there's richness in the struggles of life, but it's only when we experience nothing that we realize how long it's been since we've truly, truly rested—lifetimes at least. I mean rested like the wispy clouds rest as they sweep through the sky, like the Earth rests as it sweeps through the solar system, like the universe itself rests in endless, timeless space—a primordial tranquility that can restore and regenerate all things.

Just like the true size of the universe, the depth of this awake, alive nothingness is still unknown and always will be. It's immeasurable by its very nature. Some spiritual adepts insist that it is so deep that not even awareness or the brahmaviharas can escape from it—a sort of metaphysical black hole at the center of us. This is a version of the Buddhist concept of *cessation*: the liberating experience of the total stopping of all phenomena, even consciousness itself.[6] It's a letting go that even transcends letting go.

BECOMING WHAT WE LONG FOR

As you might have noticed, words struggle and will ultimately always fail to describe the deepest refuge. The concepts above are simply pointers toward a preexisting place of ultimate safety and connection within and around each of us. In this "place," if we can call it such, we receive the unconditional embrace that our wounds have longed for since the original impacts so long ago. However, the healing here is less of a transformation into something new, and more of a dissolving out of form altogether, like offering bits of paper to an eternal fire. In this way, we could say that our wounds don't just heal but alight with insight, awakening to their empty essence. They *become* the safety they've longed for.

Cultivating emotional safety through compassion allows us to release our self-protection and relax. When we relax entirely and stay fully awake, we naturally sink into the vast field of awareness. This field then embraces and illuminates our remaining pain, and any new pain that arrives. Once we've experienced this, it doesn't need to be limited to times of relaxation but can begin to integrate into the rest of our lives.

We began this process by shining mindfulness and compassion on *emotions* in the body. Now our mindfulness widens into a panoramic gaze, all-inclusive and without borders. We relieve our attention of our own anxious agenda, allowing it to return to awareness again and again. In time, it remembers how to hold everything in our experience all at once. In doing so, everything reveals itself as connected but also empty. We are empty together with all things.

Just as the deepest protection of interconnection restores our faith in the goodness of life, the deepest refuge of awareness restores our faith in the ultimate resolution of all pain. Since our access to awareness is through letting go, and because the nature of our pain is essentially empty, then we—and all beings—are destined to return to this refuge someday. Our effortful, conditioned patterns of clinging and resistance can't sustain themselves indefinitely—at least not after we hear the Dharma. It may be years from now; it could be many lifetimes. But just as with the five forces of healing, we can be assured the unyielding laws of nature will bring us back home.

An Unlikely Marriage

Of all the paradoxes we encounter on the spiritual path, often the hardest to reconcile is the coexistence of the personal and universal dimensions of ourselves—I know it has been for me. How do we merge the very mundanely personal reality of our daily lives with the vastly impersonal realities of deep spiritual experience? Said differently, how do we integrate the first two and second two turnings of the wheel?

One day we're in the grind of negotiating challenges at work, juggling dozens of minute details. The next day in meditation, we're having an expansive, heart-opening experience that dissolves the boundaries of self. Again and again on the path, we oscillate between feeling contracted and defended and fluid and open. If we're not careful, this can further aggravate our aversion as we try harder to grasp the spiritually pleasant and push away the unpleasant of the mundane. However, if we see it as a classical spiritual paradox, we know that somehow the density of our lives and luminosity of spiritual experience must just be two sides of the same coin.

To embody a paradox like this, we must forfeit our usual strategies. It won't help to try harder, analyze the problem, or avoid the challenges of life. Instead, it asks us to release our mental fixation and drop into the inclusive field of the heart. We are asked to welcome everything in our experience fully and equally.

When we do, we can hold multiplicity with grace. We can witness two or even more opposing views simultaneously or sequentially without clinging to either as the ultimate truth. This is an essential skill for integrating deep spiritual truths amid our lives—not to mention for navigating life, in general. It is also one of the natural fruits of cycling through the core practices in this book.

Image and metaphor can be particularly helpful here. They can seed our minds with understandings that relax our dualistic frameworks of true/false, agreeable/disagreeable, pleasant/painful, etc. In turn, they can help us feel how the multiplicity of our selves or of a moment coexist as complementary aspects of the same unified reality.

LIKE A RADIANT DIAMOND

I like to think of any moment, or this practice itself, like a rotating diamond with many facets. Each side reflects a different understanding, yet the diamond is always singular, whole, and complete. In this way, a single moment can be seen from our surface-level narratives, from the depths of our subconscious, from the perspective of the collective, or from the universal.

Take a simple meditation. On the surface, we are perceiving ourselves as just sitting and watching the sensations of the breath. On a deeper level of our psyche, we are interpreting whether this is a safe or unsafe activity, subtly scanning the environment and communicating with our physiology. On the collective, our breath is an echo of everyone who has ever breathed and a hologram of everyone breathing across the globe right now. In the universal, our experience is just vast, empty space breathing itself into existence. All aspects can coexist peacefully.

LIKE A DEEP LAKE

The truth of any moment can be thought of like a deep lake. Its surface ripples and waves with the impacts of life, like pebbles thrown in. Underneath, larger creatures move within the deeper currents of our subconscious. On the bottom, the remains of the collective past rest. The water itself is the universal medium through which we experience life.

I love the fluid feeling of this metaphor, especially the sense that our awareness is more like a living liquid than an empty space. It's an energy and substance that flows around every part of us, helping us feel buoyant and connected. This is actually resonant with some of the newest unified field theories in physics that, at the infinitesimally small scale, the vacuum of space is actually a fluctuating river of energy.[7]

There's also a reflection on equanimity here. A pebble thrown into a puddle is much different than a pebble thrown into a deep lake or a vast ocean. The initial impact is the same, but the effect is worlds apart. The wider and deeper we allow our heart-mind to be, the more space the impacts of life have to reverberate within before churning up the water.

LIKE A VAST ECOSYSTEM

We might imagine ourselves like an ecosystem. Our personal heart-minds are like a node in the web, perhaps a single tree. The interactions of all the nodes combined is the collective, like the community of an old-growth forest. The universal is the space through which the ecology evolves and information is transferred around the web.

In ecosystems, each node is interdependent with everything else, just as our personal lives are interwoven with everything around us. Every thought we think is dependent upon the ecology of the moment, the multiplicity of moving parts. Instead of us acting upon the environment, we and the ecology cocreate the shared, collective experience in each moment. And all of this creation moves effortlessly through the limitless space within and around us (i.e., the universal). In sum, we are both the elements and space; we span life and death.

So when our personal heart-minds are affected by life, we can imagine allowing the web of connections we're embedded in to help absorb those impacts. Just as in the metaphor of the pebble in the ocean, an impact contained in a small space is much more dramatic than an impact that is transferred across the web of life. This view itself can catalyze a marked difference in our felt experience.

LIKE A GREAT RIVER

I also like to imagine the totality of who we are to be like a great river flowing to the ocean. The wide banks and river bottom (i.e., the universal) gracefully hold the torrent of life energy (the collective) flowing across the landscape. On a far edge, a powerful eddy forms, taking on a unique shape and form (the personal). Our individual embodiment is like this eddy: the same substance as the river, just suspended temporarily as a vortex of energy. We seem solid and continuous because we have a center of spin that funnels our perception inward. However, we are never made of the same water from one moment to the next, constantly infused with the larger energy of the river of life. It's only a matter of time before the currents shift and our form will be released back into the flow.

In this metaphor, and the others before it, we are reminded that death is a part of life, a dimension of who we already are. We don't transcend the river or the web or the lake of life. We are the elements themselves always in the process of transforming into something else.

So when we become entangled in a thought or emotion that constricts or divides us, we can pause and simply remember the larger flow of energy that's moving through us. When we can graciously hold the wholeness of a moment without pitting any of the parts against each other—and then relax there—a sacred alchemy occurs.

THE AWAKENED HEART

A thorough self-compassion practice returns us to interconnection within the world of form. The resulting safety and connection help us release into the deepest refuge of the formless: awareness. However, even when we've experienced the fruition of both realms, they can still remain separated at some level of our experience. The task is then to weave together the worlds of form and the formless so all of experience becomes a seamless and unified whole.

We could imagine practicing this weaving in various ways. For example, we could do it as a walking meditation. With the first foot, we feel the solidness of the Earth under us, and with the next foot, we feel the endless space within and around us—and repeat. Or, in a meditation practice, we care deeply for a troubled emotion on the in-breath and then dissolve back into spaciousness on the out-breath—and repeat. Or, in our lives, we alternate between intensive secluded practice and intensive immersion in life. For me, each time I've traversed the boundaries of form and formless, I've learned something new. Mainly, I've learned how to more thoroughly and graciously let go.

As we learn to release both the world of form and the world of the formless, we become disenchanted not just with the empty promises of the world (e.g., if you just get this or that, you'll be happy) but also with the vast array of shiny spiritual experiences. I know I spent many years chasing after mountaintop experiences, thinking they were ends in themselves. However, the seeking after bliss, the mystical unions, the revelatory insight, etc., can themselves be a type of stress.

Eventually, we realize we didn't really want to have special experiences or be someone special anyway, as that would just be more to have to maintain and we know now how tiring that can be. We just want to *be*.

We want what's real to be enough. Hence, even after decades of ardent spiritual effort and meaningful spiritual experience, we must let go even of our own search for awakening. The jewels of our journey can only be kept by constantly giving them back to life—not looking forward or back.

In this release of both form and the formless, a new nondual consciousness can arise—one that exists at the seam or threshold of the two. To one side is the observable tumult of thoughts, emotions, sensations, and the world around us, whose essence has revealed itself as care or love. To the other side is awareness, whose essence is vast, empty space. Poised with grace between the fullness of interconnected form and the emptiness of awareness, the awakened heart has access to both but is dependent on neither.

If this awakened heart can be said to abide anywhere, it is *within* non-clinging itself. In this way, it's like falling through open space, but without ground beneath you: at first your stomach drops, but as you look down and realize there's no bottom, falling simply becomes the nature of experience. As instructed in the Buddhist texts, the practitioner "abides independent, not clinging to anything in the world"[8]—not the world, but also not liberation; not form, but also not the formless. This means not even clinging to the deepest protections or refuges we've experienced.

I know we've all heard spiritual teachers say you are not you, you *are* awareness. However, I won't be limiting myself by that identification, either. To return to the metaphor of the marriage between the personal and universal, experiencing the awakened heart is more like being a wedding officiant. As form and formlessness are reunited in their sacred bond, we consecrate an ancient and eternal love and vows to serve that love indefinitely. In this unique position, we can gracefully navigate both form and formlessness without getting entangled in either.

In the chorus of this heart, the pervading hum of contentment is layered underneath the varied melodies of the human realm, creating the most brilliant of harmonies. Here, it's possible to care freely and act authentically as we're no longer afraid to lose. We've already let go of everything and everything is already holding us. We can move with all the rich rhythms of life, including the painful ones, and yet not be beholden to any of them. We can relax as the awakened heart rings and reverberates its full and compassionate sound through the open time and space of our lives.

A Universe Awakening

It's important to remember that no concept will ever be True with a capital *T*. Especially when describing experiences that reach beyond the self, words will always be more symbolic than precise. They are placeholders, pointers, or simply there for inspiration. In this way, the explorations of this chapter need only be as true as they are helpful and timely for you. If these teachings soften your heart and draw you open, then follow them. If not, set them down. Spiritual concepts are not to be clung to but instead tried on, like you would a light piece of clothing.

For me, exploring the larger-than-self stories of the universe is a beautiful adventure. If we are not just *connected to* everything but actually *are* everything, as various spiritual traditions and scientific inquiries have suggested, what would it feel like to live this interconnection in its fullest expression? If the star clusters and supernovas of the Webb telescope are an aspect of *me,* that brings a whole new feeling to this universe-body I dress every morning. I'm not only much larger than I thought, but my consciousness itself isn't an isolated accident. It's an emergent property of the cosmos itself.

$\cdot$ $\cdot$

We've all heard the story of the Big Bang. In the beginning, there was nothing. Then, miraculously, there exploded forth the ten thousand things— heat, dust, stars, and planets . . . oceans, mountains, atmosphere . . . and eventually living beings, *including their joy and sorrow.* Sure, that first moment sounds unbelievable. What's even more impressive is that that first moment of creation is still happening in us and around us right now.

We know we've done these things before, the putting on of clothes and the feeding of our bodies, but in a real way, these experiences are emerging into creation for the very first time. When we feel this, each task somehow becomes the most relevant and meaningful one we've ever done. We sense we are part of a vast, ancient, and mysterious purpose that we don't need to understand but just expresses through ourselves.

In this light, healing and spirituality are particularly awe-inspiring. It's revealed that the self-compassion we've been growing is not really ours. It belongs to the same source as do the oceans, the mountains, the trees, and the flowers. The same is true of our wounds and their causes. They were just nature coevolving through us.

While, in the beginning, it felt like a lot of effort to get the wheel of healing turning, we realize now it wasn't our effort at all. It was the cosmos unfolding through us. Our longing for freedom was more like gravity, a mathematical certainty, a structure of the universe itself. In a baffling but beautiful performance, life divided itself, longed for itself and, with the progression of healing and insight, returns to itself in celebration.

From this perspective, even our confusion, which has unfolded lawfully, is somehow forgivable—even trustworthy—as part of this grand design. If we didn't forget our universal origins, we could never know the joy of remembering them. Perhaps even those first protective layers over our original wounds—the ones that would cause us to forget who we were—weren't a mistake. A seed of compassion lives within them, for they allow us the beauty of returning home to ourselves someday.

Taken together, this process of forgetting our essence has caused much grief in our societies and world—much desire, aversion, and delusion. Yet it also played a part in propelling evolution through the ages and creating the precious diversity of living creatures on this planet. One living being, in particular, has shown itself to be a miraculous alchemist.

We humans can consciously turn our attention around to realize our true origins and translate that experience into pure feeling. When we remember we *are* everything, a very pure and exquisite kind of love is born in the heart—something perhaps never before created. From the vast nothingness before the Big Bang, over billions of tumultuous years, *finally through us, the universe has made love from nothing.* I personally can't imagine a greater alchemical miracle than this.

• •

When we feel ourselves as the universe unfolding, things can become very silent and still inside. Like kneeling before a towering peak or an ancient old-growth tree in nature, we are humbled into an awe-filled unity. Just by being, we are expressing a purpose beyond our comprehension.

On an emotional level, this can feel like gaining immeasurable support and companionship. Discovering an indestructible inner dimension of life and feeling the profound fulfillment of its embrace, we realize we have nothing to fear. Our authentic expression can flow without interruption or diminishment. We know we can risk it all and lose, yet never be destroyed.

In turn, we stop demanding fulfillment from all the people, places, and things in our lives that were never designed to provide it. Our friends, partners, and families no longer have to try to provide our essential well-being for us—and inevitably fail. Instead, they, too, are permitted to be free while they're here.

We still want what is good and wholesome and direct our lives in those ways. We still want a loving partner and friends, an inspiring job, connection to nature, solution to the global crises at hand, etc. We just know now to never entirely depend on those things for our happiness. The ups and downs remain but rest within a wider reassurance of safety.

It's this independence of well-being, born from the realization of our universal origins, that we might call *sovereignty*. Developing it is an ongoing practice of returning to the deepest protection and deepest refuge within us while still embracing our lives. It's also the natural state of the awakened heart.

• •

The spiritual ideas described in this chapter are for us to explore in our own unique ways and in our own time. With insights, the best approach is "easy come, easy go." When you realize something profound, don't expect or need it to stay forever. Instead, assume you'll evolve, and assume you'll be triggered back into your default mode at times and that's OK. I say that from experience.

As we know, spiritual realization is much more than an idea or a moment of lofty insight anyway. It's also how we make those insights *real* in our lives, here and now. That's why this entire section of the book—part 3—is entitled "The *Real*ization." In the following two chapters, we explore how to integrate the insights described here into the messiness of our human relationships and ailing world.

Summary, Prompts, and Practices

CHAPTER SUMMARY

- In learning to relax our protective strategies, including the protective shell of the self, we open to the deepest protection of interconnection and, from that place, can effortlessly radiate essential heart qualities.

- Relaxing and letting go even further, we come to rest within the deepest refuges of the heart-mind—namely, the silence, stillness, and spaciousness of awareness that underly all things.

- As we weave these profound experiences back into our daily lives, we learn to hold the paradox of the personal and the universal, or form and emptiness. When we marry the two within us, we experience what I call the awakened heart.

- Living this understanding can inspire the feeling that the universe is living through us. Feeling the support of this vast presence, our sense of well-being can become unshakable, increasing our resilience in our daily lives.

JOURNAL PROMPTS

- What is the most common form of self-protection you know in your life right now? What forms of protection have you outgrown to get here? What is an even deeper protection that could keep you safe with even greater ease? What might support you in embodying this deepest protection?

- What is a comfortable and familiar refuge you go to regularly in your life? How does it support you? Is there an even deeper refuge that your heart longs to inhabit? What might support you in resting there instead?

- What is the metaphor that you most resonate with that brings together the universal and personal in you? Why? Or what's one of your own?

- In what ways can you already see the universe unfolding through you? What ways would your life change if you were to fully allow this universal expression to flow freely?

GUIDED PRACTICES

Please complete the meditations in the four turnings before completing the two guided practices for chapter 8. The first meditation is an exploration of the deepest protection, in particular, the other brahmaviharas besides compassion. The second explores the awakened heart, converging awareness with our humanness to support a unified and sovereign consciousness. This second meditation is also the last of fourth turning meditations. Access the guided meditations at www.justinmichelsondharma .com/thedharmaofhealing/practices or www.shambhala.com/dharmaof healingpractices.

9

FREEDOM IN RELATIONSHIP

Relationships are perhaps the most significant parts of our lives, both the source of great wounding and great wisdom. As such, our healing and liberation must always include them. In this chapter, we put spiritual insights to the test against the reality of relational life. We examine what a self-compassionate approach to relationships might look like, including discovering new ways of being with, seeing, and speaking to others. Then, we explore how we might creatively embody the insight of interconnection in our relational lives.

· ·

No matter how deep we might journey in spiritual practice, we always return to relationship. At its most fundamental level, this is how life itself is wired. From the first moments of our lives, we are forged from intimacy. As we grow, our hearts and minds come to know themselves through mimicry. Still today, every breath is a conversation with the plant kingdom as we inhale oxygen and give back carbon dioxide. Every meal is an alchemy of life into energy, as living things become fuel for our bodies. We are made from an intimate web of togetherness and kinship.

It's no wonder that people often identify their relationships with other beings—plants, pets, or partners—as the most meaningful parts of their lives. Relationships speak to the core of us. It's also very telling that, without them, our happiness, physical health, and even our lifespan dramatically decline.[1]

Simultaneously, however, relational experiences are often some of our most profoundly confusing and painful experiences. As adults, this is because they powerfully trigger our earliest wounds and our strongest self-protective instincts. This is not necessarily a bad thing, though.

For example, for me, each intimate relationship I've had has awakened dormant parts of my psyche—both pain and joy—that had been invisible to me. Even though at times I clung to my practice like a life raft amid a flood of emotion, I was eventually able to make each connection a profound catalyst for spiritual growth. Without the revealing nature of relationship, it's unlikely I'd ever have been forced to heal my deepest pain.

Not all of us are so lucky. Perhaps we get hurt more deeply than we know how to repair, or perhaps we just weren't resourced or interested in growing in the ways we needed to. When this is the case, relationships can also reinforce lasting confusion and wounding.

Fortunately, the medicine of self-compassion doesn't just heal ourselves but can intuitively teach us relational healing and wisdom as well. It can soothe the source of our reactivity in relationships, build empathy and understanding, and lay the foundation for authentic connection. The principles in this chapter have and continue to help me navigate my most important relationships, as I hope they do for you.

The Most Precious One

For many years, I was perplexed why the Buddha, who uniquely proclaimed the truth of nonself, also said, "You can search the whole universe and find no one dearer than yourself." Eventually, I discovered that when spiritual insight occurs within an integrated psyche, one result is that a person comes to love themselves more. Indeed, when compassion guides our practice, insights into the universal and interconnected nature of self don't negate our personal emotional or physical needs. They just place our humanness within a broader and more powerful field of care.

Said differently, we can experience ourselves as the vastness of the universe and still find nowhere more sacred and profound than the colors and textures of our own embodied expression. We delight in the preciousness and rarity, and we wonder at the fragility and impermanence. We graciously welcome the miracle of our lives.

Importantly, being the most "dear" or "precious" is not an assertion of superiority, as I initially thought when encountering this teaching. It's simply a function of proximity. Our relationship with ourselves (and our present-moment experience) is the most intimate relationship we can have. Therefore, our love can always shine upon us with the greatest richness and strength—if we don't deny ourselves the privilege.

Perhaps, at this point in the book, we've even discovered firsthand that we can fall in love with ourselves with even greater depth and richness than we've experienced with loved ones. It's as though the entire universe is joining us in loving us. Or perhaps we haven't let ourselves take in the full extent of our own passionate care out of fear of being selfish.

THE STIGMA OF SELFISHNESS

In many progressive, religious, and spiritual circles, being "selfish" is just about the worst label we could be given. In relationships, being labeled a "narcissist" is a similar curse. However, it's partially these ingrained stigmas that condition many of us to neglect ourselves in sacrifice to others. Many students have told me that's why they never did self-compassion before; it just felt selfish or self-centered. Instead, they aspired to become "selfless." While the intention is honorable, of course, the tragic irony is that by not giving ourselves kind attention, it creates and sustains the internal deficits that eventually lead to the selfish behavior we wanted to avoid.

Part of the confusion is that we falsely view selfishness as a function of the *amount* of attention we give ourselves when it's often more a result of the *quality* of attention. If our attention toward ourselves is unkind or neglectful, we are more likely to disregard or disrespect others[2] which is a key piece of the dictionary definition. According to Merriam-Webster: *selfishness* is "excessive concern with oneself . . . *without regard to others.*" If our self-attention is truly kind, we are much more likely to be kind to others. Studies have shown that self-compassionate people are more likely to be affectionate and generous in relationships.[3]

We may need a new word for someone who is very self-absorbed in self-kindness but also holds others in very high regard. To play off the definition of selfishness above, this person may be greatly "concerned with oneself" but also remains considerate and generous. The research is showing this to be possible, but psychologists are still trying to understand how.[4]

While it doesn't fit our Western paradigm, it can be seen again and again within those that have devoted themselves to cultivation of a kind heart.

Students of mine have stated it simply: Self-compassion softens the heart so it's naturally less aggressive toward others. It attunes us to our own suffering so we're able to notice others' suffering. It resources us so we can be more present with the other person. It validates our experience so another person doesn't have to—to name just a few mechanisms.

In my experience, when we sincerely nourish ourselves with our care, we can generate an unparalleled inner fullness. This not only brings out our innate gifts, but it also overflows into our relationships and the world. This is because true self-compassion meets the core needs for attention, approval, affirmation, safety, connection, etc., that we typically spend a lot of time trying to *get* from others. Thus, paradoxically, it frees us up to consider others as they are and on their terms. We could say that by being selfish or self-indulgent with self-compassion, we allow a balanced selflessness to emerge. We deeply honor ourselves and yet don't let that self-focus disconnect us from others or the world.

Therefore, devoting ourselves to self-compassion is the first foundation of healthy relating. Not doing so is the cause of so much relational distress, as I and many others can attest to firsthand. We can overfocus on the other person, pouring ourselves into them, only to wake up at the end of a day or a marriage and realize we've somehow never filled our own cup. Our needs never actually got met and now we're resentful; we may have even overlooked countless transgressions that hurt us along the way. Perhaps we were afraid to lose their approval or reassuring presence. Or we may have just thought it was an honorable way to relate, that it's our duty to take on the other's burdens and carry them as a labor of love.

As we'll dive deeper into in later sections, it's this lack of mindfulness and self-compassion that sets us up for relational challenges. In other words, if we become emotionally vulnerable to someone else *before* we have learned to do this with ourselves, or if we fall in love with someone else before we also establish love for ourselves, the relationship will bear the burden of our unknown and unloved parts. We'll project our salvation onto others, take on other's wounds at our own expense, and fall into a tumultuous codependency—just like in all the movies. Alternatively, consciously investing in our own emotional and spiritual well-being buffers us against these tendencies.

On the whole, an overemphasis on selflessness can actually become a net loss, not just for us but our relationships and the world. Not only can we be left drained and diminished, but we can inadvertently enable others to neglect developing their own self-support systems to help them thrive in the long term. Instead, a more sustainable and liberating way to engage in relationships is to deeply honor ourselves first, sincerely support others when we can, and, if possible, help those around us to become more self-sufficient so they can do the same.

RADICAL RESPONSIBILITY

Every choice we make has an effect on those around us, whether helpful, hurtful, or neither. That includes what we choose to think, feel, say, and do in relationships. By acknowledging our impact, we prevent self-compassion from becoming a mindlessly self-affirming exercise. Instead it becomes the foundation from which we can address the relational patterns that affect others.

We've all blamed others for why a relationship didn't or isn't working. We perhaps thought this would preserve a position of emotional safety, perceived power, or moral authority for us. However, the opposite is often true. The protective blame not only disconnects us from others but also from ourselves and what we can learn. It risks leaving us feeling powerless over our well-being, and it's rarely fully true.

Taking responsibility starts with humility and self-understanding. It starts with knowing how wounded we've been and likely still are. I know I could recite a litany of things I said or did in relationships that I wish I didn't, that came from a place of unconscious hurt. By taking responsibility, we can not only learn to forgive ourselves but also reclaim our agency for the future. We each have the capacity to cocreate beautiful and harmonious relationships that include healing, insight, and joy.

In service to this, I want to bring back Diagram 4.3 (page 111) to refresh our memory of the emotions involved in relational dynamics and explore how we can use this model to assess the health of our relational lives.

Using this diagram as a guide, let's start at the beginning, exploring *why* we engage and reengage in various relationships in the first place.

The emotions on the top of the diagram represent a variety of wholesome orientations to relationships. For example, we might start or continue a relationship because we want to learn from someone, appreciate their presence, feel silly and playful with them, or simply feel safe or calm in their embrace. We might just love them or love caring for them. In the context of healing, the most fundamental orientation we need for a healthy relationship is an openness to self-discovery.

Without that desire to grow, our relationships likely won't survive the challenging moments that require us to transform. With it, however, relationships can be the perfect teacher to show us the wounding we didn't know we were holding. Then we can address it with self-compassion and guide it to liberation. In this way, a safe and conscious relational container can be a powerful support on the path.

However, if we don't intentionally approach relationships from the top side of the emotional diagram, or at least with a willingness to look at our wounds, we will probably find ourselves sliding to the bottom. We'll move into relationships like we move into other aspects of life, including spiritual practice—away from what is unpleasant and toward what is pleasant. We can unconsciously use others to avoid our pain or seek shelter from the world. I know I did this for most of my life, not seeing that one of my hidden intentions was for my partner to take care of or reassure my most insecure parts—which objectively they can never really do.

Unfortunately, acting from any unwholesome emotion in the bottom half of the diagram will inevitably undermine our ability to feel connected because the emotion itself arises from disconnection. For example, we might lack self-worth, experience shame and doubt, and then find ourselves longing for approval or attention from a relationship to resolve it. This rarely works, at least for long. Even if we have an unconditionally affirming person now, when the relationship changes, we may be left with an amplified version of the original pattern we wanted relief from.

However, perhaps the most common unwholesome motivation for relationships is that we just feel a general sense of being alone. Loneliness is not an emotion but an idea with such gravity that it collects all manner of unwholesome emotions, and in doing so, becomes heavy and awkward in our hearts. It's so painful that we understandably engage in relationships to escape or resolve this feeling. Of course, again, this strategy rarely works for long. Even for those that it seems to, it also creates a dependency that burdens the relationship and prevents us from healing our core belief of separateness and the wounds that orbit it.

Take a moment to consider an important relationship in your life and reflect on why you started it but also what motivates you to continue. Sometimes to uncover this, we have to ask a hard question: "How would I feel if this relationship were to end?" Sometimes the feelings that arise are precisely the ones we've been trying to avoid.

· ·

The diagram can also remind us of the pathways to relational healing. This happens when we or the other person in a relationship can recognize a challenging pattern and then relate to it with the healing emotions of curiosity, gratitude, or compassion. Just like in our personal healing journey, applying healing emotions to unwholesome emotions in relationships restores trust, softens our armor, and transforms relational wounds.

To do so, we must first learn to recognize our reactivity. In other words, we recognize the ways we use protective emotions to shield our vulnerability from the other person(s). We might use frustration or indifference to prevent ourselves from feeling or expressing a disappointment or hurt we hold. Or we might use anxiety or longing to prevent ourselves from being abandoned or feeling distant. Noticing this with curiosity, both people can practice gratitude for these forces, and then compassion for the tenderness underneath (shame, doubt, sadness, fear, aloneness, etc.). This helps restore safety and connection in ourselves and in the relationship.

In the end, we are each responsible for studying our own painful emotional patterns in relationships and committing to their healing. Only we can admit to the ways we evade true vulnerability and connection, and bring ourselves back into balance when we're reactive through practices like those in this book. Ultimately, we are the source of our own sense of inner safety and connection. It's easy to think what others should be doing differently or try to convince or control them in some way, but that orientation to relationship rarely changes anyone. Instead, we first sincerely love ourselves and, through that, learn to relate to others with the same unconditional care.

In practice, this just means a devotion to applying curiosity, gratitude, and compassion to our own emotions *and theirs*, just as they are. We might find this necessitates conscious work toward forgiveness for hurts we've sustained (see the meditation at the end of chapter 7). When sincere, these practices reliably result in increased intimacy, greater ease and joy, and mutual fulfillment. They can also result in clear seeing about what changes we might need to make in a relationship to take better care of ourselves as well as the strength to draw those boundaries with kindness. "I'll always love and care about you," we might say sincerely, "and I also need this or that to change." We enact compassion for them *and* ourselves.

Again, take a moment to consider a challenging pattern of interaction in one of your present relationships. What emotions are you responding with, both to yourself and them? Are you bringing compassion to the anxiety or just more judgment? Are you bringing gratitude to the longing or just more fear?

BECOMING SOVEREIGN

Sovereignty is a self-sufficiency of well-being arising from a deep internal support system. As described in chapter 8, this can be born from the realization of our universal origins. However, it can also grow from our simple devotion to self-compassion and radical responsibility. If we're lucky, it can also kindle from the stabilizing influence of a very secure relationship. The hallmark of sovereignty in relationships is the resilience to remain present, vulnerable, and connected in the face of relational challenges—even those that threaten emotional security.

Modern culture trains us to predicate our well-being upon our desired circumstances and conditions. For example, in our intimate relationships, we learn to think, *I'll be whole and happy when or if I find another person who loves me no matter what, who will never leave me, who completes me, or who meets my image of the ideal partner.* In making our internal state dependent on relational ideas or outcomes, we puncture the integrity of our internal systems, draining our energy. In the process, we lose control of our contentment.

While it can simply feel like a natural longing after connection, paradoxically, this emotional overdependence on the other person actually maintains disconnection. By trying to control relationships, we distort them, and by distorting them, we can't authentically meet them—nor let them be what they naturally are meant to be. We primarily interact with our *idea* of the person and how they might benefit or harm us, not with who they are as a sovereign being.

Psychologically, one way to understand the process of becoming sovereign is a transference of early attachment patterns from people/places/things back to ourselves and deeper internal forms of support (i.e., awareness). We gradually develop a secure attachment to ourselves and life itself. From this more profound sense of security, we feel free to take wise relational risks—which inevitably include getting hurt—as we're held by the indestructible part of us. We know that relationships may end, but they are never the end of us.

In healthy relationships, this sovereignty is naturally strengthened through the friction of two seemingly opposite capacities: *loving* and *letting go*. As we love another being, we extend outward into connection. As we let go, we return home to loving ourselves. By naturally navigating between the two, our capacity for each can grow. In sovereignty, we learn to let them coexist.

Granted, aspiring toward sovereignty in relationships is a humbling practice. It's not perfect, nor ever complete. We still affect and are affected by others. We still feel deeply. We are just not as threatened by relational changes or conflicts. This frees us up to act with less fear, and we can have confidence to be ourselves.

In this place, we have much less to defend. If others judge or don't agree with us, it doesn't jeopardize our emotional security. Moreover, we demand less of others. We will have preferences and requests, but they aren't based on a deeper sense of lack. We're really just there to love. We can still choose to lean or rely on someone else while also maintaining our center of gravity in our own safety and connection.

I can say from my own experience that when we're in this sovereign place, it really is a different paradigm of relating, one that promises so much more inner freedom. In my own journey with this, I've valued the question, *What would I do or say in this relationship if I felt fully safe and connected right now?* When I let myself feel into that, often the way I relate is surprisingly different. Let's just say, by pausing in this way, there's a lot of things I've been grateful I didn't say or do.

In sum, when we're sovereign, we have choice. We can choose to stay or go, to let them in or draw boundaries, to play or be serious. We can change, and we can let them change too without stopping loving. We know that whatever happens will be OK in the end.

• •

In summary, to stay free in relationship, we always start and end by returning to ourselves. By embracing our own emotional and spiritual needs, taking radical responsibility for how we feel, and working toward greater sovereignty, we can find more clarity and well-being even amid complex relational dynamics. In these ways, there is little difference between self-compassion and relational freedom. However, maintaining that freedom is not just about refining how we relate to ourselves. It's also about refining the way we *see* others in our life.

Seeing with New Eyes

As we've covered, our organism is organized to try to help us. This extends to how we perceive the world and especially how we see others. In other words, we have a habit of forming perceptions of others—often skewed—in an effort to protect ourselves.[5]

When we get hurt by others, we instinctively generate protective impulses to avoid those types of people or situations that could cause hurt again. In some instances, this can be very helpful. Often, however, it becomes an unconscious habit with declining effectiveness and accuracy over time.

For example, if we were once hurt by a person of a specific gender or race or political affiliation, we might avoid or dislike all people of that group well into the future, even the well-intentioned ones. The human mind naturally exaggerates the scope or intensity of threats to keep us extra-safe. In addition, our perceptions are readily influenced by the perceptions of those closest to us and reinforced by stereotypes in media, movies, and advertising. The ultimate effect is we quickly categorize and divide the world in ways that actually separate us from others—which also harms us.

If we notice our less-than-compassionate perceptions of others when they arise, we can have agency over whether we act from them. We can choose to release them if they don't serve us. Best of all, we can practice seeing others in novel ways that acknowledge their inherent *goodness and wisdom*. To do so, we don't need to blind ourselves to potential threats or concerns about someone; we just learn to see with more depth than we usually do. Counterintuitively, this act alone can actually make us safer, as it often invites forward the best in people.

In this section, I'll first offer a series of wise views that have helped me stay in my heart instead of in judgment when relating to other people. Then I'll offer a series of phrases and questions that can guide us to think and speak in the language of compassion. This approach can certainly benefit others, but first and foremost, it's medicine that helps our heart-minds stay free. Wise seeing and speaking are profound acts of self-compassion.

COMPASSION CONSCIOUSNESS

It's safe to assume that anyone we see or interact with knows suffering. While there is a wide disparity in conditions, the first noble truth exempts no one. Although there is indeed beauty in life, everyone is subject to certain innate features of existence: We get hurt. Things don't go the way we want. We lose the things we love—eventually everything. And we can't really control or predict much of any of it. Moreover, many of us aren't taught how to navigate these realities at all—I can't say I was until I encountered the Dharma.

Intentionally acknowledging this shared reality can help us develop a consciousness of compassion for other people. We can also seek greater understanding to ripen our compassion. For me, listening to people's stories and studying cultural histories have helped me appreciate the wounding that has shaped people. Letting this information in, I naturally soften and open my heart more. I realize that if someone weren't suffering themselves, they'd never try to hurt anyone. If they could find a supportive connection to their own pain, they'd never choose to cause harm.

Seeking a greater understanding of others' challenges is an especially important exercise for those of us in privileged circumstances. It's easy to avoid truly feeling the pain of those around us, not to mention the pain of the inequality we benefit from—directly or indirectly. When we do consciously, however, it not only works to evolve our capacity for compassion but helps us reconnect with those in our community who are less fortunate. In this way, developing a consciousness of compassion requires both our curiosity and our willingness to feel together.

Once we see another's pain, it easier to see their goodness and the wisdom that lives underneath it. Just as the five forces of healing support us, so too do they support everyone. The following reflections can help us see others in this way—ultimately the way we, too, would like to be seen. As you read through them, you might consider a particular person you struggle with (use a light or easy example to start), imagining how each could be true for them.

1. They are *trying to help* themselves—even if it's actually hurting them or others.
2. They *care deeply* about something/someone—even if they're not acting in a caring manner.
3. They *long for harmony* and connection—even if they're creating conflict.
4. They *desire to heal* and be happy—even if they're choosing to suffer now.
5. They have *the inner wisdom* to free themselves—even if they are confused on the surface.
6. They are already *whole and complete*—even if they feel conflicted and insufficient inside.

It may take some reflection or contemplation to consider how these might be true for another person in their unique situation. For me, when I do, they transform my heart from cool judgment to a sweet warmth. Even if the person may have made mistakes or hurt me, I can take it less personally, refrain from trying to change them, and more readily trust in their innate evolution. Consequently, I can stay connected to them while still caring for myself, whether that means taking space, offering support, or both. When these reflections aren't enough, I usually need the forgiveness practice at the end of chapter 7.

In other words, learning to see others with compassion helps us too. We all know that when others harm us, wield power over us, or otherwise irritate us, we can spend countless hours possessed by anger, ill will, or the like. While this may feel wholly justified, it also hurts us. Seeing that each of us is doing the best we can with what we have—our varying degrees of wounding, self-knowledge, and support—can be a great relief from our tendency toward judgment and division.

A vital aspect of these reflections is that they keep us equal to the other person. We don't look down in pity or judgment. We instead offer them compassionate dignity. We preserve the possibility of their highest expression emerging. Being good and wise at the core, each person just waits to bloom from the inside out. If they receive sustained compassionate attention, then sooner or later, the process naturally unfolds. While we can help with this through compassionate seeing, we also remember that their most potent medicine will, in the end, have to come from inside their own heart-minds.

HEALING SPEECH

Wise view and wise intention are the first and second steps of the noble eightfold path of Buddhism. The third step is wise speech. When we start with a compassionate view of others, we are naturally primed for compassionate intentions to emerge. This then leads naturally to compassionate speech in its myriad forms.

In this way, wise speech is not a particular set of words. We know from experience that even the kindest phrases can be spoken void of feeling, with impatience, or even in a sarcastic or spiteful tone. And we are incredibly sensitive to the energy behind the words we hear. Instead, wise speech arises from wholesome emotions and/or the conscious field of connection underneath them.

That being said, I know personally how humbling it is to try to repattern our speech. Language forms alongside our wounds. We fuse with a wounded or protective pattern in ourselves, and words slip out that we wish we hadn't said. By intentionally practicing wise speech, we don't just support others, though. We also protect ourselves from disconnection, regret, and relational strife.

While there are countless forms of wise speech, arguably the most helpful is speech that supports healing and, ultimately, awakening. This type of speech arises most readily from the healing emotions of curiosity, gratitude, and compassion. Most powerfully, it arises from true compassion, the compassion that includes wisdom. In other words, truly healing speech helps both the speaker and the listener *see, understand, care for,* and *support* both parties better. It's this intention that guides the following communication method.

• •

Perhaps paradoxically, the most essential tenet of healing speech is learning to listen. Listening is where we start. That doesn't just mean nodding our heads but sincerely asking curious questions and compassionately reflecting back what we hear. Many of us easily forget this step, eager to share and defend our opinions or feelings.

While there are many ways to listen, in Tables 7, 8, and 9, I offer a series of suggested questions to engage listening, examples of the kinds of answers such questions might evoke, and compassionate reflections based on the four aspects of true compassion. Finally, I offer abbreviated versions that boil the initial questions down to their basic elements. As you practice your listening skills, please use your intuition to modify or reinvent the phrases to suit your heart-mind.

TABLE 7. COMPASSIONATE LISTENING

	ASPECT	QUESTIONS	ALTERNATIVE QUESTIONS
1.	Seeing	What are you feeling right now?	Where are you feeling this in your body?
2.	Understanding	What's creating this feeling for you right now?	What's the story of the pain right now?
3.	Caring	What does this show you care about?	*Alternative for protectors*: How is this feeling trying to protect you?
4.	Supporting (inner)	How might *you* support this pain right now?	What could you do that would help you feel safer right now?
5.	Supporting (outer)	Is there anything I can do to support you right now?	How can you best be supported right now?

TABLE 8. COMPASSIONATE LISTENING: EXAMPLE ANSWERS AND REFLECTIONS

	EXAMPLE ANSWERS	EXAMPLE REFLECTIONS
1.	I'm feeling very anxious. My chest is tight, and my heart is beating fast.	I see/hear/feel you in your anxiety. I'm here with you.
2.	I just lost my job and don't know how I will pay my rent. I'm worried it's all going to fall apart.	It makes sense you'd feel that way given what you're going through.
3.	Myself, my family, my life. I guess this feeling is trying to motivate me to get up and start searching so I can protect what I love.	I see how much you care about yourself and your family. It's beautiful and moving. Thank you.
4.	I guess I can be a little easier on myself, take a deep breath, and trust something will work out. Just having your support makes me feel safer and calmer.	Those sound like wise ideas. I definitely support you in being easier on yourself and taking some time to relax and calm down before doing anything else.
5.	Thanks for asking. Just listening is helpful. I guess, if it was possible, I was thinking finding a loan for next month's rent would really take some stress off.	I do want to help. I'm glad I can do something by listening here. I'm also happy to review my finances and see if I can swing a loan. I'll let you know.

TABLE 9. COMPASSIONATE LISTENING: ABBREVIATED QUESTIONS

1.	Is there anything you'd like to share right now?
2.	Is there anything I can do to support you right now?

Listening and asking compassionate questions are often very supportive for a person, especially when they're in distress, and it's a gift many only receive in therapy, if at all. Asking curious questions helps a person discover what's happening for themselves, which they usually aren't fully aware of. While this is a great gift, this process can be just as valuable in preventing *us* from being reactive to another's pain, which often comes across as trying to quickly fix, shift blame, give advice, or somehow rush the process.

In the example in Table 8, we could imagine how different it would feel to respond, "Well if you would have showed up at work on time, this wouldn't have happened" or "I've been telling you that job was terrible anyway" or "Well, I don't know what to tell you; I can't do anything about it." While we want them to heal or feel better, it's unlikely to happen through our pressure, admonishment, or dismissal. Instead, we can steady ourselves, meet the person where they are, summon our curiosity and care, and stay present with their process as it unfolds.

As you can see from the above process, after curiously asking the questions and receiving their response, I suggest responding intuitively using language similar to the compassionate self-talk phrases in the core practices (i.e., *I see you, I understand, I care, I support*). However, when we're using these phrases in an interpersonal setting, there are a few nuances to keep in mind.

First, in the case of understanding, there will be a range of degrees to which we can *actually* understand, based on both the details we've heard and the personal familiarity we have with what they're going through. It's not helpful to say you understand when you don't or couldn't. You might say instead, "I think I have a sense of what you're going through" or "I understand the best that I can as a different person or in a different place" or "I have no idea what that's like, but it sounds really hard. I'm so sorry." We're primarily trying to validate their experience as real and significant.

In the case of caring, it's a prime opportunity to reflect to the person how much *they* must care. Especially when someone is experiencing anger, longing, or anxiety, we can be assured they are acting from a place of protective care. By naming that, we speak directly to the deeper goodness of the other person's heart-mind. In hearing that, they often realign with that part of themselves and often become more regulated. For example, in response to their distress, we might say, "Thank you for caring so much about keeping the house clean," or "I see how much you care about maintaining a safe work environment. Thank you." We might even share that we care about the same thing, creating a deepened sense of connection.

As for the last aspect of compassion—supporting—there are two parts:

how they might support their pain and how we might support them in it. The first is often an empowering question that leads to greater self-care. The second requires skillful introspection on our part. Can we support this person at all? If so, how and how much?

The primary reminder here is that we have agency. We're not obliged to support them. We can say, "I'm sorry, I love you but I can't right now," or "I'll have to take some time to think about it," or whatever is real for us. Thank them for bravely sharing what they need. As we practice, we'll get more skilled in creating parameters for our support so we can be generous but also compassionate and true to ourselves. For example, we may always hold someone in our hearts but acknowledge we can't be there for them right now. Or we may get very specific (e.g., "I can support you by listening here for another ten minutes, and then I need to take care of myself."). In situations where we disagree with the other's action, we can find a way to say no to certain requests while still affirming our care for them (e.g., "I can't give you any more money if you're going to spend it in these ways, but I will always be available if you need to talk to someone."). In situations where we feel unsafe, we may not be available to support the person in *any* quantifiable way, and we can do our best to express that kindly.

In general, the above questions and responses are a handy script we can draw from. However, in a real-life scenario, our conversations won't be formulaic. We might not even ask a question before our spouse unloads on us for twenty minutes about their day. It happens. As we're listening, we might just keep repeating silently phrases of *I see you, I understand, I care*, and *I support* to keep our hearts primed and open. Then, at the end, we might offer an intuitive series of compassionate reflections loosely following the four aspects. After they feel heard, we might choose a question or two to learn or illuminate more. Don't worry too much about the words, though—more the heart behind them. If you actually feel compassion for them, you can trust it will be felt.

..

We can also use a similar structure for sharing with others what's happening in our own experience. This requires self-awareness, and it also requires the courage to be vulnerable. So it's best if, before sharing, we take time to be with our emotional experience. We can offer ourselves compassion first, ideally securing an inner foundation of safety and connection. From there, we can share more authentically, including asking for support if we need it, and can do so without expectations or demands.

TABLE 10. COMPASSIONATE SHARING PHRASES

	ASPECT	PHRASE STRUCTURE
1.	Seeing	I feel/felt _____ [emotion] in my _____ [place in body] . . .
2.	Understanding	when _____ [circumstance] happens/happened . . .
3.	Caring	because I care/cared about _____ [something you value].
4.	Supporting (inner)	I am supporting/supported myself by _____ [form of self-care].
5.	Supporting (outer)	Can you help support me by _____ [request help]?

TABLE 11. COMPASSIONATE SHARING EXAMPLES

	EXAMPLE 1	EXAMPLE 2	EXAMPLE 3
1.	I felt frustration rise up in my throat	I felt a lot of anxiety in my belly	I felt sadness and compassion well up in my chest
2.	when I saw all the dishes left in the sink again.	when I found out I would need surgery.	when I heard about *your* painful circumstances
3.	You know I really care about keeping our agreements and keeping things sanitary here.	I'm worried because it's risky and I care so much about my family and the life I'm creating.	because I care about you so much and because I've been through something similar.

4.	So I stepped away to calm down a bit, but now I hope to find a solution. (Pause before the next question.)	I've been taking some time off work to weigh my options, talk to my kids, and now tell you. (Pause before the next question.)	I've been taking a break from my work to try to process it but just generally trying to breathe and let the feelings come through. (Pause before the next question.)
5.	Can you first support me by letting me know how this happened? And, if you have ideas, how we might be able to prevent it in the future?	Would you be open to first just giving me a hug? Then, if you have time, can you help me think through these different health treatments?	It would feel like a relief if I could find some way to support you. Can you tell me more about your situation and what you might need?

In the examples above, we can see how the basic framework can be applied to a variety of emotions and situations. They might be personal or interpersonal challenges (examples 1 and 2) or even expressions of wholesome emotions (example 3). In each, using the four aspects of compassion as a structure helps us see, understand, care, and support ourselves better, while also giving a chance for others to do the same. Again, the key principle that allows this to happen is taking personal responsibility over how we feel instead of blaming others. This is practiced through the use of "I" statements (*I feel, I care, I support*, etc.).

Our primary intention in sharing is not to achieve a particular outcome—even though we likely have solutions in mind. The intention is to authentically explore and deepen the unfolding intimacy together. It's all too easy to rush to a demand (e.g., "*This* is how I need you to support me."). Though it may be expedient, it tends to weaken the connection over time.

That's one reason why, in the sharing practice, I encourage stating how you're supporting yourself *first* before asking the other person to support us in some way. Often if we are sincere in the first four steps, and we pause there, the listener may voluntarily offer a way they can support, and that often feels better than having to ask. Even when we do ask for specific support ourselves (the last step), we practice honoring the sovereignty of the other person and being open to receiving a no or a maybe instead of demanding our desired outcome. We can even make it collaborative, saying, "It would be supportive if we could brainstorm together how to address this challenge."

TRANSFORMATIVE INQUIRY

As we all know, some relational patterns are very tenacious. They often take much longer to relax and transform than even our internal conflicts. However, if we are in a trusting relationship and are both in a supportive mindset and safe setting, we might consider inquiring more deeply together with transformative inquiry.

While it's very tempting to give our "wise perspective" on someone else's issues, in this practice we're guiding or being guided into discovering it ourselves. Of course, it's essential that the recipient consents to inquiry and feels resourced to consider the questions. Again, it's also paramount that the questioner can ask the questions from a curious and compassionate place in themselves instead of trying to create a predetermined outcome.

The questions are divided into two sections based on which type of emotional pattern is at hand. As a reminder, protective emotions are indifference, anger, longing, anxiety, and their variations. Their signature expression is tension, contraction, or numbness in the body. The wounded emotions are shame, guilt, sadness, fear, and their variations. Their signature expression is a softness, rawness, or tenderness.

The questions we ask another person are the same as those we asked ourselves in chapter 5. However, the responses we give in return may be different. Some responses that can help to deepen the receiver's experience are written in the rightmost column. In sum, we are helping the person to take their time and fully feel their emotions in their body. It's often necessary to encourage them to return to and stay with their present-moment experience—so long as it's not overwhelming to them.

In addition, if we are to ask these questions of another person, it's good to be prepared to hold compassionate space for anything else that might come up. We don't give advice or shift the focus to us, unless it's asked. We patiently reflect with self-compassion phrases and offer any support that seems appropriate to help them discover more.

NOTE: For people familiar with self-dialogue practices like IFS or Voice Dialogue, the word you *can be replaced with* that part of you.

TABLE 12. TRANSFORMATIVE INQUIRY FOR PROTECTIVE EMOTIONS

	TRANSFORMATIVE INQUIRY QUESTIONS FOR PROTECTIVE EMOTIONS		ALTERNATIVE QUESTION	OPTIONAL RESPONSE
1.	Notice the Impact	Do you notice the impact this [protective emotion] is having on you **right now**? Describe.	Where do you feel the pain of this response in your body **right now**? Describe.	Feel the impact fully, if you can. Offer yourself some compassion.
2.	Explore a Deeper Protection	Where is a place in your body that feels strong but relaxed **right now**? Describe.	Can you imagine what it would feel like to be completely protected from all harm **right now**? Describe.	Breathe and let yourself sink into it. Let yourself enjoy.
3.	Consider a New Approach	Is there another response/ approach that might be easier and protect you even better **right now**? Describe.	If you could choose, what new emotion or strategy might you rather use to protect yourself **right now**? Describe.	Discover what this new approach feels like in the body. Affirm it.

TABLE 13. TRANSFORMATIVE INQUIRY FOR WOUNDED EMOTIONS

TRANSFORMATIVE INQUIRY QUESTIONS FOR WOUNDED EMOTIONS			ALTERNATIVE QUESTION	OPTIONAL RESPONSE
1.	Explore a Deeper Refuge	What is the deepest and safest refuge you can feel within you **right now?** Describe.	Can you imagine a place within you that is completely and absolutely safe **right now?** Describe.	Breathe and let yourself sink into it. Let yourself enjoy.
2.	Consider a New Feeling	If you could choose, how would you wish to feel **right now?** Describe.	Can you imagine your most liberated internal expression **right now?** Describe.	Again, let yourself feel into what you would be like. Let yourself enjoy.
3.	Imagine the Release	What might it feel like **right now** for this wound to heal and be liberated? Describe.	What might it feel like in your body **right now** to set down the weight of this pain? Describe.	Healing is possible for you. Feel the wisdom in your wound.

In transformative inquiry in pairs, the power lies in being able to relax and effortlessly receive the prompts. On our own, it's all too easy to get in the way of our own process or enact hidden aversion. Here, we can let the question land, discover what authentically arises, and feel held by another person we trust.

The intention is that, little by little, when a person goes through this process, they regain their agency and choice. They find a place of ever-present safety within and finally feel what it's like to embody a liberating response to a challenging circumstance. However, they don't do so from a place of willpower but from the gentle strength of compassionate suggestion. Over time, our consciousness itself may choose to take a seat at the center of ourselves.

··

It's safe to say that for most of us, these interpersonal communication practices differ significantly from how we currently communicate. To begin incorporating them, I recommend first starting alone. Grab a journal, recall current relational situations that are challenging you, and write both what you *really* want to say (which helps to be aired somewhere) and then the compassionate approach based on these methods—but in your own words. Then, after doing that, see if you can get a neutral friend or person to make time to practice together. You can role-play for each other or use small but real-life issues between the two of you. After gaining some confidence and modifying it to suit you, it can start to become accessible in the times you need it most.

Relational healing skills are worth investing in for anyone on the healing or spiritual path. This is not just because relationships are the most meaningful part of most of our lives, and as such, we want them to thrive. Nor is it just because others can act like mirrors for us, a potent, relational form of mindfulness for our psyches. It's also because healing together, especially when done within a deep bond of safety and connection, has the profound capacity to rewire our past relational wounds. In turn, spiritual insight can also begin to integrate into our relational lives. So while other people could never replace our own devotion to ourselves, they can be powerful catalysts for real-life transformation.

A CRACK IN THE WALL

The combined power of compassionate consciousness and healing speech should not be underestimated. I regularly witness transformations in people from being seen and responded to in these ways. Given supportive circumstances, I don't believe there is anything that inherently prevents transformation in even the most troubled people on the planet.

Most people are hard to reach because they have thick protective walls around their pain. The critical catalyst for those folks is finding a way to soften the armor *so they can see and feel for themselves that they are suffering.* "It seems like you're having a hard time. Are you OK?" we might say. "Is there something I could do to help?" Startled by the rare compassion, it could be the miraculous moment where they finally turn their attention around to feel their pain. "Yes, I guess I am having a hard time. Thank you," they might reply. A crack opens in the wall, and love can begin to leak in. Once a person truly opens to their own pain, they can never entirely go back into hiding. In some way, the healing journey has begun.

Ultimately, however, the benefit of seeing and speaking with compassion is primarily our own. Just like our protective layers over our own pain create a barrier between us and our original hearts, our protective barriers toward others do the same between us and life. The depth and breadth of the inner refuge we can experience depends, in part, on the inclusiveness of our relational hearts. Even if we choose to never see someone again, we never have to keep them out of our hearts—doing so only hurts us. Hence, healing our perception of others can help liberate us, too.

The Relational Self

When we gain some fluency in the relational concepts and practices offered thus far, we can then harness the power of conscious relating for even deeper healing, insight, and joy. We can relax into the collaborative synergy between us, expanding and amplifying the wholesome together. However, this process is greatly supported by transforming our perspective on ourselves. When we embody the relational nature of the self, wise relating can unfold effortlessly.

Indeed, while it may appear that we are acting in our lives with individual agency, we are constantly cocreating within a larger relational web or system, much of which is invisible to us. As I've mentioned, we only breathe because the plant kingdom breathes along with us. We only speak because we learned from others. In other words, each person's contribution—in a friendship, family, or society—works in synergy to cocreate the higher-order character of that relational system. When this understanding is embodied, a relationship can feel almost as though a new entity has been created. I call this the *relational self* or *relational selves*.

The larger relational systems we inhabit generate a consciousness that can be supportive and life-affirming—or the opposite—depending on the quality and character of the relating. When we infuse our relationships with healing emotions as we've been practicing, the relational self brightens. We feel safer and more connected, naturally relaxing our sense of self outward. We access an intelligence and strength greater than our own. In this way, being subject to our web of relationships is not just a source of significant vulnerability but also a source of great transformative power.

SURRENDERING TO THE DANCE

When a relationship is infused with wholesome emotion, we can soften our walls and enter into a larger dance. For some of us, we might experience this in an intimate relationship. If we're fortunate, we might feel it throughout a healthy community of people. For some, we might mainly feel it away from humans, perhaps in nature or the garden, where we feel connected and safe with the plants and animals.

Regardless, when we relax into the safety of supportive collaboration with one another, we not only feel more resourced to heal but also activate our essential creative impulses. We inspire one another by exchanging and reflecting ideas, feelings, movements, and the like. In a way, we access a shared field of possibility and surprise ourselves with what comes through. We delight at how neither of us could have created it alone. Of course, this is only true because of the deep interconnection that characterizes our reality.

For me, I find this most vibrantly through improvisational partner dance. Each vibrant cocreation is never the same, always a fresh discovery. However, for you, it might be through philosophical conversations, work collaborations, or even healthy competition like team sports. It could even be found in the ways we engage in the natural world—in tending to animals, for example, or walking through a forest. Regardless, when we stop overthinking it and let go into the dance of that relationship, we come out enlivened. Indeed, relational creativity is an essential aspect of our humanity.

In practice, however, sustaining creative relational dynamics in our lives depends on our sense of sovereignty. If we're psychologically whole, we have access to our unique authenticity and, from this place, can collaborate with another whole person to synergize something new. If we instead engage out of emotional dependency or hesitate out of disconnection, the dance will be dampened in some way. If we're overly concerned about what the other person will think, what we look like, or whether we're doing it right, we'll trip and miss our cue to respond. The ever-awaiting magic of the moment will pass us by.

However, surrendering to the dance of relationship isn't ultimately dependent on other people. If others aren't engaged or can't relate in a supportive way, we can still offer ourselves over to a yet even larger field of relationship. This could be with nature, as we've said, but it could also be with something as vast as awareness itself. When we allow ourselves to play this big, we can feel a sense of collaboration everywhere. We can dance to the rhythm of our relationship with the whole.

THE FIELD OF CARE

We exist within a living field of energy and information. Whether we realize it or not, everything we do affects everything else. One name for this is the *butterfly effect*, a term coined by American meteorologist Edward N. Lorenz to describe how even the minutest actions can affect entire global systems. Another term from quantum theory is *entanglement*: tiny particles change in tune with one another across space and time. At every level, communication is constant and pervasive. Studies have even shown that our hearts constantly send and receive information to and from the environment[6] around us, including other people.[7]

To visualize this, we might imagine we exist within a three-dimensional field or network filled with connections and communication. When we relax the conceptual boundaries of ourselves and feel the space between and around us, we can access this larger field of intelligence. This can be practiced and embodied perhaps most readily through spontaneity and improvisation. If we are willing to live on the edge of each new and mysterious moment, we can act in ways that aren't entirely defined by our past. When our activity arises from the intelligent interactions of the field itself, we can find ourselves on adventures, small or grand.

I notice this most readily with public speaking. The attention in the space is gathered, the field of energy is potentiated, and I find the words can freely emerge as an expression of the space we've cocreated together. The listening cocreates the speaking, and the speaking informs the listening. The system co-organizes, and I can trust the "rightness" of what comes through. In this way, each moment is unique and arises from something greater than I am. It's constructed freshly from the conversation between innumerable factors in the present-moment field.

The most powerful thing is that our *intention* radiates through that field. It's transmitted without words. That's why practicing mindfulness and self-compassion together in groups is so powerful. When we share the sincere intention to radiate care, we create a thick and rich field of it that nourishes everyone. In turn, that potentiates the safety and trust needed to access even more.

In other words, there's magic in creating relational containers that have room for exploration, that aren't ever fully planned. This way, we create room for inconceivable expressions of the moment to emerge. When they do, we watch the mind trying to claim ownership over this magic. "It's something special about me, about us, about this place," we want to exclaim. But instead, we smile and let ourselves surrender again, knowing it's always about all of that and much, much more.

RELATIONAL FLOW

This experience of relaxing into a field of care can evolve into a sort of warmhearted, relational "flow state." A flow state is often described in psychology as an experience of near-total absorption within an activity and seen as a state of optimal functionality and enjoyability. Within it, we are not plagued by distracted or self-critical thoughts but are fully melded with our present-moment experience.

Accessing a field of care is similar but more explicitly relational. It arises in an engaged union with the world or other people and is guided by wholesome emotion. While general flow states come about through intense concentration or passion, relational flow states arise through the continual perception of interconnection. Instead of focusing on a particular object or activity, we sink our attention into the interstitial space between us. For example, we might imagine the center point of ourselves migrates out of our heads and rests *between* us and another person (say in a dance), or between us and our computer screen when we're working, or between us and Earth when we're hiking. Or, on the inside, we might shift our attention from the solidity of the body to the fluids pulsing through us that connect our organs or the edge of our skin where our body dialogues with the world. In doing so, the locus of our consciousness shifts from our separate, solid selves into the relational field itself.

Dynamic flow is the language of the field. We realize we are not acting or being acted upon alone but arising together with everything else in each new moment. In this way, a flow state emerges.

In human relationships, a form of this can naturally occur in a new romance or friendship. In falling for another, we allow ourselves to become absorbed, trusting and surrendering deeply. We can spend hours enraptured in the simple feeling of being together. Essentially, we temporarily surrender to the relational field, allowing it to animate us. In time, we often fall out of this place through relational hurt or clinging, but even after this time of surrender passes, it's worth remembering the feeling of it. In those moments, our protections are fully down and our trust in life is impenetrable—an inherently spiritual experience.

In some form, that awake and buoyant energy can return to any old relationship. However, it requires fully letting go of what the relationship has been and what it will become. Usually it's from a place of hurt or fear that we inadvertently step out of the flow. But in doing so, we lock ourselves into the pain, making ourselves into a rock instead of moving with the river. Thus, we may need deep relational healing to recover our freshness and aliveness that existed before the disappointments arrived.

You might imagine for a moment that the space between you and another person is not empty but thick like water. Let your attention dive into the eddies between and around you. Then, together, ride the cocreated currents of your shared authenticity. It may test the gravity of your connection, but it can also energize the mystery and magic. If we keep trusting the process and are compassionate to ourselves, we may flow swiftly into a new and untraveled parts of the river together.

When we zoom out, we see that relational flow isn't just for the good times. It's also for the inevitable rapids and waterfalls in our lives. Typically, we try to speed the river up when it's hard and slow it down when it's pleasant, but in reality, the river just flows. We dream of a future, ideal relationship, but the river won't stop there either—at least for more than moment. Relationships keep changing; the only reliable thing is how we show up for them. In the end, we all have a choice: either we can stand on the shore while our lives pass us by or we can point our bow downriver and get soaked to the bone, riding rapid after rapid until we're released, once and for all, into the ocean.

SHARED RESPONSIBILITY

Living within the larger sense of the relational self is a creative heart-exercise that stretches us to embody a more expansive version of ourselves and, in doing so, act with greater ease, clarity, and resilience in relationship. Re-establishing a relational flow is a gift to the others involved, but it is first and foremost an act of self-compassion—as it provides the basis for our freedom of heart in relationship. Using the metaphors and examples in the last section, consider what ways the relational self has come alive for you in your life, how you might cultivate it more today, and what that might feel like in your body now.

Needless to say, relationship is a humbling process—especially today. This is because, through the digital realm, we are more connected than ever to our collective human drama. We're not just in relationship with a single person, but in some way, with all the people on the planet in all their states of being. As we lean into this shared field of care, it becomes border-less, extending outward in all directions. As it does, it transforms into a shared field of responsibility as well.

In this way, the relational self is not just a concept that helps us harmonize our closest connections; it's a foundation for action and a motivation for catalyzing broad, positive change for all.

Summary, Prompts, and Practices

CHAPTER SUMMARY

- Relationships are fundamentally meaningful to us as social animals. They're the source of our core wounding and, often, our greatest wisdom. Thus, we must always include them on the healing and spiritual path.
- Staying centered in our own experience is essential in healthy relationships. It includes learning to care deeply for ourselves, taking full responsibility for our experience and action, and grounding into the spiritual support systems that keep us feeling safe and connected.
- When relating to others, cultivating a consciousness of compassion and practicing healing speech keep us calm and connected, even when others are acting in ways that are challenging. It helps to encourage the

healing process in all those around us. (Please reference lists and tables above.)

- When we infuse our relationships with healing emotions and expand to embody their interconnected nature, we access a greater creativity, care, and flow that keeps all our relations feeling alive and whole.

JOURNAL PROMPTS

- In what ways do you overgive to others and overlook yourself? How might you rebalance that?
- In what ways do you engage in relationships from an unwholesome instead of a wholesome place? What would it mean to reverse that?
- Who in your world have you shut out of your heart-mind? Use the six reflections to practice seeing them in a new way.
- Write out the compassionate sharing phrases for a situation that troubles you. Consider someone in your life you could practice sharing and asking questions with.
- What people, places, or activities help you expand into a wholesome relational self? In other words, when do you naturally enter a flow state in relationship? How might you create conditions for that more often?

GUIDED PRACTICES

There are two meditations for chapter 9. The first is to radiate compassion toward others in our lives, especially the more challenging ones. The second practice is establishing sovereignty in our relationships to allow for more clarity and freedom.

Access the guided meditations at www.justinmichelsondharma.com /thedharmaofhealing/practices or www.shambhala.com/dharmaofhealing practices.

10

WAKING UP AS THE WORLD

In the past two chapters, we explored the personal and relational wisdom that can come from dedicated healing and spiritual practice. However, we can't sustain our well-being without establishing these insights within the chaos of the modern world. More than ever, our personal lives are inevitably entangled with the triumphs and tragedies of our larger human community. No matter what we do, there is no escape from this intimacy. We know by now, however, that if we want to stay free in our hearts, closing down or lashing out are not options. The only way forward is to keep evolving and expanding ourselves to include it all.

To do so, in this final chapter, we'll consider the vital importance of grief, healthy hope, and the paradox of acceptance and agency. We'll explore how generosity and inclusivity aren't just niceties but necessities—even for our own freedom. And we'll consider ways to cultivate an unshakable steadiness amid tragedy—such as expanding our sense of self to include the whole of planet Earth.

Reclaiming Our Well-Being

Even for the most practiced among us, the daily news of global suffering, especially combined with the relentlessness of daily life, can easily wear us down. We may have done substantial work to feel at home in ourselves, but we can still feel saddled with the weight of the world. Healing and spirituality not only can't bypass this reality but they also can sometimes amplify our heaviness.

Indeed, since we were in our mother's womb, our nervous systems have registered the disconnection and stress that pervades and reverberates through the world. As we recover our sensitivity through self-compassion, we begin to uncover that stress and see how it's woven through every layer of our wounding. Though we heal and relieve our personal burdens, each release also reveals how far our human community has strayed from their original hearts. As we return home, we're shown with excruciating intimacy the sacredness that has been lost, the incredible potential we all have, and what is truly at stake.

While waking up in a world of crisis day after day is extremely challenging, if we stay overwhelmed, we will give away not just the power to make change but our inner freedom as well. Hence, a crucial piece of the spiritual path is healing *as a global citizen*. It requires tuning and retuning our hearts to the most skillful and wholesome orientations to pain. Only then can we free our own minds from the oppressive nature of the world and reclaim our well-being and our agency amid it all.

THE GRACE OF GRIEF

Grieving is an essential act of self-compassion in the world today. As described in chapter 4, it differs from unwholesome sadness in that, in its release, it brings us back into connection. By letting grief cleanse and reopen our heart-minds time and time again, we allow it to protect us from accumulating and storing unwholesome emotions and restore our capacity for joy. This is why grieving, albeit painful, can ultimately feel like grace in our lives.

For me, grief—especially grief for the world—has been a regular part of my adult life. But I haven't always been willing to feel it. Many of us carry thick protective layers that cover our grief. These are the many faces of aversion to the painful tragedies we witness—all of which disconnect us from the power of this wholesome force. Witnessing the instability of the world, we might think, *Now I really can't relax. I have to stay even more vigilant* (anxiety). Seeing injustice, we might think, *I now have a duty to be loud and defiant* (anger). Finding a potential solution, we might think, *This has to work out or else everything is lost* (longing).

At the core we often hold a simple and understandable judgment that keeps us from taking it all in: *This shouldn't be happening.* Adjacent to this judgment lives a simple fear: If we don't maintain some contention with what's happening, we won't have the motivation to fix it. Unfortunately, not only are the tragedies indeed happening but wishing they weren't isn't actually as helpful as we think. As we now know, true compassion can respond with even greater effectiveness and ease.

By feeling the protective energies held in our bodies and relating to them compassionately, we can reveal the depth of feeling we hold inside and let it flow into grief. These feelings can be existential. We can feel shame at being alive and human; we can doubt the rightness of life itself and how it's come to this; we can fear the complete destruction of this rare jewel of a planet in this vast universe. We can even tap into the collective well of grief that spans all species on Earth.

This is naturally overwhelming. However, when the pain is too big for us to hold, it can actually be an opportunity. That's when grief can shift from a healing process into an act of spiritual realization. As the weight grows within us, we are forced to let go. The dam of our heart gives way and the grief spills out everywhere. We are carried on this raging river back to its source, and as the water settles, find ourselves floating in the resilient ocean of the heart of life. Only the field of interconnection can hold a pain as vast as the world itself.

I can say with certainty that my heart is broken. In fact, I don't expect my grief for the state of the world to ever leave. This willingness to be broken, though, is not a weakness to get over or even heal from, as I once thought, but actually an essential vulnerability. It's through the crack in our hearts that grief can deliver us home. And if we let it do so over and over again, guided by compassion, we can feel a renewed resilience bubble up from that place. In this way, grief is not just a catharsis but can become a regenerative and transformative force. Paradoxically, the deeper the pain, the deeper our healing and insight can be.

To explore this in greater depth, revisit guided meditation 7 in chapter 6.

SURRENDERING INTO CHOICE

Working regularly with grief can help us transform surrender from a temporary act to an enduring state. On more and more levels of our lives, we come to terms with what *is*—with compassion instead of resignation. Facing our reality heart-on is the spiritual version of "getting sober." We surrender our addictions to aversion, longing, and distraction to finally meet life on its terms—it's messy, unpredictable, unfair, and far beyond our control.

This type of surrender isn't a giving up, as we might fear. Guided by compassion, this surrender threads the needle between numbness and overwhelm, between aversion and desire, between the past and the future. Through that passageway, our hearts become energized instead of crushed. Paradoxically, aligning our whole being with the way things are leaves us with an ever-greater sense of choice and agency in our lives. It creates the opposite of apathy, resignation, or complacency, all of which are unhealed protective layers that can disguise themselves as surrender.

By honoring all potential outcomes with compassion—from discomfort to death or collapse to extinction—we unbind ourselves from the sticky energies that unconsciously control us and our relationship to what is. This includes the old worldviews, the old hurts, and the "shoulds," "can'ts," and "have-tos" around our lives. For me, this has been a regular practice of acknowledging and releasing my fear of any potential painful outcomes. I find the more I can let go of, the freer I am to respond authentically and courageously to life as it presents itself.

In the insight tradition, one of my favorite practices of surrender is called the five remembrances. We remember every day that we are of the nature to (1) become sick, (2) grow old, (3) pass away, and (4) lose *everything* we care about. Everything includes the people we love, the world we try to save, our spiritual ideas and practices—and much more. After grieving this truth, we finish with the fifth reflection: we alone are responsible for our actions, and we are the heir to their consequences. In other words, *we have choices about how we relate, and those choices matter immensely.*

The remembrances suggest that, when we build a life based on clear seeing and acceptance, we distill it to its essence. We rest on a simple and sober foundation that isn't constantly in conflict with the nature of life. In this way, the tragic chaos of the world doesn't have to oppress us but can actually be the fodder for our liberation. It helps us remember that our capacity to choose *how* we relate to this moment is our greatest power. A single choice to surrender might sound small, but repeated over time, it can bring us greater inner freedom *and* lead to positive, practical change in our lives.

As someone whose personal wounding has related to feeling trapped or helpless, this understanding has meant a lot to me. It's been liberating to realize that no matter what the world looks like or where we are, we are never actually helpless. We always have some agency within our little realm. Even if we are somehow completely stuck, we can always choose to relate with wisdom and compassion to that stuckness, and that can mean *everything* to our well-being.

EMBODYING HEALTHY HOPE

Coming to terms with the way things are in the world and our lives creates a foundation for developing a new brand of hope. Conventionally, our conception of hope is often just a mixture of anxiety and longing, often arising from an experience of internal lack. We tend to think this longing makes salvation more possible or, at least, might make the present moment more bearable. Instead, it keeps us in a state of perpetual dissatisfaction, separate from what is. Hence, it's simply a false refuge, just another protective strategy that can't truly nourish or sustain us.

Healthy hope, on the other hand, is grounded in connection and equanimity. It doesn't lean on an idealized future. It instead sources from the goodness that is already here, within and without. While the media triggers our anxiety for views and clicks and teaches us that there are "evil" people out there, we must remember what's truly at our core as humans. Looking out at the world, we can also notice the countless life-affirming movements already underway—like those involved in healing, insight, repair, and regeneration. Then we might take the first step of healthy hope: opening to the possibility of real, positive change.

Who knows, the world or our lives could make a massive turn for the better, perhaps even starting tomorrow. Of course, we can't know this *will* be the case, but we can feel it's possible. Things might go wrong, but they might also go very right. This is like optimism but simpler and more honest. It is the logical upside of the unpredictability and uncontrollability of the world: sometimes, we're surprised with good fortune.

It's possible that we'll heal. It's possible the world will heal. It's all possible. When we consciously keep ourselves in this state of possibility, it helps our heart-minds stay buoyant. Now, we are open to the good that could come and are ready to receive it and amplify it if it does. We're open to exploring, trying new things, and investing our positive energy when we're in this place. For me, this is often a natural outgrowth of surrendering to grief.

Of course, disappointments will still happen. Before long, we may find ourselves assuming again that things probably won't work out for us or the world. After all, in addition to the gloomy global news stream, each of us has a natural negativity bias that's wired into our biology, pulling us toward worry and fear. We might find ourselves focusing on all the potential negative outcomes again. Our friend, self-doubt, may return to try to help by preventing us from taking risks that could hurt us.

So, to recover and sustain this state of possibility, it can help to call on two other healing emotions: curiosity and gratitude. *How could things go right?* we might ask ourselves, or *I'm curious to see what happens.* When we do, our heart cracks back open just a bit. Then we can follow with gratitude to reinforce the sentiment.

"Thank you for the possibility of grace," we might say. Indeed, living in a world where spontaneous good can happen is amazing. We might even explore practicing gratitude for a brighter future—as if it were already here. We might ask ourselves, *What would it feel like in our bodies to live in the outcome we want?* Or, broader still, *What would it feel like to live in a healed heart, relationship, or world?* Feel the answer in your body and say thank you.

This exercise can have an insightful result. We realize we've clung for years to specific outcomes, but essentially, we actually wanted the *feeling* we thought those things would bring such as wholeness, peace, satisfaction, or ease. When we liberate those feelings from the future circumstances they seem to hide behind, we can enjoy them now even if conditions don't change. In other words, what we *really* want might not be the circumstances but the liberated feeling, which we'll only ever get if we shift our priorities to that above all else.

Healthy hope is a state of possibility supported by curiosity and gratitude. It helps us orient toward a brighter future without demanding it meet our expectations or dreams. It keeps us connected to the highest potential outcome while not sacrificing our contentment or wholeness in the present. It naturally leads to wholesome action, unburdened by the passivity of despair. Even if things take a turn for the worse, it doesn't degrade into hopelessness, as it's not predicated on specific conditions.

In its maturest form, healthy hope can evolve into insight and devotion, as these two emotions are the most elevated forms of curiosity and gratitude. The state of possibility can mature into a state of discovery (insight), and our gratitude can grow into a wholehearted devotion to the essential goodness of life. We are open and responsive to what may come but remain rooted in what is.

THE FOUNDATION OF RESILIENCY

Through grief, choice, and healthy hope, we begin reclaiming our well-being amid the world's chaos. This is a challenging task, especially for those in the most adverse circumstances. However, if we can muster a wise attitude amid the hardship, the intensity can actually deepen and hasten the reclaiming process. In our courageous intimacy with the uncontrollable nature of life we share, we can learn more quickly to grieve and begin again and, in the process, develop true resiliency. In this way, reclaiming our well-being is an act of self-compassion with global import. It creates a foundation from which we can energize and sustain the crucial service work needed everywhere.

The Heart of Service

There are countless forms of service work in this world and each of our expressions will look unique. Helping others could be our career or it could look like raising our kids or volunteering in our community. It could even just be calling a friend to see how they're doing. It's less important what we choose to do and more important *how* we do it.

In the world today, as a well-intentioned person, it's easy to get mixed up. We can unconsciously take on the burden of the world and act for many years from a hidden mixture of anxiety, guilt, and low self-worth. We can easily fall out of balance, give too much, and become resentful. In our passion, we can burn bridges instead of make coalitions. I know I've had to learn some of these things the hard way, as many of us do. I pushed myself for many years to "save the world," running on underlying desperation until I burned out and had to find another way.

Fortunately, when we're devoted to self-compassion, our lives naturally transform into service from the inside out, not from an obligation or righteous idea. Helping in some way becomes inevitable as it's a natural outgrowth of the beneficial connection we've reestablished inside. However, strengthening, focusing, and sustaining this service orientation requires additional skill-building and heart-stretching.

This section explores perspectives and practices that synergize our generous impulse with our journey of healing and insight. If we can harness the heart of service within us, we can become a powerful force for positive change in the world.

THE SPIRIT OF GENEROSITY

Just like compassion, generosity is much more than an idea or even an act. It's an intimate emotional process. Without care, it can be easily corrupted. Giving can be enriching, or it can be dry, or even manipulative.

To recover its original function, we can start by looking deeper within. Helping is wired into our biology. In fact, being generous can trigger similar pleasure regions in our brains as if we were acting in self-interest, only stronger.[1] It's evolutionarily designed to feel powerfully good.

However, for many of us, this naturally beneficial behavior has been deactivated through disconnection. We not only feel separate due to our own wounds and our addiction to unwholesome emotions but also by living in an atomized, individualistic society built on the threat of scarcity. When we go against the grain and reconnect, suddenly generosity starts to become natural again. Over time, we can learn to reclaim the holy grail of service work: *helping others while nourishing ourselves.*

At their core, giving and receiving are actually part of the nature of life. The in-breath receives a gift from the trees around us, and the out-breath gives back. We receive this body from the elements for a time and will soon enough have the opportunity to give it back. Hence, generosity doesn't have to be overly effortful or stressful. Maybe it can be more like a long breath out.

This image reveals another benefit of generosity: it helps us let go. Unconsciously, we cling to our possessions, or even our time and energy, thinking they will keep us safe and happy. Yet, deeper down, the very act of clinging itself confines our heart-minds. Generosity helps us let go, bringing us back into nourishing connection.

This is the simplest explanation of how generosity sustains itself. Through letting go, generosity helps us return to the embrace of interconnection, and feeling connected inspires us naturally to give again. If we then add a few more healing emotions, we have the recipe for a lasting, generous spirit.

The first emotion I suggest is joy (mudita), which you'll recall was the third brahmavihara we explored in chapter 8. *Mudita* is often translated as "sympathetic joy," "altruistic joy," or "joy in the joy of others"—a joy that comes from *witnessing* goodness and well-being. For example, when we give attention, encouragement, or support to another person, we can rejoice too. We rejoice in our own goodness, the goodness of giving, and the well-being it creates for others. This enhances the nourishing effect of generosity on our psyche.

The second emotion I suggest is gratitude. Witnessing the joy created, we readily feel grateful for being able to give and for the opportunity to let go. Moreover, gratitude helps us see our abundance instead of the scarcity in our lives, preparing us to give again. Gratitude further establishes this pleasurable feedback loop.

Too many times I've done something generous and not even taken the time to feel its goodness. *Oh, it's not about me*, I'd think, or *I don't need the attention.* Now, I try to pause and reflect on the people affected, the merit of my own letting go, and then breathe the joy and gratitude into my body. I might even wish them well in my heart before moving on. When I do, I can almost feel the neural pathways of generosity syncing up and strengthening through my brain.

In this way, giving consciously leads to deeper connection, joy in the result, and gratitude for the opportunity. The synergy of the three creates a cycle of sustainable generosity. Over time, this can mature into a wholesome sense of purpose in our lives and a trust in the goodness of people and life. Helping create joy through giving is so fulfilling that it can feel like what we're here to do—or at least an important part of it. This isn't because it gives us worth—we already have worth. It's because generous acts reaffirm the deepest protection that exists beneath the strategies of comfort, convenience, or possessing material things. They remind us that we have an innate place within the larger flow of giving and receiving that characterizes life itself.

CARING FOR THOSE WHO HARM

Our generosity brings us into even deeper intimacy with the pain of the world. Naturally, this also brings us into contact with the perpetrators of that pain. This can challenge our capacity to care.

Most of us naturally feel compelled to sympathize with victims, but we can have a hard time opening our hearts to those who hurt others. By opening I don't mean to encourage putting ourselves in harm's way. We all wisely choose to avoid contact with certain people at certain times. I'm speaking to whether we still feel care for them nonetheless. If we are to sustain the healed and awakened heart, our inner radiance must shine without limits. If we are to transform the world together, our service has to include the perpetrators of harm.

As someone who regularly mediates interpersonal conflicts and who has always found themselves pulled into the peacemaker role, I witness firsthand how hard it can be for folks to find resolution with those who have hurt them. While there are many valid reasons for this, a big one is an unconscious belief that the other person's reformed actions, or their punishment, will resolve the pain we feel. When we instead reclaim responsibility for our healing, we can eventually see the perpetrator clearly without the mirage that blame and hatred create. Then we can finally appreciate the harm that doing harm creates.

Despite how it may seem, when someone hurts another—especially knowingly—they register the pain of their act. Their consciousness inscribes the misalignment with their essential goodness and wisdom. In this way, they don't just hurt the victim. They further fracture their connection to themselves—sometimes in irreparable ways—even though it's often deeper down and out of view. A lack of remorse doesn't mean they're bad or evil but instead shows the tragic extent of internal division.

While in the moment of impact the pain of the victim is greater, in the broader context of healing it's sometimes the case that the perpetrator wounds themselves even more significantly. By reinforcing their own internal disconnection, they make their journey back home much harder. If this person now wants to heal, they must go through additional steps that are often too painful to bear. Let me explain.

When someone knowingly causes harm, their protective layers tend to *thicken* in response—an attempt to shield against the additional pain they've caused and may have to now feel. For those perpetrators who find the safety to feel what's underneath, they must first experience the victim's pain. Only then can they attend to their own remorse, broken self-trust, and fractured sense of self-worth. If they are thorough, they can come to a place of self-forgiveness. Often, however, they feel they must wait for forgiveness from the victim or others before they fully do. Only after all this can they begin to access the actual wound that triggered the harmful act and finally start meaningful personal healing.

This process is so arduous internally, and often without instruction and support, that the perpetrator can find it easier to justify, defend, or normalize their harmful behavior. External judgment or punishment can actually provoke a more robust protective response and, thus, can even increase the likelihood of the harm continuing. If the harm is allowed to repeat over and over, the perpetrator can reach a point of saturation where they would rather do anything than face feeling all the layers of pain they've created. Absent a significant compassionate intervention, this is a hard place to recover from.

This dynamic is important to understand partially because *each of us has been, and is, a perpetrator of harm* in some sense, and we don't always realize how we shape ourselves in the process. More globally, however, the healing of perpetrators is the most significant leverage point for wholesome change. As we all know, there are large-scale players whose decisions have an enormous impact on vast swaths of the population. Unless their pain is addressed, they are unlikely ever to transform, cease causing harm, and create the wholesome along with us.

Opening our hearts to those who cause harm doesn't mean we forgo accountability. It means considering how we might support them through the healing process with care. Given compassionate conditions, everyone can eventually heal and become a force for good. Even in our less-than-compassionate prison system, there are countless stories of healing and reformation; they just aren't often celebrated as widely as we need them to be.

In the ancient Buddhist texts, there is a story of hope regarding a serial killer–turned–enlightened being named Angulimala. When no one else would go near Angulimala, the Buddha initiated a skillful and compassionate encounter that reformed Angulimala. The murderer took up robes, practiced diligently, and eventually became a healer and an *arahant* or enlightened being. The story reminds us that everyone is redeemable no matter what they've done.

For us, we can start smaller. Perhaps we can practice opening our heart to a friend or family member that we've cast out or soften our judgment of someone who hurt us in the past. Eventually maybe we can have a courageous conversation, possibly even someday forgive. At the least, we can always keep the door of our heart cracked open for the possibility of healing and transformation for all beings—including ourselves with all our own transgressions.

As a simple practice, we might put a picture of someone on our altar who has caused us or someone we love harm. We might practice imagining the pain they might carry from doing that and embodying a genuine wish for their healing every day. This could even be a political or corporate figure we see doing great harm globally. If we'd like to deepen this capacity, we can draft letters to these people—and if we'd like, actually send them—practicing communicating the compassion we are learning to feel for their pain.

Of course, despite our best intentions or efforts, many folks may not choose healing and that will have to be OK. What we can rely on is that bold practices like these will stretch and reshape our hearts into a larger and deeper refuge for ourselves. They'll embed both humility and the truth of interconnection even deeper in our hearts. In this way, caring for those who harm is a fundamentally self-compassionate act that also addresses the source of our global distress. If we could join together in this effort, we could have a chance to finally uproot the cycles of harm.

COMPASSIONATE ACTIVISM

We're at a time in the world when there is more urgency to fix social and ecological issues than perhaps ever before. However, if we come from an underlying sense of anxiety and spread that to others—and especially forcefully impose our solutions upon others—our approach risks reactivating the collective wounds that cocreated our global predicament in the first place instead of healing them. Thus, how we enact our generous agenda is vitally important. *Compassionate activism* is an action or set of actions that comes from a heartfelt experience of true compassion *for all involved.* An underlying principle of this approach is inclusivity.

Inclusivity is a helpful concept for merging the spiritual and societal aspects of ourselves. On the spiritual level, it can refer to an ever-expanding experience of identity and connection. We can experience ourselves as not just all parts of our psyches but all parts of society and nature as well. In activism, it can refer to a similarly expansive embrace of all people with their differing viewpoints, lifestyles, and backgrounds. We may not agree with or understand people, but we honor them in how we think, feel, speak, and act. When we merge these two aspects of inclusivity—feeling part of everything and honoring everything—we can imagine an activism that can also liberate us.

To make sense of this practically, we must make a discernment between our overarching view and experience of interconnection *and* the granular differences in perspective and approach that are expressed in social and political discourse. Compassionate activism is grounded in the former so that the latter doesn't lead to division and polarization. In other words, we work to see and feel our connection and compassion for everyone, and from that place of mutual respect, we debate and engage in the many passionate differences of opinion and action that lead to social and political change.

This spirit of discourse is hard to find in the public sphere today. This may be because compassion itself is not the primary end most of us are seeking. Understandably, we're trying to enact all sorts of other important and valid agendas to keep ourselves or our communities safe, but we're usually happy to sacrifice being kind if we can get them. In compassionate activism, the priorities are flipped. A compassionate world is the end we seek and less so a particular set of policies, politicians, or conditions. In other words, what the world looks like is less important than how we relate as a collective—which includes our actions too. Nonetheless, by prioritizing a compassionate response above our particular agenda, we initiate connection and healing across the board, which eventually leads to lasting beneficial outcomes for everyone. In fact, there is evidence to suggest that when groups of people consciously emanate heart-centered states of being, others may benefit immediately, even across vast distances.[2]

In our personal activism, we might think of compassionate activism as a balancing act. If the stress of our service work prevents our healing or undermines our capacity to be compassionate, we may need a shift. If, conversely, our healing work becomes so all-encompassing that we can't be of service in the world, we may need a different shift. While our attention will, of course, fluctuate through our lives, we can make our activism and our healing two sides of the same coin. When we establish ourselves in safety and connection through compassion *and* continue being of service in our authentic way, we are more clear seeing, resilient, and effective. As a good faith, practical expression of this, there are a few simple things we might each try in our personal lives.

First, we can try to resist the name-calling, pejoratives, and demonization of others—both individuals and groups. When we hear one of the endless monikers employed to disparage and discredit like "right-wing extremist," "conspiracy theorist," "bigot," "commie," or "snowflake," it's a cue to pause and remember our intention to stay connected. If we're with a friend who uses such language, we might even suggest some alternative ways to speak less divisively.

Second, we can practice using the four aspects of compassion in speaking about those we disagree with. For example, this could be a practice of acknowledgment, honoring, and/or appreciation for a different person's experience *before* disagreeing. When hearing a friend disparage someone on the "other side," we might respond, "I see how they could have come to that, given what they've been through. I can appreciate their struggle and want them to be well. That being said, I think their perspective or action is leading to more harm than good because . . .". This is a good alternative to the common judgment we so often default to these days: "Yeah, I just *can't understand* why anyone would do that."

Third, we can practice reintegrating our social lives to include more diversity of thought and opinion. To do so, we must resist the immense pressure to disavow those who hold opposing beliefs or even who have or continue to make mistakes that affect us. We remember that the view someone holds, or even their momentary behavior, is not their whole self; we can disagree strongly with people but still love them. Often these people are our family members, dear friends, neighbors, doctors, or store clerks whom we see often and actually have much more in common with than not. By continuing these relationships, we can be like bridges, helping to span gaps between groups and keep the social fabric together.

The three simple actions above, if multiplied across millions of people, would be a good start toward depolarizing our world. They suggest that powerful activism sometimes looks more like mediation, and that if more of us acted like mediators instead of taking sides, we might put out each new spark of conflict before it raged into a wildfire. Instead of letting ourselves be riled up into infighting by the media and politicians, we might come to understand, respect, and maybe even love each other a little more. Of course, we'd still have our opinions and disagreements, but we could also unite enthusiastically around the many things the majority of us do agree on—like that we want to live in a peaceful country, end corruption, have a clean environment, or finally solve poverty. These are things we can only make happen if we stand in united, nonviolent opposition to business as usual.

To really get on board with this inclusive approach, we must truly see that repairing the social fabric will make us safer than division ever could. We must see that the world is too interwoven now to exile those who disagree with us or have wronged us without creating—sooner or later—an even greater threat. Acting with anything but love toward our enemies will, in the long run, only hurt us and the very people we're trying to help. The greatest danger to our personal and public safety may not be a pandemic or a climate catastrophe. It may not be war or wealth inequality. It may be what's underneath all of them: the division we perpetuate within human consciousness—for it prevents solving anything else.

..

As many of us know, taking on big issues requires a deep grounding and security in ourselves. If we fuse with fear, we will be tossed about by one news headline after another. We'll be swayed by the methods of manipulation and control surrounding us. We'll let the security of fitting in override finding our authentic path or speaking our truth. We'll justify acting cruelly to protect ourselves and those we love. Before long, our values will degrade into status symbols and even "being compassionate" will be weaponized to further divide us.

In these polarized times, true compassion toward others is radical. To refuse to condemn others, to keep the channels open for dialogue, to not abandon the hearts of those who cause harm—these acts can risk our ostracization from the group we're in. To find the unwavering courage we need to enact true compassion, most of us have to reach beyond ourself, to sink our anchor down into a deeper and securer place. We've already explored the refuges of interconnection and awareness. It's time we also try calling on the support of the Earth herself.

The Planetary Self

Simply by virtue of our birth in this human body, each of us retains an inalienable belonging to life. Without lifting a finger, saying a word, or even "being good," we are part of the ancient lineage of the Earth. Having reverence for this fact is a profound act of self-compassion. It restores an innate dignity and gives us strength to face the world heart-on.

Environmental scientists have long documented the vast network of interactions that create this planet. From the interior tectonics of the planet to the water, ice, and atmospheric systems, each interacts with the others to create the living Earth. In his 1979 book *Gaia: A New Look at Life on Earth*, the environmentalist and futurist James Lovelock hypothesized that these interacting Earth systems function as a single intelligent organism—a notion that has since gained traction with a number of other thinkers.

This suggests that, just as cells cooperate to make up our physical form, we are cells within a greater body of Earth. Just as our cells receive information from the environment so we may sense our reality, the Earth, too, may collect and organize our individual perceptions to perceive its reality. Scientists still can't locate our own consciousness in any part of our body, heart, or mind, so it may very well be part of a *much* larger process. Our organism may be like a node in a vast web of information that connects the planet. If this were so, we could imagine that each of us has access to a planetary consciousness or is part of a "planetary self."

Whether scientifically provable or not, it is a concept approximating a liberating spiritual experience we each subjectively can have. As my teacher's teacher Buddhadasa Bhikkhu said, "The entire cosmos is a cooperative. The sun, the moon, and the stars live together as a cooperative." Physicists like Stephen Hawking have theorized a similar concept, that the entire universe acts like a giant neural network or self-organizing entity.[3]

Such realizations are particularly valuable, because they stand at the intersection between healing, insight, and activism. They help us heal, awaken us to the deepest protection, and support a compassionate composure as we come up against the great challenges of the future. For this reason, exploring it is perhaps the most important act of self-compassion yet.

THE EARTH AS OUR WITNESS

According to the stories passed down, in the final moment before Siddhartha achieved awakening and became the Buddha, he was challenged by Mara, a demon-like entity who personifies delusion. Mara, trying to inspire doubt, asked the young prince why he thought he could awaken or by whose authority he could do such a thing. Sitting devotedly underneath the bodhi tree, Siddhartha simply reached down and touched the Earth. Mara vanished, and the Buddha became enlightened.

Precisely what the ardent spiritual seeker intended when he put his hand on the Earth can't be known. Many have said he was calling the Earth herself to witness or authorize his awakening. It's also possible that this act signified the profound transformative power of synergizing one's being with the larger consciousness of the planet and beyond, a profound act of embodied interconnection that expands our small, conventional identities. In the language of the Dharma of Healing, perhaps the Buddha was placing his heart back into the heart of life itself.

Either way, it's particularly instructive that the Buddha didn't conquer the "armies of Mara" through argument, judgment, or conflict. He did so by aligning with a reality that *included* Mara. Perhaps his Earth-touch may have actually been a compassionate message: "Not just me, but you, too, are part of this Earth."

In this way, the Buddha's touch may not have signified an awakening *from* the world, but instead an awakening *as* the world. As such, it naturally led to generous action. Indeed, when the Buddha awakened, he didn't become complacent. He got up and skillfully helped whoever would listen, and did so tirelessly, traveling and teaching for the next forty-five years. However, if he had relinquished his separate sense of self, then it's fair to say that it was no longer him doing this. It was the Earth or the cosmos teaching herself the Dharma.

A healthy cell in a body acts intuitively, naturally synergizing its innate cellular wisdom with the body's wisdom as a whole. When a cell becomes overly independent and loses touch with the body, we call it cancer. We can witness the plethora of mental illness and confusion that occurs when we lose touch with the whole. In this way, the Buddha's touching the Earth can serve as a potent affirmation of the power and value of returning the cells of our selves to the body of the Earth. If it catalyzed a profound devotion to compassionate activism for him, we can surmise that, as each of us return, we'll produce the precise realignment needed to steer the planet back into collective harmony.

..

In practice, we might experiment with a few eco-somatic exercises to feel how these ideas could support us. In meditation, we might imagine placing our attention not just on our body or emotions but *into* the body of the Earth, feeling ourselves animated by this greater, ancient presence. We could even sit with a being in nature, like a tall tree or an old mountain. We could place a bare hand or foot on it and imagine our energy systems merging at the point of contact. We might breathe into that point, exchanging support back and forth. We might even ask if that part of the Earth could hold our pain or offer us guidance.

As we continue to play with this, we could imagine letting go and letting the Earth breathe, the Earth read, the Earth walk, the Earth cook, the Earth help. *What would the Earth do now?* we might ask and then move intuitively. We might even narrate a few moments of our day to remind ourselves: *The Earth is feeling upset. The Earth is feeling joy.* This is one of my favorite practices, especially when doing personal retreats in nature.

In this playful way, we can invite our experience to break out of the same confining boxes of self-protection that tend to define our lives. In our decision-making, we can quiet the cost-benefit equations and the moral assessments and expand into a heart-based intuitive guidance system sourced from the greater field of interconnection. For me, this is a fluid and harmonious mode of living akin to the relational flow described in the last chapter.

When you try it, you'll likely find that things go better. I know I always do. Or, as I like to say, "The Earth does it better." For me, this isn't much of a surprise, though. The Earth embodies the intelligence of billions of years of evolution.

As someone who's been anxiously involved in Earth activism, I love the implication of this. If the Earth does it better, then whatever we invite it to do *through us* is likely superior to what we've been trying to do *for it.*

Relaxing into this elemental wisdom might supersede the modern, preconceived ideas of "what the Earth needs." At the very least, it can prevent us from falling into the pernicious, self-deprecating view that sees humans as an unnatural blight on the Earth. Such views only increase separation and prevent the larger healing that's needed. "How does the Earth want to help the Earth?" we might ask. When we fully reconnect our hearts, we may find ourselves, our lives, and our activism changing in unexpected ways.

THE PLANETARY NERVOUS SYSTEM

The body of the Earth is trillions upon trillions of times larger than our body.[4] It's also been here millions of times longer than our body has. The Earth literally constructed our bodies from her body, just like our mothers did. It's no huge leap to suggest the Earth had a similar formative role in fashioning our nervous systems as well as continuing to support them. If we were to try to identify that regulating force, we might look to the electromagnetic resonances of our planet and our own bodies. Amazingly, the Earth vibrates in the same frequency range as our brain waves in deep relaxation and has been shown to affect and be affected by human activity—including our thoughts and emotions.[5]

Not too long ago, we may have intuitively coregulated with the Earth, balancing our internal state through its vast and ancient presence. Yet this nurturing bond has broken down through the countless modern wounds of separation, the resulting loneliness, and the chronic anxiety that comes from it. Perhaps if we can relax and retune to the Earth's nervous system—the humming and pulsing energy of our planet—we can reassure our tiny systems of their vast primordial parentage. Like a fish in an aquarium being reintroduced to the ocean, we can recollect the vast mystery of life we've always been a part of. This is the essential skill of the spiritual path generally: recognizing what's always already been here but has been hidden from our view.

Coregulating with the Earth may sound like a strange concept, but it can have profound practical implications. If we do it, we can theoretically face even the most cataclysmic events without losing connection to the deeper protections and refuges. For example, we are actually in the middle of what many experts call the Sixth Great Extinction.[6] Even though it's horrific from a human perspective, it's likely not so stressful for the Earth. She's been through it at least five times before.

By plugging our heart-minds back into the Earth's nervous system, we can share in the fruits of this view. We can recognize that, even though the future threatens everything we've known as humans, we can't kill the Earth. We can't kill this larger intelligent dimension of ourselves. Even moon-sized asteroids, volcanic disasters, and great floods haven't. Contemplating this view can provide a vast protection for our heart-minds in this age and, as such, be a profound act of self-care.

Of course, this is hard to do when the alarm bells are going off in our systems. We hear the voices, *No, we must use any tool we have to do something now!* Remembering the story of the Buddha, however—this passionate demand could just be the final persuasion of Mara. It could be one more voice in a long line of voices that has convinced us to stay anxious and separate. If we follow the parable above, our response would not be to obey or resist. It would be to touch the Earth, remember our connection, and let a larger wisdom move through us. This doesn't mean we don't act. It just means we act from a different place.

This is the great spiritual challenge of our time. As the dust of panic blows through the world, it's easy to get lost in the sandstorm. The voice of Mara is at its most convincing right now. But if we act from it, we just create more of Mara's anxious and angry world. We oppress ourselves with the very longing that we think will liberate us. To experience a peaceful world, we can't justify peace only when things go how we want or when what we care about isn't threatened. We must justify peace amid unimaginable loss, even as everything is falling apart.

· ·

The concept of the planetary self is an expansion of the relational self that we explored in the last chapter. We could imagine a "universal self" in a similar, yet even more expansive, way. These are creative heart-exercises that stretch us to embody larger versions of ourselves and, in doing so, act with greater ease, clarity, and resilience in the world. Effectively, we expand the definition of self-compassion to include the whole world *as ourselves*, and in doing so, we stay connected and whole in this age of no escape. As our sense of self transforms, we naturally come into contact with the conceptless space of awareness that underlies everything.

Moreover, these exercises can help to ease the chronic debilitating sense in our lives that things are "out of place" or shouldn't be happening. We can learn to relax into a greater sense of support and, therefore, trust. We end up saying yes to our lives as they are and the world as it is while placing our trust in a greater wisdom. Lo and behold, this supports us in making precisely the changes we need to make—but from a more wholesome place inside.

However, it's critical to remain devoted to true compassion through the four turnings while practicing these creative exercises. This ensures that we don't use the exercises inadvertently to bypass our wounds, thus delivering us back into old patterns. Turning the wheel of healing, we may very well discover these larger ways of being emerging as a natural outgrowth of a wise and compassionate heart.

THE MEANS ARE THE ENDS

It doesn't really matter how long we've practiced, how many books we've read, or how hard we've tried. It doesn't matter what spiritual ideas we hold or even what past awakenings we've had. It only really matters how we devote ourselves to *this* moment. The means we use are the ends we achieve. In other words, the most important outcome is always now. A wholehearted and wholesome embrace is the alchemy of awakening.

In the Soto Zen tradition that I also practiced within for a time, the enactment of this truth is called *practice-enlightenment*. We don't practice *for* enlightenment; we enact it. We engage entirely with each moment as if it is the only moment that ever existed. We do so because it is.

In the Dharma of Healing, this correlates with *true* compassion. We don't care for something because it serves us. We wholeheartedly devote ourselves to intimacy with our suffering. We pour ourselves completely into ourselves as if we were the most precious thing we'd ever see. We do so because we are.

We can practice for decades from the mind of progress and feel disappointed with every return of pain and confusion. Or we can stop practicing to end suffering and practice like the moment is worth our complete attention regardless of how it looks. The eventual effect will be less suffering, but we won't care so much by the time that happens. We'll be looking at a new, perfectly imperfect moment, peering deeper into the embrace.

To practice in this way is to humbly accept that there may always be suffering—*always*. We can't expect to heal every last wound within us or humanity. Even if we someday eradicated suffering from our being, we would still awaken next to others who are deeply confused, and that would trigger us again. We can, however, heal and perfect our *relationship* to pain. I don't mean that we will ever *like* it; I mean that we can learn to fall in love with caring for it. We can then feel at home no matter how life unfolds.

Once we grasp the fundamental principles of this path, we are not so different than the spiritual masters of history. Each of us is already whole, just at different stages of remembering. Each of us struggles with the universal pains of life; we're just at varying levels of resilience to them. To advance is not to know anything new but to live the unknown even more completely. Each of us has our limits, but when we practice wholeheartedly, they continually expand like the universe itself.

We turn the wheel of healing to understand this for ourselves, but also to join the community of humans devoted to this journey. We turn the wheel so, someday, every last person might discover the paths of healing and insight and celebrate together an end to the cycles of harm. We turn the wheel so all living things, the Earth, and the universe itself can discover their nature through us and with us. By aligning ourselves with these profound intentions, we carry an inner strength with us even in the darkest moments.

• •

The richest aspects of the journey aren't the big spiritual experiences. They're where the mystery meets each moment of our daily lives. Experiencing deep healing and insight there doesn't require practicing harder or longer. It just requires that we *prioritize* presence. Our practice comes alive when we prioritize presence above the deeply ingrained urges to self-protect.

We all know that something could go wrong in everything we do. Someone might reject us; we might not make enough money; we might become sick; we might lose what we love, or worse. By obsessing over avoiding these earthly hazards, we trade the wholeness of this moment for an elusive safety in the future. On this altar, we sacrifice our joy, authenticity, and nourishing sense of connection. Now we know we don't have to.

Instead, we can inquire with ourselves. Of everything we "should" or "have to" do, we can ask, *What would happen if I didn't, or if it didn't go right?* Feeling each potentially painful consequence, we can continue to ask, *And what would happen then?* Before long, we will have followed the architecture of our fear to its deepest foundations (e.g., being alone, being in pain, death, and dying).

Yet, as each fear challenges us, we reassure ourselves that even if (or when) it came to pass, it could never take our connection to life itself. We will *always* have a home in awareness. No one and nothing can take that truth.

In this way, we can grieve our worst-case scenarios now. We can soothe our gravest insecurities. And then live the day we already had planned to live—or the one we dream of—but from this fearless and connected place.

THE UNIVERSAL GOOD NEWS

Whether we acknowledge it or not, we are certainly on a grand journey together—one of universal proportions—and no one knows where it's going. We may be headed toward cataclysmic destruction. It's also possible that we are on the verge of global harmony. Healthy hope would invite us to hold the doors of our heart open to the latter.

While we can't know the future, we can notice patterns within and around us. When we do, we see many foreboding prospects and also many encouraging signs. For example, when we zoom out to analyze the last two hundred years, we are still trending toward increasing global education, health, and democracy, decreasing global famine, poverty, and war, and we continue to innovate in every sector to address our collective challenges.[7] However, there's one trend, in particular, that always stands out to me: the increase in global interest in healing and spirituality. Interest in mindfulness and meditation has grown rapidly,[8] making its way into every aspect of society—even business, sports, and medicine. Self-compassion is also gaining momentum, as are many other forms of healing.[9] There has arguably never been such a high degree of interest in healing and spirituality in recorded history—at least in the West—and there's no end in sight to this growing trend.

This is significant in and of itself. However, in addition, polls have shown that more and more people are awakening to transformative spiritual or religious experience.[10] They are reconnecting with the universal dimension of themselves, called by many names. We could say this is a lucky accident or due to some special quality of a certain few. Instead, however, what if it were a natural, causal unfolding of the evolution of the Earth itself? As physicists know, we live in a mathematical universe. If self-realization is happening, it is likely to be a lawful result of interactions we just can't yet fully define.

As we explored with the five natural forces of healing, we are each organized for our own benefit. Now, if we combine that with the view of the planetary self, we can then imagine that the Earth, too, is organized in this way. If so, our collective rise in healing and spiritual growth may be an emergent property of the Earth's self-organized systems—a part of the design. What's more, we might have the honor to *be* the vehicle through which the Earth is evolving her own self-discovery and growth.

There is a concept in Buddhism of the *boddhisattva*. In the Mahayana tradition, these are people that devote themselves to awakening for the welfare of all sentient beings. In fact, they may devote themselves so thoroughly that even after they awaken, they vow to return again and again to the earthly plane until everyone is liberated. In essence, it is a vow of eternal compassion. I can't help but consider the possibility of the same spirit embedded within the fabric of the universe itself.

Despite the seeming rarity of our planetary circumstances, just in our galaxy alone, NASA has found over *300 million planets* that could harbor life[11] and there are over 100 billion galaxies in the universe. Perhaps the network of living planets are like the cells of the body of the universe, each in some part of the process of self-discovery. Perhaps awakening itself is designed into the evolution of the entire cosmos, part of the vast play of life. This is a wondrous thought.

This possibility means that for living beings to realize their universal origins is not an accident but an inevitability. It may not happen tomorrow or even in this lifetime, but if we are in an awakening universe, we are guaranteed to wake up someday in some form. It would follow, then, that using mindfulness and compassion to turn our attention around for our own self-discovery would be the enactment of an infinitesimal—but critical—part of this miraculous universal process.

TURNING THE WHEEL TOGETHER

Before we end, let's slow down and take a final moment together. Take a deep breath and bring your attention to the simple sensations of holding this book.

Don't try to do anything special. Just listen to the silence, feel the stillness, and open to the spaciousness around you.

Then, place a slight smile in the corners of your mouth and wait. Slowly feel the warmth seep into the space, staying here until your smile widens on its own.

Imagine this simple radiance is not just yours, but an age-old prayer of the Earth itself. The warmth emerges and seeps into the collective ether, travels the globe like weather, and blesses every being in their day. Before long, it escapes into the vacuum of space, traveling the outer arm of our spiral galaxy, dusting each planet and star in its path.

As it does, it feeds a vast wheel of healing that stretches across the universe. The countless emissaries of compassion across space and time help in its turning. Our countless ancestors and the bodhisattvas of the ancient past are here. There are humans, but there are also the mountains and the oceans. There are the elements. There are the comets crossing the night sky. We're all turning the wheel together.

Take a long and deep breath, again. Let it out slowly and feel yourself relax. All things are with us on this journey; we've never been alone. In fact, everything is rooting for us.

As my teacher Joan Sutherland says, "The world has a stake in your awakening." Perhaps the universe does, too. If this is true, then there will be no being left behind in the end. Everyone will eventually awaken and be free.

We may not see the end. The Earth may not see the end. But this self-aware universe is destined to awaken itself to itself in all ways, always.

We may as well surrender to the dance.

Summary, Prompts, and Practices

CHAPTER SUMMARY

- Learning to engage in the world without losing our calm and connection requires an inclusive, heart-centered approach.
- Initial aspects of this include learning to grieve, reclaiming our sense of choice, and cultivating a healthy hope that revitalizes our heart-minds.
- Sustainable engagement in service work requires an intimate understanding of the nature of generosity within us and engagement that's

not complete until we learn to stretch our care to include even those who cause harm or oppose us.

- In the process, the Earth itself can be an indispensable support. Through creative practices, we can access its grounding presence as a stabilizing force for our nervous systems and a foundation from which to enact positive change.
- This is a powerful moment in the evolution of the Earth, a time when more and more people are awakening to their essential nature and remembering their participation in the mysterious unfolding of this self-aware universe.

JOURNAL PROMPTS

- What are one or two things regarding the state of the world that you need to grieve? How might you make space for this natural cleansing process in your life?
- What is something that helps others but also feeds your heart? Practice enacting this as a way of exploring sustainable generosity.
- Who is someone that you have cut out of your heart? What is an issue that you care so deeply about that you sacrifice kindness? In both cases, what would it take to welcome kindness back in? Brainstorm some ideas.
- Imagine for a moment you felt the world through the elemental nervous system of the Earth. You've been through dozens of cataclysms, five extinctions, etc. What would you say to humanity at this time?
- Do you believe you will heal and awaken someday? Or not? Do you hold this possibility for yourself? Why or why not?

GUIDED PRACTICES

We have two guided practices for the final chapter. The first is a compassion meditation that includes all beings on this Earth and beyond. The second is an exploration of the "planetary nervous system," which provides a deep grounding presence for these times and to which we are inevitably connected. Access the guided meditations at www.justinmichelsondharma.com/the dharmaofhealing/practices or www.shambhala.com/dharmaofhealing practices.

Notes

Introduction

1. "Global Emotions Report," Gallup.com, July 21, 2023, https://www
.gallup.com/analytics/349280/gallup-global-emotions-report.aspx.
2. Angelica Misitzis, "Increased Interest for Mindfulness Online," *International Journal of Yoga* 13, no. 3 (2020): 247–49, https://doi
.org/10.4103/ijoy.ijoy_15_20.
3. Michael Lipka and Claire Gecewicz, "More Americans Now Say They're
Spiritual But Not Religious," Pew Research Center, September 6, 2–17,
https://www.pewresearch.org/short-reads/2017/09/06/more-ameri
cans-now-say-theyre-spiritual-but-not-religious.
4. Shaun Callaghan, Martin Losch, Anna Pione, and Warren Teichner, "Feeling Good: The Future of the $1.5 Trillion Wellness Market"
McKinsey and Company, April 8, 2021, https://www.mckinsey.com
/industries/consumer-packaged-goods/our-insights/feeling-good-the
-future-of-the-1-5-trillion-wellness-market.
5. Dexing Zhang, Eric K. P. Lee, Eva C. W. Mak, C. Y. Ho, and Samuel Y S.
Wong, "Mindfulness-Based Interventions: An Overall Review," *British Medical Bulletin* 138, no. 1 (2021), 41–57, https://doi.org/10.1093/bmb/ldaboo5.

Chapter One: The Age of Compassion

1. Intergovernmental Panel on Climate Change, "Climate Change 2022:
Impacts, Adaptation, and Vulnerability," IPCC, accessed January 17,
2024, https://www.ipcc.ch/report/ar6/wg2.

2. Ali M. Alshami, "Pain: Is It All in the Brain or the Heart?" *Current Pain and Headache Reports* 23, no. 12 (2019): 88, https://doi.org/10.1007/s11916-019-0827-4.

3. Rollin McCraty, Mike Atkinson, and Raymond Trevor Bradley, "Electrophysiological Evidence of Intuition: Part 2. A System-Wide Process?" *Journal of Alternative and Complementary Medicine* 10, no. 2 (2004): 325–36, https://doi.org/10.1089/107555304323062310.

4. Dacher Keltner, Jason Marsh, and Jeremy Adam Smith, eds., *The Compassionate Instinct: The Science of Human Goodness* (New York: W. W. Norton, 2010).

5. Kathryn L. Sowder, Laura A. Knight, and Jaclyn Fishalow, "Trauma Exposure and Health: A Review of Outcomes and Pathways," *Journal of Aggression, Maltreatment and Trauma* 27, no. 10 (2018): 1041–59, https://doi.org/10.1080/10926771.2017.1422841.

6. Robert C. Scaer, *The Trauma Spectrum: Hidden Wounds and Human Resiliency* (New York: Norton, 2005).

7. C. Benjet, E. Bromet, E. G. Karam, R. C. Kessler, K. A. McLaughlin, A. M. Ruscio, V. Shahly et al., "The Epidemiology of Traumatic Event Exposure Worldwide: Results from the World Mental Health Survey Consortium," *Psychological Medicine* 46, no. 2 (2016): 327–43, https://doi.org/10.1017/S0033291715001981.

8. Ali Jawaid, Martin Roszkowski, and Isabelle M. Mansuy, "Transgenerational Epigenetics of Traumatic Stress," *Progress in Molecular Biology and Translational Science* 158 (2018): 273–98, https://doi.org/10.1016/bs.pmbts.2018.03.003.

9. Tori DeAngelis, "The Legacy of Trauma," *American Psychological Association* 50, no. 2 (2019); https://www.apa.org/monitor/2019/02/legacy-trauma.

10. Kathryn M. Magruder, Katie A. McLaughlin, and Diane L. Elmore Borbon, "Trauma Is a Public Health Issue," *European Journal of Psychotraumatology* 8, no. 1 (2017): 1375338, https://doi.org/10.1080/20008198.2017.1375338.

11. The Cigna Group, "The Loneliness Epidemic Persists: A Post-Pandemic Look at the State of Loneliness among U.S. Adults," Cigna Group Newsroom, accessed September 17, 2024, https://newsroom.thecignagroup.com/loneliness-epidemic-persists-post-pandemic-look.

12. US Department of Health and Human Services, "Social Connection—Current Priorities of the U.S. Surgeon General," accessed June 12, 2024, https://www.hhs.gov/surgeongeneral/priorities/connection/index .html.

13. Frances M. Carlson, "Significance of Touch in Young Children's Lives," *Young Children* 60 (2005): 79–85.

14. Shannon Sullivan, "Inheriting Racist Disparities in Health," *Critical Philosophy of Race* 1, no. 2 (2013): 190, https://doi.org/10.5325 /critphilrace.1.2.0190.

15. G. Straker, D. Watson, and T. Robinson, "Trauma and Disconnection: A Trans-Theoretical Approach," *International Journal of Psychotherapy* 7, no. 2 (2002): 145–58, https://doi.org/10.1080/13569080 21000016828.

16. Eric L. Garland, "Pain Processing in the Human Nervous System," *Primary Care: Clinics in Office Practice* 39, no. 3 (2012): 561–71, https://doi.org/10.1016/j.pop.2012.06.013.

17. Matthew Kimble, Mariam Boxwala, Whitney Bean, Kristin Maletsky, Jessica Halper, Kaleigh Spollen, and Kevin Fleming, "The Impact of Hypervigilance: Evidence for a Forward Feedback Loop," *Journal of Anxiety Disorders*, 28, no. 2 (2014), 241–45, https://doi.org/10.1016/j .janxdis.2013.12.006.

18. Peter A. Levine, *Waking the Tiger: Healing Trauma: the Innate Capacity to Transform Overwhelming Experiences* (Berkeley, CA: North Atlantic Books, 1997).

19. Antonia Ypsilanti, Lambros Lazuras, Phillip Powell, and Paul Overton, "Self-Disgust as a Potential Mechanism Explaining the Association between Loneliness and Depression," *Journal of Affective Disorders* 243 (January 2019): 108–15, https://doi.org/10.1016/j.jad.2018.09.056.

20. Ricks Warren, Elke Smeets, and Kristin Neff, "Self-Criticism and Self-Compassion: Risk and Resilience: Being Compassionate to Oneself Is Associated with Emotional Resilience and Psychological Well-Being," *Current Psychiatry* 15, no. 12 (2016), https://link.gale .com/apps/doc/A474714850/AONE?u=oregon_oweb&sid=google-Scholar&xid=dd3a8a76.

21. Christina Alexandra Löw, Henning Schauenburg, and Ulrike Dinger, "Self-Criticism and Psychotherapy Outcome: A Systematic Review

and Meta-Analysis," *Clinical Psychology Review* 75 (2020), https://doi.org/10.1016/j.cpr.2019.101808.

22. Darko Manevski and Zenger News, "Adults Say Over a Thousand Negative Things about Themselves Each Year," *Newsweek*, July 6, 2022, https://www.newsweek.com/adults-say-over-thousand-negative-things-about-themselves-each-year-study-1722350.

23. Raj Raghunathan, *If You're so Smart, Why Aren't You Happy?* (New York: Penguin, 2016).

24. John Ramos, *Internalized Oppression: The Psychology of Marginalized Groups* (New York: Springer Publications, 2014).

25. Katherine W. Unthank, "How Self-Blame Empowers and Disempowers Survivors of Interpersonal Trauma: An Intuitive Inquiry," *Qualitative Psychology* 6, no. 3 (2019): 359–78, https://doi.org/10.1037/qup0000136.

26. World Health Organization, *World Mental Health Report: Transforming Mental Health for All*, June 16, 2022, https://www.who.int/publications/i/item/9789240049338.

27. George M. Slavich, "Social Safety Theory: A Biologically Based Evolutionary Perspective on Life Stress, Health, and Behavior," *Annual Review of Clinical Psychology* 16, no. 1 (2016), https://doi.org/10.1146/annurev-clinpsy-032816-045159.

28. P. Grossman, L. Niemann, S. Schmidt, and H. Walach. "Mindfulness-Based Stress Reduction and Health Benefits: A Meta-Analysis," *Focus on Alternative and Complementary Therapies* 8, no. 4 (2010): 500, https://doi.org/10.1111/j.2042-7166.2003.tb04008.x.

Chapter Two: Mindfulness Alone Is Not Enough

1. The Buddhist term for the concept of heart-mind is *chitta*. For more information, see Bhikkhu Bodhi, trans., *The Connected Discourses of the Buddha: A Translation of the Samyutta Nikaya* (Boston: Wisdom Publications, 2000), 769–70n154.

2. For one example from the suttas, see Digha Nikaya 19, verse 6.8, https://suttacentral.net/dn19/en/sujato.

3. For further discussion of Buddhist patriarchy, see Serinity Young and Rita M. Gross, "Buddhism After Patriarchy: A Feminist History, Anal-

ysis, and Reconstruction of Buddhism," *Buddhist-Christian Studies* 14 (January 1994): 248, https://doi.org/10.2307/1389850. See also Bernard Faure, *The Power of Denial: Buddhism, Purity, and Gender* (Princeton, NJ: Princeton University Press, 2003).

4. Analayo, *Compassion and Emptiness in Early Buddhist Meditation* (Cambridge, UK: Windhorse Publications, 2015).

5. Kristin Neff, *Self-Compassion: The Proven Power of Being Kind to Yourself* (New York: HarperCollins, 2011).

6. Kristin Neff and Marissa C. Knox, "Self-Compassion," *Mindfulness in Positive Psychology: The Science of Meditation and Wellbeing* 37 (2016): 1–8.

7. See Wendy J. Phillips and Donald W. Hine, "Self-Compassion, Physical Health, and Health Behaviour: A Meta-Analysis," *Health Psychology Review* 15, no. 1 (2021): 113–39.

8. See, for example, Randolph M. Nesse, *Good Reasons for Bad Feelings: Insights from the Frontier of Evolutionary Psychiatry* (London: Penguin Books, 2020).

9. Jack Kornfield, "Magandiya Sutta and Majjhima-Nikaya" *Inquiring Mind*, April 24, 2022, https://inquiringmind.com/article/0601_07_sutta-jack-kornfield.

10. For an excellent overview of the four noble truths, see Bhikkhu Bodhi, *Noble Truths, Noble Path: The Heart Essence of the Buddha's Original Teachings* (Boston: Wisdom Publications, 2023).

Chapter Three: The Art of Healing

1. For example, one recent study found that 89.7 percent of participants surveyed had experienced a traumatic event. See D. G. Kilpatrick, H. S. Resnick, M. E. Milanak, M. W. Miller, K. M. Keyes, and M. J. Friedman, "National Estimates of Exposure to Traumatic Events and PTSD Prevalence Using DSM-IV and DSM-5 Criteria," *Journal of Trauma Stress*, 26, no. 5 (2013): 537–47, https://doi.org/10.1002/jts.21848.

2. For more information, see Antonia V. Seligowski, Nathaniel G. Harnett, Julia B. Merker, and Kerry J. Ressler, "Nervous and Endocrine System Dysfunction in Posttraumatic Stress Disorder: An Overview and Consideration of Sex as a Biological Variable," *Biological Psychiatry:*

Cognitive Neuroscience and Neuroimaging 5, no. 4 (2020): 381–91, https://doi.org/10.1016/j.bpsc.2019.12.006.

3. See, for example, Beth Jacobs, *The Original Buddhist Psychology: What the Abhidharma Tells Us About How We Think, Feel, and Experience Life* (Berkeley, CA: North Atlantic Books, 2017).

4. "Lifting the Lid on the Unconscious," *New Scientist* 239, no. 3188 (July 2018): 36–37, https://doi.org/10.1016/S0262-4079(18)31354-X.

5. J. Tseng, and J. Poppenk, "Brain Meta-State Transitions Demarcate Thoughts Across Task Contexts Exposing the Mental Noise of Trait Neuroticism," *Nature Communications* 11 (2020): 3480, https://doi.org/10.1038/s41467-020-17255-9.

6. Karen Jensen, *Three Brains: How the Heart, Brain, and Gut Influence Mental Health and Identity* (Coquitlam, BC: Mind Publishing, 2016).

7. See, for example, Christof Koch, "What Is Consciousness?" *Nature* 557, no. 7704 (2018): S8–12.

8. Stephen Johnson, "Jung's Autonomous Complexes: The Mini-Personalities That Can Take Over Your Life," Big Think, accessed February 17, 2024, https://bigthink.com/neuropsych/jung-autonomous-complexes-mini-personalities.

9. For an overview of the topic, see Ashleigh E. Hillier, Carol Smith, Susan Maher, "How to Stick with New Habits—or Kick Old Ones," CNN, April 16, 2023, https://www.cnn.com/2023/04/16/health/brain-how-habits-form-wellness-partner/index.html.

10. For more information on disowned selves in Voice Dialogue, see Hal Stone, "Voice Dialogue—Discovering Our Selves," Voice Dialogue International, accessed September 17, 2024, voicedialogueinternational.com/articles/Voice_Dialogue-_Discovering_Our_Selves.htm.

11. For more information on IFS parts work, see Derek Scott, "Grief and the Internal Family System," in *Principles and Practice of Grief Counseling*, ed. Howard Winokuer and Darcy Harris (New York: Springer, 2012), 168–69.

12. See, for example, Ervin Laszlo, *The Interconnected Universe: Conceptual Foundations of Transdisciplinary Unified Theory* (Singapore: World Scientific Publishing, 1995).

13. See, for example, Nama Friedmann and Dana Rusou, "Critical Period for First Language: The Crucial Role of Language Input During the

First Year of Life," *Current Opinion in Neurobiology* 35 (2015): 27–34, https://doi.org/10.1016/j.conb.2015.06.003.

14. See, for example, Pamela M. Cole, Laura M. Armstrong, and Carol K. Pemberton, "The Role of Language in the Development of Emotion Regulation," in *Child Development at the Intersection of Emotion and Cognition*, ed. Susan D. Calkins and Martha Ann Bell (Washington DC: American Psychological Association, 2010), 59–77, https://doi.org/10.1037/12059-004.

15. See, for example, Jennifer L. Goetz, Dacher Keltner, and Emiliana Simon-Thomas, "Compassion: An Evolutionary Analysis and Empirical Review," *Psychological Bulletin* 136, no. 3 (2010): 351–74, https://doi:10.1037/a0018807.

Chapter Four: The Heart of the Matter

1. R. McCraty et al., "Cardiac Coherence, SelfRegulation, Autonomic Stability, and Psychosocial Well-Being," *Frontiers in Psychology* 5, Article 1090 (2014).

2. See, for example, C. S. Carter and R. Dantzer, "Love and Fear: A Special Issue," *Comprehensive Psychoneuroendocrinology* 11 (2022): 100151, https://doi:10.1016/j.cpnec.2022.100151.

3. For more information, see V. Rajmohan and E. Mohandas, "The Limbic System," *Indian Journal of Psychiatry* 49, no. 2 (2007): 132.

4. See, for example, Rollin McCraty, "Heart-Brain Neurodynamics: The Making of Emotion," *The Neuropsychotherapist* 6 (2003): 68–89, https://doi:10.12744/tnpt(6)068-089.

5. Alan S. Cowen and Dacher Keltner, "Self-Report Captures 27 Distinct Categories of Emotion Bridged by Continuous Gradients," *Proceedings of the National Academy of Sciences of the United States of America* 114, no. 38 (2017): E7900–7909, https://doi:10.1073/pnas.1702247114.

6. For more information on the biological and cultural variability of emotion, see Jozefien De Leersnyder, Michael Boiger, and Batja Mesquita, "Cultural Differences in Emotions," in *Emerging Trends in the Social and Behavioral Sciences: An Interdisciplinary, Searchable, and Linkable Resource*, ed. Robert Scott, Stephen Michael Kosslyn, and Marlis C. Buchmann (Hoboken, NJ: John Wiley and Sons, 2015), 1–15.

Chapter Five: The Living Expression of Compassion

1. Thanissaro Bhikku, trans., "Jata Sutta: The Tangle," Access to Insight, accessed October 24, 2023, www.accesstoinsight.org/tipitaka/sn/sn07/sn07.006.than.html.

Chapter Six: Turning the Wheel of Healing— Surface and Depth

1. Thanissaro Bhikku, trans., "Dhammacakkappavattana Sutta: Setting the Wheel of Dhamma in Motion," *Access to Insight*, accessed October 24, 2023, https://www.accesstoinsight.org/tipitaka/sn/sn56/sn56.011 .than.html.
2. For more information, see "How Do Your Emotions Affect Your Physical Health?" News-Medical.net, accessed February 17, 2024, https://www.news-medical.net/health/How-Do-Your-Emotions-Affect-Your-Physical-Health.aspx#1.
3. In Buddhism and the insight tradition, the closest concept is *chitta*, which contains the unconscious reservoir of all our past impressions. See Peter Harvey, *The Selfless Mind* (London: Curzon Press, 1995), 112.

Chapter Seven: Turning the Wheel of Healing— Collective and Universal

1. See, for example, A. Combs and S. Krippner, "Collective Consciousness and the Social Brain," *Journal of Consciousness Studies* 15 (2008): 264–76.
2. For more information, see Alice C. Schermerhorn and E. Mark Cummings, "Transactional Family Dynamics: A New Framework for Conceptualizing Family Influence Processes," *Advances in Child Development and Behavior* (2008): 187–250, https://doi.org/10.1016/s0065-2407(08)00005-0.
3. Laith Al-Shawaf, Daniel Conroy-Beam, Kelly Asao, and David M. Buss, "Human Emotions: An Evolutionary Psychological Perspective," *Emotion Review* 8, no. 2 (2015): 173–86, https://doi.org/10.1177/1754073914565518.

Chapter Eight: The Joy of the Awakened Heart

1. For more information, see M. S. Mahler, F. Pine, and A. Bergman, *The Psychological Birth of the Human Infant: Symbiosis and Individuation* (New York: Basic Books, 2008).

2. Palden Gyatso's complete story can be found in *Fire under the Snow: Testimony of a Tibetan Prisoner* (London: Harvill, 1998).

3. Acharya Buddharakkhita, trans., "Karaniya Metta Sutta: The Discourse on Loving-Kindness," Access to Insight, accessed January 17, 2024, https://www.accesstoinsight.org/tipitaka/kn/snp/snp.1.08.piya.html.

4. "Due to the Space Inside Atoms, You Are Mostly Made Up of Empty Space," *Interesting Engineering*, accessed February 17, 2024, https://interestingengineering.com/science/due-to-the-space-inside-atoms-you-are-mostly-made-up-of-empty-space.

5. For more information on the mechanics of time and black holes, see Robert M. Wald, *Space, Time, and Gravity: The Theory of the Big Bang and Black Holes* (Chicago: University of Chicago Press, 1992).

6. For a scientific study of Buddhist cessation, see Ruben E. Laukkonen, Matthew D. Sacchet, Henk Barendregt, Kathryn J. Devaney, Avijit Chowdhury, and Heleen A. Slagter, "Cessations of Consciousness in Meditation: Advancing a Scientific Understanding of Nirodha Samāpatti," *Progress in Brain Research* 280 (2023): 61–87.

7. For a general article, see "The Vacuum Catastrophe," www.resonancescience.org, accessed June 8, 2024, https://spacefed.com/astronomy/the-vacuum-catastrophe/

   Or, for a more detailed explanation, see Nassim Haramein and Amira Val Baker, "Resolving the Vacuum Catastrophe: A Generalized Holographic Approach," *Journal of High Energy Physics, Gravitation and Cosmology* 5, no. 2 (2019): 412–24, https://doi.org/10.4236/jhepgc.2019.52023.

8. For more information about this instruction, see Joseph Goldstein, "The Four Foundations of Mindfulness: A Direct Path to Liberation," *Lion's Roar*, accessed June 8, 2024, www.lionsroar.com/the-four-foundations-of-mindfulness-direct-path-liberation/.

Chapter Nine: Freedom in Relationship

1. For more information, see L. Tay, K. Tan, E. Diener, and E. Gonzalez, "Social Relations, Health Behaviors, and Health Outcomes: A Survey and Synthesis," *Applied Psychology: Health and Well-Being* 5 (2013): 28–78.

2. Antonia M. Werner, Ana N. Tibubos, Sonja Rohrmann, and Neele Reiss, "The Clinical Trait Self-Criticism and Its Relation to Psychopathology: A Systematic Review—Update," *Journal of Affective Disorders* 246 (March 2019): 530–47, https://doi.org/10.1016/j.jad.2018.12.069.

3. For example, see K. D. Neff and S. N. Beretvas, "The Role of Self-Compassion in Romantic Relationships," *Self and Identity* 12, no. 1 (2013): 78–98, https://doi.org/10.1080/15298868.2011.639548.

4. Angélica López, Robbert Sanderman, Adelita V. Ranchor, and Maya J. Schroevers, "Compassion for Others and Self-Compassion: Levels, Correlates, and Relationship With Psychological Well-being," *Mindfulness* 9, no. 1 (2017): 325–31, https://doi.org/10.1007/s12671-017-0777-z.

5. Lee Daffin and Carrie Lane, "Module 4: The Perception of Others—Principles of Social Psychology," *Pressbooks*, accessed January 17, 2024, https://opentext.wsu.edu/social-psychology/chapter/module-4-the-perception-of-others.

6. Rollin McCraty, "The Resonant Heart," *Shift: At the Frontiers of Human Consciousness*, no. 5 (2005): 15–19.

7. Rollin McCraty, Mike Atkinson, Dana Tomasino, and William Tiller, "The Electricity of Touch: Detection and Measurement of Cardiac Energy Exchange Between People: Is a Biological Science of Values Possible?" in *Brain and Values* (New York: Psychology Press, 1998), 21, https://doi:10.4324/9780203763834-16.

Chapter Ten: Waking Up as the World

1. For more information, see Amy Novotney, "What Happens in Your Brain When You Give a Gift?" APA.org, December 9, 2022, https://www.apa.org/topics/mental-health/brain-gift-giving.

2. See, for example, Rollin McCraty and Abdullah Alabdulgader, "Con-

sciousness, the Human Heart and the Global Energetic Field Environment," *Cardiology and Vascular Research* 5 (2021): 1–19, https://doi:10.33425/2639-8486.S1-1002.

3. Bobby Azarian, "The Case for Why Our Universe May Be a Giant Neural Network," *Big Think*, June 13, 2023, bigthink.com/hard-science/the-universe-may-be-a-giant-neural-network-heres-why.

4. The Earth is actually even bigger than that! According to NASA, the Earth is 1.08 quadrillion kilometers cubed (a quadrillion is a thousand trillion), while an average human body is 0.07 cubic meters. See David R. Williams, "Earth Fact Sheet," Nasa.gov, January 11, 2024, https://nssdc.gsfc.nasa.gov/planetary/factsheet/earthfact.html.

5. See again McCraty and Alabdulgader, "Consciousness, the Human Heart and the Global Energetic Field Environment."

6. For an excellent overview, see Elizabeth Kolbert, *The Sixth Extinction: An Unnatural History* (London: Picador, 2015).

7. For more information, see Max Roser, "The Short History of Global Living Conditions and Why It Matters That We Know It," *Our World in Data*, November 13, 2023, https://ourworldindata.org/a-history-of-global-living-conditions.

8. Angelica Misitzis, "Increased Interest for Mindfulness Online," *International Journal of Yoga* 13, no. 3 (2020): 247–49, https://doi:10.4103/ijoy.IJOY_15_20.

9. Global Wellness Institute, "Research Report—the Global Wellness Economy: Looking Beyond Covid—Global Wellness Institute," *Global Wellness Institute*, December 1, 2021, globalwellnessinstitute.org/press-room/press-releases/2021-gwi-research-report.

10. G. H. Gallup Jr. "Religious Awakenings Bolster Americans' Faith," *Gallup News*, January 14, 2003, https://news.gallup.com/poll/7582/religious-awakenings-bolster-americans-faith.aspx.

11. Jessie Yeung, "Our Galaxy Holds at Least 300 Million Potentially Habitable Planets, NASA Finds," CNN, November 6, 2020, https://www.cnn.com/2020/11/05/world/nasa-300-million-habitable-planets-intl-hnk-scli-scn/index.html.

About the Author

JUSTIN MICHELSON is a teacher in the insight meditation tradition with over twenty years of training at centers such as Spirit Rock Meditation Center, Insight Meditation Society, Vipassana-Metta Foundation, and Cloud Mountain Retreat Center. He is currently the cofounder and lead teacher for Eugene Insight Meditation Center in Eugene, Oregon, where he offers his unique style of Dharma with an emphasis on emotional healing and nature-based practice. Whether in the wilderness, retreat center, or online, his greatest passion is to cocreate spaces where our pain can be honored, cared for, and even celebrated—in service to the awakened heart that lives within each of us and nature itself.

Justin offers online courses and meeting groups, in-person retreats, and additional writings through his website at www.justinmichelson dharma.com. His teachings can also be found on Facebook and Instagram @justinmichelsondharma. Following the traditions of his Buddhist lineage, he is dedicated to keeping the teachings of the Dharma accessible to all regardless of financial means.